CW0054410

mùtûm àl'aaduu dà dàbìiuu yaak'ìi
Tamata Bula Vakavanua i Valu
duine dualchas cogadh
Umuntu Isintu Impi
Człowiek Kultura Wojna
Dyn Diwylliant Rhyfel
Menneske Kultur Krig
人、文化、战争
MOKHO NAMUN KELE
मनुष्य संस्कृति युद्ध
hiɓɓɛ walde konu
òme coltiva guèrra
ਮਨੁੱਖ ਕਲਚਰ ਯੁਧ
Homo Kulturo Milito
Ihminem Kulttuuri Sota
Ἄνθρωπος Πολιτισμός Πόλεμος
DEN BREZEL SEVENADUR
Menneske Kultur Krig
война культуры человека
Mens Cultuur Oorlog
Man Culture War
Homme Culture Guerre
Mensch Kultur Krieg
Člověk Kultura Válka
Hombre Cultura Guerra
إنسان- ثقافة- حرب
iti tangata peu tupuna tamakianga
Homem Cultura Guerra
Tagata Mahani Tau
人 文化 戦争
duine cultúr cogadh
Uomo Cultura Guerra
Människa Kultur Krig
insan kültür savaş
Tangata Maoritanga Pakanga
nahpew pimahtisiwinsechikewin nootinkewin
anini pimahtisiwin mihkahtink

DOMINIEK DENDOOVEN
PIET CHIELENS

WORLD WAR I

FIVE CONTINENTS
IN FLANDERS

LANNOO

Gloire à la plus grande France

9387

Postcard of a *tirailleur sénégalais* with his trophies. French propaganda described the West Africans as big children who were instructed in civilization by the mother country.

TABLE OF CONTENTS

INTRODUCTION
AS-TU TON GRIS-GRIS, FATOU?

PIET CHIELENS — DOMINIEK DENDOOVEN

At the height of the Second Battle of Ypres in early May 1915, when the British-French command in the Ypres Salient decided to make a strategic retreat, the British Generals French and Plumer voiced their concern about the strength of the French wing. The French commander General Foch assured them that the British flank in the North would be secured by 'really good troops'. Plumer explained that according to him this should mean: 'Not less than three regular French divisions should be kept between the British left and the Belgian right, and that French troops (not coloured) be placed on the immediate left of my troops. The Indian troops which were on my left have now been relieved by white troops.' Or in other words, if we manage to get rid of the weak coloured units, then so must you. Foch fully agreed with this: 'The part of the front in the immediate vicinity of the English troops is to be occupied only by French troops, to the exclusion of Algerians, Colonial and Native troops.'[1]

Such latently present or explicitly voiced racist thinking was omnipresent in the armies of the First World War. The deployment in the conflict of large groups from the colonies was deemed necessary, just as necessary as the colonies were, yet was still always approached with critical distrust. Barked at and punished, men from all over the world were deployed as labourers, as storm troops and as cannon fodder. It would be pointless to reproach these same generals for using these bad troops as eagerly as the reliable units for their degrading war of attrition. Simply add up the figures: coloured troops fell in the same proportion and, if deployed, in the same numbers, i.e. as courageously and honourably as their white colleagues. But in nationalistic, colonial and imperialistic thinking penetrated by European supremacy and superiority there was no other option but that the other was inferior, primitive, different.

Different assuredly, but mainly equal. Amidst the storm of the siege of Diksmuide (Dixmude) in early November 1914, the French Chiefs mockingly asked their West African soldiers whether they had their gris-gris[2] on them? *'As-tu ton gris-gris, Fatou?'* After which they were exterminated together by the deadly fire. Meanwhile, a little further away Belgian sergeant Maurice Goebbels was gathering an impressive collection of lucky dolls from many (allied) countries. However, in the end they would not save him. In Dikkebus, parish priest Achiel Van Walleghem noticed that whenever British soldiers departed for the

The Muslim cemetery of the prisoner of war camp Halbmondlager in Zossen-Wünsdorf near Berlin.
(© Bildarchiv Preußischer Kulturbesitz, Berlin)

After the First World War many African villages encouraged the population to wear a 'Flanders poppy' on 11 November.

front line they visited the graves of some executed soldiers. 'This might well be superstition,' thought the priest. Whereas each page of his enormous diary is full of prejudiced and self-righteous opinions, he also narrates many facts in which everyone is absolutely equal in the face of unending death and war.

This book explores the borders between equality and difference throughout the history of the First World War in Flanders. Who were these troops who came here, how did they get here and what did they think of this great uncontrolled tragedy of evil Western rationale and military and political perseverance? How were they prepared for this and how did they fare?

This is the first exhaustive overview of who was present. This information was first confirmed during the preliminary research for the exhibition Man — Culture — War (In Flanders Fields Museum, 1 May - 7 September 2008) and for the book by the same name. Where we previously spoke of 'more than 30 different nationalities', we found that there were certainly 'more than 50 different ethnic groups', in some cases represented by massive contingents and in other cases by barely a few individuals. A second very important finding is that the concept 'nationality' is not unequivocal and was inadequate. Other concepts also like *people*, *ethnic group*, *nation* .... always seem to wrong some group. In order to avoid classifying

people systematically, we have mainly opted for the neutral yet somewhat vague 'culture'. In a similar perspective the designation of the population groups must be approached with caution, all the more because history has many pitfalls in store. Thus the Chinese in the Flanders' Westhoek were and are usually referred to as 'tsjings', but this word is derived from the highly insulting English word 'chink'. If other such designations are found in the book this in no way demonstrates any ill intentions of the author. It merely indicates how persistently some words survive albeit unconsciously and how there is an occasional lack of good alternatives to designate one or the other group.

To a certain extent the same applies for the geographical descriptions that are also intentionally vague. The British spoke of France & Flanders, without giving any indication of where the one started and the other ended: many soldiers started their letters with 'Somewhere in France' when in fact they were stationed near Ypres. This was quite logical to a certain extent: the operational area behind the front in Flanders extended right up to the French Channel ports and 'Flanders' extended on either side of the 'schreve' (the line — as the border is called here). The concept of Westhoek designating the area around the West Flemish towns and cities of Veurne, Ypres, Diksmuide and Poperinge is just as vague. Except in the case of Ypres (Ieper), where the French name of the town is well accepted in English literature, the names of towns and villages are in the current official spelling, thus Veurne (Furnes), Diksmuide (Dixmude), Nieuwpoort (Nieuport), Poperinge (Poperinghe), etc.

The historiography of the First World War is still all too frequently a national, even a nationalistic and quite certainly a Eurocentric (white) event that continues to be nurtured by the outdated and highly restrictive battle history. Whereas in many other scientific disciplines such as archaeology and anthropology interest for the First World War has been aroused and has grown, many First World War historians seem to fall back on old certainties and are hesitant to broaden their field of research. Consequently, many often far more socially relevant subjects remain unexplored territory, the multicultural aspects of the Great War is just one such subject.

Long forgotten historiography, surprisingly well

The *Victory Medal* was awarded in all allied countries apart from China and Montenegro. It explicitly stated that the war was being fought 'for civilisation'. This specimen is the South African version. Every South African who contributed to the victory of the allies whether in battle or behind the front received such a medal. The medal was only withheld from the (black) members of the South African Native Labour Corps.
(In Flanders Fields Museum)

documented presences together with massively forgotten and vanished aspects of our past are called up as witnesses of a war that drew in five continents in a never seen blood bath. It affected Europe and the world to such an extent that since then questions as to its survival or revival have never subsided. Had this been the war for our civilization? Was this what our Western civilization was capable of? This question was often honestly and rightly asked. Victory medals were struck to continue reinforcing the civilized aspect of the disastrous enterprise. Yet no one bothered to ask the non-Western participants what they thought about it. Would such an approach and outcome have been possible in their so-called primitive cultures?

This book allows us to finally put this last question, even though we may not be able to answer it conclusively. Many aspects broached here must be further investigated. Many witnesses disappeared and were silenced long before they had the right to speak. However, today we can list their names, who they are, and we often summon their dead body as the sole witness to their presence in this war, thus giving us the opportunity to grant them their right of speech. In this way we will finally also (briefly) gain insight into their ideas on handling conflicts, about acts of violence and fighting, about death and remembrance, and thus we will attempt to understand how 'we' thought then and now. Finally, now Europe is again faced with so many different cultures and groups that were already present at the time, it also gives us the opportunity to state that we already shared a common history whether we like it or not. For many cultures present during the First World War the front region is the only place and the only moment when their history and ours touched. This gives us an opportunity to meet. The horrible bloodshed could thus become a fertile soil for a future of mutual understanding.

1. The National Archives, Kew: WO 158/201: Second Army: Plumer's force: Operations April 27-May 11, 1915, quoted by Julian Putkowski in *Toxic Shock, the British Army's reaction to German discharges of poison gas during the Second Battle of Ypres* (paper presented at the conference *1915: Innocence Slaughtered?*, Ypres 17-19 November 2005).

2. A grigri or grisgris is a talisman that protects the wearer from evil and/or brings him luck. It is usually a small cloth containing a mixture of herbs, stones, oils, bones, hair, nails etc.

Army organization

Troops are divided into different units according to their (relative) size, but mainly according to their position within the command structure. There were major differences per country and even per province or county (particularly in the British Armies), according to their army corps (infantry, cavalry, engineers...) or to the period (1914, 1918).

A **contingent** is a general word for a military force, it has no tactical or organizational connotation. This simplified overview is limited to the infantry.

— **company** (150-200 men, led by a Captain), subdivided into 4 **platoons** (40-50 men, with a sub-lieutenant) and subdivided into **sections** (e.g. 10 men, with sergeant)
— **battalion** (800-1000 men, led by a Major), with staff and 3 or 4 companies
— **regiment** (2000-3000 men, led by a Colonel) with staff and 3 or 4 battalions
— **brigade** (4000-6000 men, led by a Brigadier General), with staff and 2 regiments
— **division** (15000-18000 men, l d by a Major General), with headquarters and 2 or 3 brigades (later 3 regiments). Moreover, 1 or more cavalry squadrons, 1 or 2 artillery regiments, one engineers battalion, transport and medical units also belonged to a division

During the First World War there were large units like army corps, army and army groups. An **army corps** consisted of 2-4 divisions and had between 40,000 and 60,000 men. Two to four army corps formed an army (100,000-250,000 men); an **army group** included two to three armies.

In the British armies a regiment was mainly an organizational unit (as opposed to the above-mentioned tactical division). A British regiment was often linked to a geographical recruitment area or referred to a former role or 'patron'. Some regiments only consisted of one battalion whereas others comprised tens of battalions. In wartime they were not organized in regiments but in various brigades, and consequently they were often deployed in different scenes of battle. A British Infantry brigade therefore had 4 (later) 3 battalions that usually originated from different regiments.

In 1915 Arthur Wardle designed this recruitment poster for the British Empire.
The mother country is depicted as an old lion and the overseas territories as
the young lion cubs. This could be interpreted in two manners: either the dominions
and colonies are still young and full of energy as opposed to Great Britain,
or the overseas territories are like inexperienced children.

MILITARY COLONIALISM
IN FRANCE AND IN THE BRITISH EMPIRE

CHRISTIAN KOLLER

During the First World War more than 600,000 colonial soldiers including 270,000 Maghrebians, 153,000 Indians and 134,000 West Africans fought in the ranks of the Entente Powers in the European theatre of war. The presence of non-Europeans in previously unknown numbers resulted in serious discussions in the countries having deployed these soldiers as well as in Germany. This article is intended to reveal the background of colonial policies in France and in the British Empire and to confront these discussions with the reactions of the German Empire.

— French colonial troops

After war had broken out in August 1914, the French started conscripting troops from their colonies on a large scale. The first West African units were warmly welcomed when they set foot in France; the enthusiastic crowds greeted them with cheers like: 'Bravo les tirailleurs sénégalais! Couper têtes aux allemands!' (Well done Senegalese tirailleurs! Decapitate the Germans!) However, during their first deployments the colonial troops suffered some catastrophic losses. This led some sections of the officer corps starting to question their military value. During the year 1915, however, General Charles Mangin, who had been strongly in favour of a strong 'armée noire' (black army) just before the war, launched a campaign for further recruitments in Africa. The announced target figure was half a million soldiers from the colonies. The French press welcomed Mangin's proposal with great enthusiasm, however, there was some scepticism in colonial political circles. To a certain extent the government took this criticism to heart. In the late autumn of 1915, it decided to extend recruitments in the colonies, but they did not meet the expectations of Mangin's supporters.

Initially, the image of the colonial soldiers with which Mangin had made propaganda for the extension of the 'armée noire' in the pre-war period prevailed in public opinion, i.e. Africans are primitive and belligerent and are therefore ideally suited to be used as shock troops at the front in a European war. In February 1915 a caricature was published in the 'Midi Colonial', a Marseille magazine, in which a Muslim soldier could be seen with a chain of cut off ears with the legend 'Taisez-vous, méfiez-vous, les oreilles

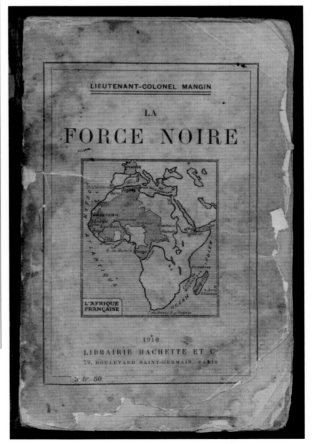

Charles Mangin (1866-1925) was a French general. In his book La Force Noire of 1910 he advocated the massive incorporation of West Africans in the French Army.
(In Flanders Fields Museum)

Le Petit Journal

ADMINISTRATION
61, RUE LAFAYETTE, 61

Les manuscrits ne sont pas rendus

On s'abonne sans frais
dans tous les bureaux de poste

15 CENT.
29me Année

SUPPLÉMENT ILLUSTRÉ

DIMANCHE 1er JUIN 1919

15 CENT.
Numéro 1.484

ABONNEMENTS

	SIX MOIS	UN AN
France et Colonies....	5 fr.	8 fr.
Étranger	8 fr.	10 fr.

LE DRAPEAU DES TIRAILLEURS SÉNÉGALAIS

déjà décoré de la Légion d'honneur, vient de recevoir la fourragère aux couleurs
de la Médaille militaire et la Croix de guerre à quatre palmes.

Dans les médaillons : le général Faidherbe, organisateur des premiers bataillons sénégalais. — M. Diagne député du Sénégal, commissaire général des effectifs coloniaux
qui recruta un grand nombre de volontaires pour la guerre. — Deux chefs illustres des troupes sénégalaises, les généraux Mangin et Marchand.

ennemies vous écoutent!' (Shut up, be careful, enemy ears are listening!). This image of colonial soldiers as bloodthirsty savages resulted in the local population being less than supportive of African troops spending the winter on the Côte d'Azur. Lucie Cousturier, who had got to know a number of injured 'tirailleurs sénégalais' while she nursed them during and after the war at the military hospital of Fréjus, wrote in her book 'Des Inconnus chez moi' in 1920 about the mood among the civilian population:

> In April-May 1916, we credited our future friends with many acts of horror. All the peasants indulged with us. There is no crime they were not accused of. After the devastation of the forest, the ugliness of their barracks, of their camps and of their hospitals, they were accused of drunkenness, theft, rape, and of causing epidemics. — 'What is to become of us?' moaned the farmers' wives, we will no longer be able to let our poultry run freely among these thieves, or dry our laundry on the hedges or let the fruit ripen on our trees. We will not dare let our young daughters walk the paths among these savages. We will not dare go out ourselves to cut the grass or gather wood. Just imagine! If we got caught by these gorillas.

To pacify these fears among the population while simultaneously refuting the accusations propagated by German propaganda, another image of the Africans was conveyed by the authorities as from 1916. They should no longer be seen as bloodthirsty savages but as big children, as descendents of 'races jeunes' (young races), who due to their intellectual inferiority were fully dependent on their white masters.

Still in 1916, colonial officer circles discussed how to resolve the ever-growing shortage of soldiers. The commander of the Somalian battalion said he was willing to recruit 6,000 Somalis, 6,000 Yemenites and 12,000 Ethiopians to fight in Europe, a proposal that apparently was never given much serious consideration by the competent authorities. The ever growing supporters of an 'armée jaune' (yellow army) were more successful. The deployment of Indochinese soldiers in Europe was indeed intensified during the second half of the war.

In the course of 1917, the fate of the 'armée noire' remained closely linked to General Mangin in person.

On 16 April General Nivelle launched an offensive in Champagne, in which the Second Colonial Corps (to which 35 West African battalions belonged) under the command of General Mangin also participated. The German counteroffensive, launched the following day, entailed many losses: almost half of all the deployed West African soldiers died. Because of this Mangin, who shortly before had asked for even more intensive recruitment in the colonies, became known as the 'butcher'. At the end of April he was relieved of his command.

From then onwards an ever-growing number of people claimed that the soldiers' reservoir in the colonies had been depleted. In September 1917, the Governor-General of French West Africa, Joost Van Vollenhoven, ordered a temporary recruitment stop. Van Vollenhoven put forward two arguments against further recruitments. First, he stressed the priority of the economic usefulness of French West Africa above its military usefulness. Second, he stressed the resistance to recruitments. In the public discussion in the mother country, however, the deployment of colonial troops in Europe was allocated a significance that was fundamental for the French colonial empire. The loyal involvement of the colonial peoples in the world war was, it was claimed, evidence of the advanced stage of the civilization process, and proved that the colonial peoples had understood that their interests were identical to those of France. At the same time the common war experience was ascribed an assimilating effect.

In fact, recruitment in the overseas territories

Back in the 19th century most European countries had colonial troops in their service. This picture shows different French colonial soldier types around 1900. (Collection Philippe Oosterlinck)

Le Petit Journal of 1 June 1919 pays tribute to the tirailleurs sénégalais and their defenders: General Faidherbe, the Senegalese Member of Parliament Blaise Diagne and the Generals Mangin and Marchand. (In Flanders Fields Museum)

presented enormous problems. The authorities in West Africa were faced with countless forms of opposition, ranging from incidental cases of self-mutilation and fleeing into the bush or to Liberia, Gambia, Portuguese Guinea and to the Ivory Coast, to armed rebellions against the colonial administration. A revolt in Bélédougou in 1915 undoubtedly opposed recruitment; during the great revolt in West Volta in 1915-1916 and numerous rebellions in the north of Dahomey between 1916 and 1917 recruitment was at the very least a major trigger. In Algeria also all kinds of opposition were witnessed. Back in the autumn of 1914 the persons concerned and their families had held protest actions against conscriptions in various locations. Resistance to recruitments culminated in the winter of 1916-1917 in a major uprising in the South Constantinois. In Tunisia there were a few minor revolts in 1915 and 1916.

However, in spite of this in January 1918, the French government again raised the issue of recruiting more troops in Africa. Prime Minister Clemenceau was found willing to recruit 200,000 mercenaries in Ethiopia, but he received little support from President Poincaré. Clemenceau had more success with his demand to have both French West Africa and Algeria send 50,000 men to the Western Front. The government entrusted the organisation of the recruitment in West Africa to the Senegalese delegate Blaise Diagne. In September Diagne was able to confirm the recruitment of 77,000 soldiers to Paris; this exceeded expectations by far. The end of the war spared these soldiers from actually having to fight at the front. However, as from 1919 many of them were stationed as occupation soldiers in Rhineland where many became sick or died.

— British Colonial Troops

In Great Britain also the issue of the colonial troops was a frequent subject of discussion. Already on 5 August 1914, one day after Britain had declared war on Germany, the war council presided by Prime Minister Asquith decided to send an Indian division to Egypt and to keep a cavalry brigade plus an extra division on stand by for deployment overseas. Three

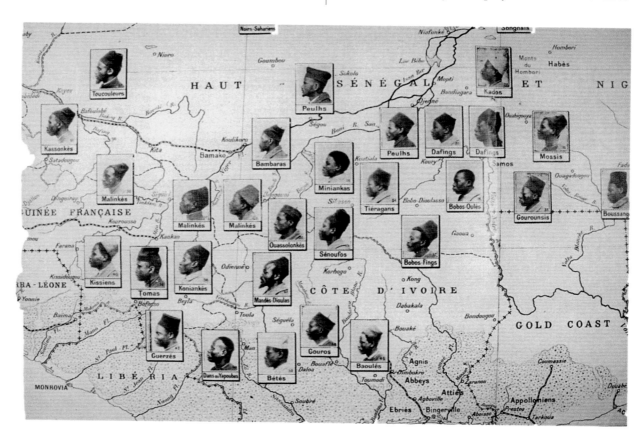

Not all ethnic groups were considered to be equally suited to military service. A map of French West Africa was shown in an article in La Dépêche coloniale illustrée of February 1917, with an indication of the names and characteristics of the main 'martial races'.

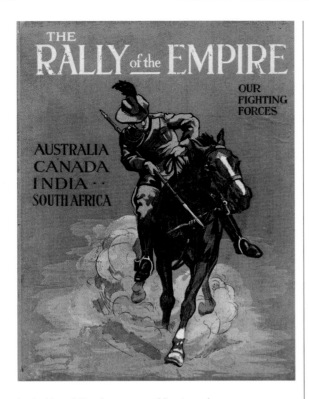

In the United Kingdom many publications chose mobilisation of the empire for their headline.
The same applies for this beautiful published book of 1914.

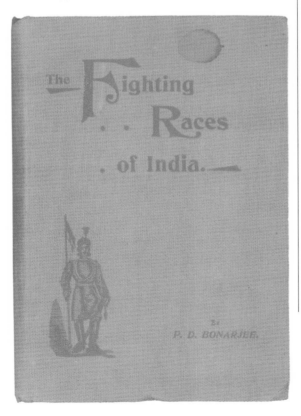

In 1899 Pitt D. Bonarjee published this 'Hand book of the Fighting Races of India'. In this influential book the author explains which ethnic groups in the Indian subcontinent are cut out to become soldiers and which are not.
(In Flanders Fields Museum)

weeks later, on 28 August, the government decided to move these units to Marseille. This decision was unanimously approved by both parliament and the press. Many writers of readers' letters also applauded the deployment of Indian troops in Europe. In September the then Indian Viceroy Lord Curzon articulated the vision of one day marching into conquered Germany with Indian troops. Shortly later in a speech at the 'Indian Empire Club' in London he described the arrival of the Indians as 'a dramatic moment in the history of the Indian Empire', yes, even as 'a landmark in our connection with India'.

On 26 September 1914, the first Indian soldiers stepped onto French soil. In the following weeks the interest for the Indian troops reached a climax. The Indians were cheered up with letters from the mother country and their first deployments in the war were extensively praised in the press. A fund set up in October for Indian war invalids and their relatives was flooded with gifts. In November some Indian soldiers even escorted King George V to the state opening of parliament.

In the course of 1915, the Indians gradually disappeared from front page news. When in December 1915 most of the Indian troops were withdrawn from the European war, the press merely printed the royal message with almost no comment. The attention of the British was increasingly focusing on the Africans. As opposed to France, Great Britain had already sent African troops to the non-European theatres of war, but not yet on the Western Front.

During the year 1916, a 'Black Army' lobby was formed, mainly supported by people with a colonial background. In May 1916 Winston Churchill demanded in the House of Commons that African units and ten to twelve Indian divisions be trained for deployment in Europe. Churchill motivated his proposal as follows:

> Let us [...] think what historians of the future would write if they were writing a history of the present time and had to record that Great Britain was forced to make an inconclusive peace because she forgot Africa; that at a time when every man counted [...] the Government of Great Britain was unable to make any use of a mighty continent. [...] It would be incredible; but it is taking place. [...] What is going on while we sit here, while we go away to

*dinner, or home to bed? Nearly 1.000 men —
Englishmen, Britishers, men of our own race —
are knocked into bundles of bloody rags every
twenty-four hours. [...] Every measure must be
considered, and none put aside while there is
hope of obtaining something from it.*

In October of that same year Major Stuart-Stephens published an article entitled 'Our Million Black Army!' in the 'English Review'. In it he called for the depletion of the reservoir of 'black fighting material' in Africa and the deployment of half a million of 'big, lusty, coal-black devils' on the Western Front, just like the French, in whose army 'thousands of fanatic Moors' had fought. In line with the Europeans and North Americans the British also imagined a hierarchy of 'race' in which the 'whites' were situated at the top of humanity, the 'blacks' right at the bottom and with the Indians somewhere in between.

Within this vertical division there was a further horizontal division for the peoples colonized under the 'whites', which played a central role in the issue of colonial troops, namely the distinction between 'belligerent' and 'non-belligerent' races. When recruiting their Indian troops the British had always mainly based their selection on the so-called 'martial races' to whom a natural, partly climatic and partly genetic predisposition for war had been ascribed. Virtually the same properties of the Indian 'martial races' were also ascribed to the New Zealand Maori fighters. Thus, for instance the London 'Times' described the embarkation of a Maori contingent for Europe in April 1915 in the following words:

*The Maoris were magnificent fighters in their
natural state, and that they have not all been
ruined in physique by a generation of peace
was conclusively shown by a glance at their
men on parade.*

Now the propagandists of the 'Million Black Army Movements' argued that 'martial races' could not only be found in India and New Zealand but also in the African colonies. Major Stuart-Stephens described the peoples of Southern Africa in the following words:

*'There seems to be something in the disposition
and genius of the common stock from which
they come, some hereditary bias in their brain,*
*in their very blood, which fits the Zulus and
Basutos for the easy acquisition of the fighting
trade.'*

The sole condition for making this 'first-rate fighting material' usable according to Stuart-Stephens, was to place them under the strict leadership by white officers familiar with the nature of the blacks.

The objectives of the 'Black Army' lobby were met with protest from various sides: military, colonial authorities, representatives of the Left parties and the South African colonists opposed the plans to allow African troops to fight in Europe. The arguments of the opponents originated from three groups, namely the humanitarians, who believed the use of Africans in Europe was inhuman, the imperialists, who feared revolts of veterans in the colonies in the post-war period if Africans were trained on a large scale and those with a military and political inclination, who questioned the military value of West African troops in a European war.

Of the Left opponents of the 'Black Army' concept Edmund Dené Morel deserves a mention, because at the beginning of the century he had acquired an international reputation for exposing the exploitation practices in the Belgian Congo. In August 1914, Morel set up the 'Union of Democratic Control', that aimed for parliamentary control of British foreign policies and a peace treaty based on compromises. He subsequently called for the neutralization of Africa in a number of publications. He described the recruitment of Africans for military service as a crime of Europe against Africa. He also highlighted the possible negative impact on the colonial system. After the war Morel launched a campaign against the 'Black Horror on the Rhine', the stationing of colonial occupation troops in the Rhineland. Also prominent members of the 'Fabian Society' such as H. G. Wells and George Bernard Shaw criticized the deployment of black African troops in Europe.

However, a more important aspect was the opposition from Africa itself. All the governors of the British Colonies and East and West Africa rejected the recruitment of troops for deployment in Europe barring one exception. The fear of a black revolution prevailed in South Africa also. The Boer newspaper, 'Ons Land', wrote shortly after the outbreak of war:

'The deployment of Arabian, Indian and

Recruitment poster for the British Indian army by Ridgewell, shortly after 1918. This poster looks very much like similar copies created during the war. The texts are in Hindi (left) and Urdu (right) and the translation of the first paragraph reads as follows: 'Easy life — lots of respect — very little danger — good pay. Look at the three men in the picture. They have opted for the profession of a soldier. They fight for their homes and their people. They prove that they belong to a brave nation. And of the good pay they receive from the Government they send a good part to their relatives back home.'

African troops on the European battlefields brings East and West, whites and blacks in close contact with one another. We cannot but wonder what the consequences of this will be. Senior citizens, women and children of the enemy will fall into the hands of these black and yellow auxiliary troops. [...] This can only be detrimental to the image of Western culture and of the whites.'

In May 1917, in a speech to the war cabinet in London, South African delegate General Smuts, spoke of the dangers to the colonial system and to European civilization in general if black Africans were given arms on a large scale.

The British Ministry of Colonial Affairs also opposed the notion of a 'Million Black Army Movement'. At the end of 1916, under pressure of public opinion, the War Office and Parliament agreed to send a recruitment mission to West Africa, but it was far from unhappy when it did not meet the expected success. At an interdepartmental conference in May 1918 it was decided to set up a West African brigade for possible deployment in Saloniki, Palestine, Egypt, Mesopotamia or Africa, 'but not against the Germans in Europe'. In September 1918, the British High Commander on the Western Front recommended they should follow the French example for the offensives scheduled for 1919 and bring 'contingents of black troops for incorporation in the British Divisions' to Europe. The War Cabinet declined this request at the suggestion of the Colonial Office.

— The German View on Colonial Troops

The colonial troops among the opponents also soon became a standard theme of German war propaganda. In July 1915, the Ministry of Foreign Affairs circulated a memorandum entitled 'Illegitimate use of coloured troops in the European theatres of war by England and France', in which African and Indian soldiers were accused of all sorts of atrocities, like poking out eyes and cutting off ears or whole heads of captured or wounded German soldiers. That same year the brochure 'The coloured auxiliary peoples of the English and French' was published by the lawyer Hans Belius, who aimed to prove that using 'savages' against 'civilised people' was prohibited by international law. Even the liberal sociologist Max Weber

Many Germans considered the fact that the French occupier deployed *tirailleurs sénégalais* in 1919-1920 as an additional humiliation. Furthermore, the West Africans were accused of rape and of other outrages. Guido Kreutzer devoted an entire novel to this 'Black Shame'. (In Flanders Fields Museum)

Bavarian medal designer Karl Götz (1875-1950) was specialized in propaganda tokens. On this token of October 1918 he denounces the deployment of people of different races by the allies.
(BDIC-Musée de l'Histoire Contemporaine, Paris)

complained that 'an army of niggers, Ghurkhas and all the barbarians of the world' were at Germany's borders.

German propaganda qualified the colonial troops with all possible contemptuous concepts suggesting that they were not regular units. The palette ranged from a 'human medley of colours and religions', 'diabolical', 'dehumanized savages', 'dead scum of the wilderness', 'Africans slaughtering in diabolical ecstasy', 'auxiliary troop scum of all colours' and 'apes' and expressions like 'African exhibition' or 'popular show of non or insufficiently civilised gangs and hordes', which was a contemptuous reference to the custom that prevailed right up to the interbellum period of exhibiting relatives of non-European peoples in zoos, in specially constructed 'aboriginal villages' and in variety shows, to 'black flood' and 'dark mud' to 'black shame', a slogan that made a remarkable career in the twenties. Furthermore, the German propagandists ventured into apocalyptic predictions that the colonial peoples would loose their respect for white people because of their deployment in Europe, and that this would eventually lead to the end of European hegemony in Africa and Asia or even to the fall of the entire 'white race'.

But how did the German military consider the colonial troops? Statements in soldiers' letters and diaries like 'you can't really consider a nigger [...] as a comrade' or the description of colonial troops as 'scum' and 'circus' bear witness to their contempt as illegitimate opponents. The stories of atrocities circulated by the propaganda apparently also reached the front, which did nothing to improve the morale of the troops. Thus, it was generally believed the Africans took no prisoners and when German units took over a new front sector the question was often anxiously raised as to whether there were any black soldiers among the opponents. In his memoirs Senegalese Bakary Diallo described the capture of a German soldier, whose whole body started shaking with fear when he was suddenly surrounded by Africans. And a German army report of 1918 stated that a column 'quickly abandoned the front line without a shot having been fired and without the enemy appearing at the cry of "The French are attacking, the blacks are coming"'.

The intensive discussions about colonial troops continued after the war with regard to the stationing

The most famous token by Karl Götz is the one he made in 1920 against the Africans in the French occupation army in Germany. On it the Africans are portrayed as semi-savage and oversexed.
The campaign against the occupation by amongst others *tirailleurs sénégalais* was referred to as the Schwarze Schande (Black Shame) or Schwarze Schmach (Black Contempt). (In Flanders Fields Museum)

of African and Asian soldiers in the French occupation zone on the Rhine. The focus was on the so-called sexual offences against the civilian population of the Rhineland which aroused international attention particularly between 1920 and 1923 during a propaganda campaign with the slogans 'black abuse' and 'black shame'.

Leo Frobenius (1873-1938) was a famous German anthropologist who was and still is admired in Africa. However, during the First World War he published this pamphlet with the telling title: 'The peoples' circus of our enemies', in which he mocked the deployment of colonial troops, describing non-European troops as performing animals in a circus.
(In Flanders Fields Museum)

— Selected bibliography:

Deroo, Eric and Champeaux, Antoine, *La force noire. Gloire et infortunes d'une légende coloniale*, Paris, 2006.

Echenberg, Myron Joël, *Colonial conscripts. The Tirailleurs Sénégalais in French West Africa, 1857-1960*, Portsmouth, 1991.

Ellinwood, DeWitt Clinton, 'Ethnicity in a Colonial Asian Army. British policy, War and the Indian Army, 1914-1918', in: Id. and Cynthia Holden Enloe (publ.), *Ethnicity and the Military in Asia*, New Brunswick-London, 1981, pp. 89-144.

Kettlitz, Eberhardt, *Afrikanische Soldaten aus deutscher Sicht seit 1871. Stereotype, Vorurteile, Feindbilder und Rassismus*, Frankfurt/M etc., 2007.

Killingray, David, 'The Idea of a British Imperial African Army', in: *Journal of African History* 20 (1979), pp. 421-436.

Koller, Christian, '*Von Wilden aller Rassen niedergemetzelt'. Die Diskussion um die Verwendung von Koloniale troepen in Europa zwischen Rassismus, Kolonial- und Militärpolitik (1914-1930)*, Stuttgart, 2001.

Koller, Christian, 'Enemy Images. Race and Gender Stereotypes in the Discussion on Colonial Troops. A Franco-German Comparison, 1914-1923', in: Hagemann, Karen and Stefanie Schüler-Springorum (publ.), *Home/Front. The Military, War and Gender in Twentieth-Century Germany*, Oxford-New York, 2002, pp. 139-157.

Le Naour, Jean-Yves, *La honte noire. L'Allemagne et les troupes coloniales françaises, 1914-1945*, Paris, 2003.

Lunn, Joe Harris, '"Les Races Guerrières". Racial Preconceptions in the French military about West African Soldiers during the First World War', in: *Journal of Contemporary History* 34 (1999), pp. 517-536.

Lunn, Joe Harris, *Memoirs of the Maelstrom. A Senegalese Oral History of the First World War*, Portsmouth, 1999.

Martin, Gregory, 'The influence of racial attitudes on British policy towards India during the First World War', in: *Journal of Imperial and Commonwealth History* 14 (1986), pp. 91-113.

Martin, Gregory, 'German and French Perceptions of the French North and West African contingents, 1910-1918', in: *Militärgeschichtliche Mitteilungen* 56 (1997), pp. 31-68.

Mass, Sandra, *Weisse Helden, schwarze Krieger. Zur Geschichte kolonialer Männlichkeit in Deutschland, 1918-1964*, Köln, 2006.

Melzer, Annabelle, 'The "Mise-en-Scène" of the "Tirailleur Sénégalais" on the Western Front, 1914-1920', in: Melman, Billie (publ.), *Borderlines. Genders and Identities in War and Peace, 1870-1930*, New York-London, 1998, pp. 213-244.

Michel, Marc, *Les Africains et la Grande Guerre. L'Appel à l'Afrique (1914-1918)*, Paris, 2003.

Riesz, Jànos en Joachim Schultz (publ.), '*Tirailleurs sénégalais'. Zur bildlichen und literarischen Darstellung afrikanischer Soldaten im Dienste Frankreichs*, Frankfurt/M etc., 1989.

Wigger, Iris, *Die 'Schwarze Schmach am Rhein'. Rassistische Diskriminierung zwischen Geschlecht, Klasse, Nation und Rasse*, Münster, 2006.

الحُلَفَاءُ فى سَبِيلِ نَصرَةِ الحَقِّ والحُرِّيَةِ

Les Nations Alliées pour le triomphe du droit et de la liberté

THE EUROPEAN ARMIES:
NO ETHNO-CULTURAL MONOLITHS

DOMINIEK DENDOOVEN

The colonising superpowers dragged virtually the whole world into the Great War. This brought peoples and cultures from all over the world to the battlefields of Europe. In the arguments justifying the deployment of colonial troops it was claimed the mother country was well worth fighting and dying for. That mother country was represented as a nation state, i.e. a state in which there was only one dominant nation. This ancient, almost natural unity should just as naturally lead its empire.

The European countries had worked hard, espe-cially during the 19th century, to create this self image. They had created an own national awareness or had at least developed and intensified it. This was indeed necessary for their cohesion and individuality as not a single European state was monocultural and unilingual. Europe was also a patchwork of nations and peoples, of cultures and ethnic groups that sometimes populated their own region but were just as often intermingled. The pre-eminent ethnic powder keg was the Balkan, where the fatal shot that would trigger the First World War was fired on 28 June 1914.

Raoul Dufy (1877-1953): Les Nations alliées pour la Triomphe du Droit et de la Liberté. Paris, s.d., colour lithograph, title in Arabic. Other versions have a title in Russian or English.
(© BDIC-Musée de l'Histoire Contemporaine, Paris)

A group photo with different types of soldiers from the German prisoner of war camp in Soltau. Seated at the front is Albert Kudjabo, one of the (very) few Congolese to serve in the Belgian army.
(Collection Philippe Oosterlinck)

For the European nation state before and during the First World War it was a matter of finding a happy medium between wiping out 'disturbing' cultural differences within the national borders and exploiting the cultural identity of certain minorities for the benefit of the war efforts.

— The German Empire

The German Empire was one of the youngest countries at war in 1914. Although the notion 'Germany' had existed for centuries and was to a large extent a cultural reality, the German states endured a difficult unification process. It was only in January 1871 that the Prussian King William I was grudgingly crowned as the German Emperor. Since then the Empire had mainly handled defence and foreign affairs. In all other matters the federal states had remained sovereign. The German Empire comprised no fewer than 25 such federal states: 4 kingdoms (Prussia, Saxony, Württemberg and Bavaria), six grand duchies, five duchies, seven principalities and the free Hansa cities of Bremen, Hamburg and Lübeck. Alsace-Lorraine, conquered from France in the 1870 war, was governed like an imperial territory. This political mosaic was reflected in the German armed forces of 1914. Almost every federal state had its own regiments and that individuality was expressed in rank insignia, uniform parts, army organization and military culture. For instance the renowned Prussian militarism was as much a concept for the other German Länder as it was for the allies.

German postcard with portraits of some important military figures. Amongst them the Kaiser and his eldest son, and also Crown Prince Rupprecht of Bavaria and Duke Albrecht of Württemberg.
(Collection Philippe Oosterlinck)

Lieutenant Kurt Zehmisch from Plauen in the South Saxon Vogtland was the *Ortskommandant* (town major) of Warneton for a considerable period of time. His good command of French and English allowed him to communicate fluently with the local population and with the British prisoners of war.
(© In Flanders Fields Museum – Collection Kurt Zehmisch)

The German Empire, and hence the German armed forces, also included many minorities. A large section of present day Poland (that did not yet exist as a state) was formed by the then Prussian provinces Pomerania, Silesia, Posen and East & West Prussia. Many soldiers from those provinces were therefore ethnic Poles for whom German was the foreign yet official language. In Brandenburg, in the heart of the German Empire, the area around the cities Cottbus and Lausitz was populated then as it is now by Sorbs: a people of Slavic origin with its own language and culture. Some inhabitants of the Imperial Territory of Alsace-Lorraine that was only put on an equal footing with the other German federal states in 1911, spoke French, German and/or an Alsatian dialect. In 1914 the population of Wervik was surprised to have to provide accommodation for French-speaking German soldiers. Many of the German-speaking Alsatians were in favour of a return to

France. The small Grand-Duchy of Luxemburg, which hardly had an army until 1914, was occupied by German troops on 2 August 1914, but maintained its (internal) self-rule. In spite of this, however, Luxemburgers were subjected to compulsory military service in the German army. They were spread out among all kinds of units. However, a number of Luxemburg volunteers fought in the French army.

Over 30,000 'Danish' soldiers from Schleswig found themselves in the same situation. This duchy had been conquered by Prussia in 1864 with the support of Austria and the German Federation. Many pro-Danish inhabitants, including some who spoke German, left much against their wishes for a war which they believed was of no concern to them. Over 5000 would never return and today lie buried in German military cemeteries. Only one small Danish cemetery was built in Braine, near the Chemin-des-Dames. Two thousand five hundred other South-Jutland conscripts deserted to neutral Denmark. The allies too were aware of the special situation of these 'German' soldiers and opened special camps in Aurillac and Feltham, where the Danish prisoners of war enjoyed a more favourable regime. After the First World War the Northern part of the duchy of Schleswig, would again become a Danish province under the name South-Jutland. The memory of the First World War was and is kept alive there: there was a thriving association of 'pro-Danish veterans of the Great War' and there are still many war monuments. The main one is the large national monument in

This young boy from Cologne served
in the Reserve-Infanterie-Regiment 236.
(In Flanders Fields Museum)

Membership card of the Association of Pro-Danish War Veterans.
Even after the reintegration of South Jutland in Denmark the memory of
the First World War was kept alive. Despite the fact that they had served in
the German army, many war veterans explicitly showed they were Danish patriots.
(Arkivet Sønderborg)

Marselisborg that was partly inspired by the Ypres Menin Gate. Some Danes also fought sporadically on the other side. For instance Ove Krag-Juel-Vind-Frijs, a son of one of Denmark's best known aristocratic families who fought in the Canadian army, lies buried in Kemmel Chateau Cemetery near Ypres.

Some figures speak volumes about the minorities in the former German Empire: in spite of Bismarck's Kulturkampf of the 56 million German nationals in 1900 — ten years later there would be ten million more — more than 3 million had Polish as their mother tongue, over 200,000 French, 140,000 Danish, 93,000 Sorbic and 80,000 Dutch. Other languages with a large number of speakers (over 20,000) were amongst others Masurian, Moravian, Czech, Kashubian, Lithuanian and Frisian.

In addition to the ethno-cultural minorities there were also religious minorities. German Jews had only been given civil rights with the creation of the Empire in 1871. Consequently, they were subjected to compulsory military service. Over 60,000 Jews served in the German army during the First World War. At the instigation of anti-semitic politicians a Jew census was carried out in the German armed forces in order to demonstrate that Jewish citizens failed to fulfil their duty towards the fatherland. The statistics proved the contrary and the research was never made public. Yet towards the end of the First World War all kinds of deceptive stories were circulating about how the Jews, who were war usurers, inferior cowards and international conspirators, had orchestrated the German defeat. This lay a solid foundation for the anti-semitism that prevailed during the interbellum period. In the German cemeteries in France gravestones with the Star of David and Hebrew inscriptions stand out against the black or grey crosses.[1]

A group of German soldiers behind the front, 1914-1915.

—Austria-Hungary

The dual monarchy (Empire of Austria and the Kingdom of Hungary) was one of the central powers together with the Ottoman Empire (Turkey) and the German Empire. Austrians (29 %), Hungarians (or Magyars, 18 %), Czechs and Slovaks, Slovenians and Croatians, Bosnians and Serbians, Poles and Ruthenes, Rumanians (5 %) and Italians (1 %) served in its armed forces. Thus 47 % belonged to a Slavonic population group. Of the officers 75 % was Austrian, i.e. German speaking. The armies of the dual monarchy were mainly active on the Eastern Front, in the Balkan and on the Italian border. Very few subjects of the Habsburg emperor were present in Flanders. On the name tables of the Kameradengrab at the German military cemetery in Langemark there are four names of men having served in the Imperial and Royal regiments and eight of them are buried in the German military cemetery in Wervicq-Sud.

Vor dem Ausmarsch: November 1914.

Seventeen year old German soldier Ernst Alexander Leipart from Berlin poses here just before leaving for the front in Flanders. A few weeks later, on 9 December 1914 he would die near Ypres.
(In Flanders Fields Museum)

Some German infantrymen in a temporary trench, in 1915. These soldiers are equipped with the early gas masks that were carried in a bag on their chests. A dust cover protected and camouflaged their spiked helmet.
(© Bildarchiv Preußischer Kulturbesitz, Berlijn)

— The United Kingdom and the Crown Dependencies

With the Second 'Act of Union' Ireland joined the United Kingdom in 1800 and the country became officially known as the United Kingdom of Great Britain and Ireland. As the name suggests it was a unification of different countries: England, Wales that had been united with England for many centuries, Scotland and Ireland. Even though there was no such thing as an Irish or Scottish army (as opposed to Germany with e.g. the Bavarian or Saxon armies), tradition and the geographical organisation of the army had provided for clearly Scottish, Irish and Welsh units. Expressions of their own cultural identity were not only given considerable leeway in the British army but were even encouraged. So the Scots wore their own uniform that consisted of a kilt with the unit tartan and a sporran, and a glengarry or tarn on their heads. It is not surprising that the Scottish units appealed to the imagination of the German opponents, who devoted many cartoons to the 'Damen von Hölle' (ladies from hell), as well as to that of the local population who were astonished by the Scots 'who wore no underwear'.

Nor was English always the first or only mother tongue of the soldiers in the British units. Some also spoke Gaelic or Cornish or Welsh like the Welsh poet Hedd Wyn (Ellis Humphrey Evans) who lies buried in Artillery Wood Cemetery near Boezinge.

The situation of the Irish was complex and comp-

licated. In Flanders the (Protestants of the) 36th Ulster Division fought alongside the (Catholics of the) 16th Irish Division. In this last unit there were many moderate nationalists who had answered the call of their charismatic leader John Redmond, and volunteered to serve in the British army that was hated by so many Irishmen. They had been promised that after the war their efforts would be rewarded with 'home rule'. Right from the start the British military authorities distrusted and even showed antipathy towards the Irish troops, and more particularly towards the Catholic Irish. Historical research shows that in military law cases such as desertion they were more often given the maximum military punishment than their English or Scottish colleagues. The (also Catholic) Belgian population greeted the Irish with more indulgence.

After the 1916 Easter Rising in Dublin and the brutal repression by British troops, public opinion in Ireland became more radical. The moderate nationalists no longer found work and the Catholic Irish soldiers in Flanders who wore the same uniform as the hated repressors, started being considered as traitors by a growing number of Irish. Until recently they were not even mentioned in history books. This is the reason why one of the last 'national' monuments to be erected on the Western front is the 'Island of Ireland Peace Park', which as its name suggests is intended to commemorate all the Irish from the North and South. This Irish Peace Park in Messines was inaugurated on 11 November 1998 by the British Queen Elisabeth II and the Irish President Mary McAleese. It is said that on that occasion the heads of

Scots were often applauded by the local population, like this piper behind the Ypres front, July 1915.
(© Royal Army Museum, Brussels)

In front of the entrance to a shelter two British soldiers of the Royal Garrison Artillery are eating their soldier's meal, 1917.
(© Imperial War Museum, London)

state of these two countries met for the very first time. During the war the two Irish divisions suffered 60,000 losses (dead, injured, missing soldiers) in Flanders and Northern France.

In addition to the countries belonging to the United Kingdom some smaller, independent Crown Dependencies also sent their sons to the front. Most volunteers of the Isle of Man served as guards in the internment and prisoner of war camps on their island. Many other Manx soldiers went overseas with one of the two Manx Service Companies that belonged to the Cheshire Regiment, or with a unit of the King's (Liverpool) Regiment. Manx soldiers are also found in other British units. As there was no single Manx unit, it is hard to pick them out. Some years

Fallen Scots on the battlefield near Zonnebeke, September 1917 (© Imperial War Museum, London)

Two British soldiers, one wounded, returning from the trenches. Other troops are moving up towards the frontline. Ypres, 1917. (© Imperial War museum, London)

ago a small pin and a piece of decorated shell were found during an excavation near Boezinge, both items carry the emblem of the Isle of Man: a triskelion.

Inhabitants of Jersey can also be found in different British units. The local militia initially formed a Jersey Overseas Contingent that joined the 7/Royal Irish Rifles. In total over 6000 Jerseymen served overseas during the Great War in many British units. Almost 700 of them never returned.

The situation was somewhat different for troops originating from the Bailiwick of Guernsey, which includes the autonomous islands Sark, Alderney and Guernsey. The law stated that the local militia must not be deployed overseas. Yet Guernsey, like Man and Jersey, formed a contingent that was also annexed to an Irish unit. Integration wasn't always smooth as about half the Guernseymen spoke only French or Normandic. In 1916, contrary to the other Crown Dependencies, Guernsey decided to set up its own full-fledged infantry battalion. In October 1917 this Guernsey Light Infantry experienced its baptism of fire during the Third Battle of Ypres. In the spring of 1918 the battalion was also active near Ypres as a section of the 29th division under the command of Guernseyman Henry Beauvoir de Lisle. After the German Spring Offensive the Guernsey Light Infantry was decimated and the unit was ultimately disbanded. The dreadful experience of the First World War resulted in the Bailiwick of Guernsey refusing to deploy its militia in 1939.

The three legs are the symbol of the Isle of Man. This small pin was found during an exploration of the battlefield of Boezinge.
(Collection Johan Verbeerst)

A party of British officers enjoying themselves with
a grammophone in their camp near Poperinghe,
26 September 1917. (© Imperial War museum, London)

Upon their arrival at a prisoner of war camp near Berlin
these French soldier types were photographed by the camp commander.
(© Bildarchiv Preußischer Kulturbesitz, Berlin)

—France

Centralization in the French Republic, which had called itself 'une et indivisible' since the revolution, also had a greater cultural impact in France than in most other European states. This was also reflected to a certain extent in the armed forces, where the regiment names hardly include any geographical references and where the uniform leaves very little room for regional diversity. This diversity could however be expressed in other areas. Thus, for instance many Breton units played the typical biniou and bombarde. Among the troops originating from La France Métropolitaine French was the only official language but many soldiers spoke their native Occitanian, Breton, Basque, Catalan, Corsican or Flemish among themselves. Obviously, the Foreign Legion included many nationalities. These marching regiments were never deployed at the front in Flanders.

As a matter of course the French regiments were mainly recruited on a regional basis. For instance the 49th Régiment d'Infanterie was barracked in Bayonne and was therefore essentially a Basque unit. 98% of the Fusiliers Marins were Bretons. The nickname of this brigade was 'Demoiselles au pompon rouge' because it included many very young boys and because of the red pompom on their caps. The history of the Fusiliers Marins during the First World War is closely related to the Yser region. They were deployed as French reinforcements for the Belgian troops during the withdrawal towards the Yser. After the Battle

The French Minister of War, General Lyautey, visits the *fusiliers marins* on the Belgian West coast, February 1917.
(© ECPAD – Médiathèque de la Défense, Paris)

of the Yser in October 1914, they managed to maintain their position together with the Senegalese and Belgian troops until 10 November 1914 in the middle of the heavily besieged Dixmude, the only place on the right bank of the Yser that had not yet fallen into German hands. Three thousand Fusiliers Marins, approximately half their men, were eliminated. The brigade never fully recovered from this blow and that is the reason why when the French Navy demanded more personnel at the end of 1915 the brigade was transformed into a battalion. The Fusiliers Marins would remain in the French sector near Nieuwpoort in West Flanders until 1917. Their last feat of arms in

Flanders was their participation in the Third Battle of Ypres. Various Breton units were also among the French territorial troops who fell victim to the first chemical attack on 22 April 1915. This is why the memorial park has a pronounced Breton character: Carrefour des Roses in Boezinge consists of a 16th century Calvary cross from Louargat (near Guincamp), an authentic dolmen from Hénansal (near Dinan) and various menhirs, all brought over from Brittany. The First World War would hit Brittany harder than most other French regions: between 1914 and 1918 one in fourteen Bretons died on the battlefield or as a consequence thereof, about twice the rest of France!

The 15th Corps d'Armée included soldiers from South Eastern France: the Alps, Marseille and Corsica. In addition to the official language French, many men also spoke Corsican, Italian or Occitanian. The 29th Division d'Infanterie that originated from this army corps was deployed in the Nieuwpoort sector in the spring of 1917 and during the bloody Third Battle of Ypres later that same year. Just like Brittany, Corsica also paid a heavy toll during the First World War: of the 45,000 Corsican soldiers 12,000 never returned. That is approximately 25 %, as opposed to the national French average of 16.5 %. Corsica was also the only French Departement in which fathers of more than three children were also mobilised.

Catalans from the Roussillon could be found amongst others in the 53rd and 253rd Régiment d'Infanterie that originated from Perpignan. The first-mentioned Catalan unit fought during the First Battle of Ypres (October-November 1914), whereas the second occupied the trenches from May through July 1918 near Loker and Dranouter. The Catalans were also very proud that the French commander-in-chief (until 1917) Joffre, originated from Rivesaltes, and was one of them. For most of the other soldiers from the neighbouring region of Languedoc the first language was often Occitanian.

Among the other 'ethnical minorities' in France we must mention the Alsatians, who could mainly be found among the Germans (approximately 380 000), but also among the French. These were essentially tens of thousands of 'optants' or their children, who had chosen the French nationality in 1872 and had left the annexed territory. The pro-French attitude of the Alsatians of the territories reconquered by

Three French *poilus* pose briefly on the Market Square of Ypres, December 1914.
(© Imperial War Museum, London)

Even though military equipment left little room for it the French army did pay some attention to regional characteristics. L'Illustration of 3 July 1915 displayed these two Bretons of the 73e Régiment d'Infanterie Territoriale with their typical *biniou* and *bombarde* on the first page. Their unit had suffered the first gas attack a few months earlier near Ypres. (In Flanders Fields Museum)

L'ILLUSTRATION

Prix du Numéro : Un Franc.   SAMEDI 3 JUILLET 1915   *73ᵉ Année. — Nᵒ 3774.*

LA BOMBARDE ET LE BINIOU BRETONS SUR LE FRONT

Le colonel d'un régiment de territoriaux, du recrutement de Bretagne, a adjoint à ses tambours et à ses clairons
les deux instruments favoris de la vieille Armorique.

Voir l'article à la page suivante.

France in 1914 was first investigated and the most doubtful cases were interned. These Alsatians could only join the Foreign Legion and mainly served in North Africa.

French-Flemings, few in number, were accommodated in various units. Because of the irony of war some fought in their own region. Jérome Verdonck from Boeschepe served in the 39th Division d'Infanterie. He had already fought in the First Battle of Ypres, Artois and Verdun until his unit had to leave Compiègne head over heels 'pour une destination inconnue' in April 1918. When he stepped off the train after travelling during the night he was surprised to be in Poperinge. He would eventually fight at the Battle of Mount Kemmel and man trenches at 7 kilometres from his parental home. Jérôme Verdonck survived but his fellow villager Rémi Hayaert had already died on 13 November 1914. He was buried in the French military cemetery of Woesten, barely 14 kilometres from his native village, but on the other side of the 'Schreve' (the border).

I would like to briefly draw your attention to the gypsies. Soldiers with gypsy blood could be found in various armies. However, they are difficult to trace. They were often looked on with suspicion. During the last year of war German military command decided that gypsies should no longer be deployed at the front. The situation of the gypsies was probably the most ironic in France. Because of the official distrust gypsy families were interned in a few large camps, sometimes from September 1914 to July 1919, while their husbands fought at the front. Some gypsy soldiers were interned upon their return from the war.

Two *fusiliers marins* in Dunkirk, 3 September 1917.
(© Musée départemental Albert Kahn, Boulogne-Billancourt)

French *fusiliers marins* in Oostduinkerke, 1916-1917.
Mainly Bretons belonged to this famous unit.
(© ECPAD – Médiathèque de la Défense, Paris)

Volontaires luxembourgeois au service de la France
3ᵉ Compagnie 2ᵉ Peloton

The position of the so-called gypsies was not an enviable one
in any country. In France official mistrust was so widespread
that gypsy families were interned in special camps. This
happened quite frequently while the men were fighting at
the front. This photo was taken in the internment camp for
nomads at Crest (Département de la Drôme) in January 1916.
(© BDIC-Musée de l'Histoire Contemporaine, Paris)

The independent Grand Duchy of Luxemburg was occupied by German
troops on 2 August 1914. From then onwards the Luxemburgers were
subjected to German military service. However, a fairly large group
of Luxemburg volunteers served in the French army also.
(Collection Franky Van Rossem)

Belgian infantrymen and French *fusiliers marins* pose together behind the Yser front, ca 1916.

— Belgium

Back in 1914 it was already a well-known fact that the Belgian nation consisted of two national communities. The 'Field notes on the Belgian, French and German Armies' published by the British general staff just before war broke out, gives the following description:

The Belgian Nation, and Belgian regiments, are composed of two different races — the Walloons, who speak a sort of French, and the Flemings, who speak a sort of Dutch. Many Walloons can only talk French; many Flemings can only talk Flemish. On the outbreak of a Franco-German war public opinion in Walloon districts is likely to be actively pro-French, whilst in Flemish districts, though hardly pro-French, is not likely to be actively pro-German. Both are Belgians first and foremost; Walloons and Flemings only in second place.

The Germans were also very aware of this and noticed even sharper distinctions which they exploited. When camp commander Otto Stiehl made a booklet with portraits of 'Duitschlands Vijanden' (Germany's Enemies), he typified the two Belgian brother communities as follows:

... The Flemings also demonstrated a strong inclination to reservedness and dark introversion: an embittered mood that could be explained by the fact that, in spite of all the resounding words of freedom, these people are greatly oppressed by the ruling pro-French Walloons, they are deprived of higher development because their education is neglected and that consequently they have been unable for a long time to reveal their strengths...When imprisoned the Flemings were among the most difficult inhabitants of the camp because of their deep rooted aversion for discipline. Their fellow-countrymen, the Walloons, displayed the same characteristic but that was the only similarity. In all other respects these two communities brought together in an impossible manner to form one state showed the greatest oppositions... Our photos show a typical picture of this highly-flammable, nervous-excitable people.

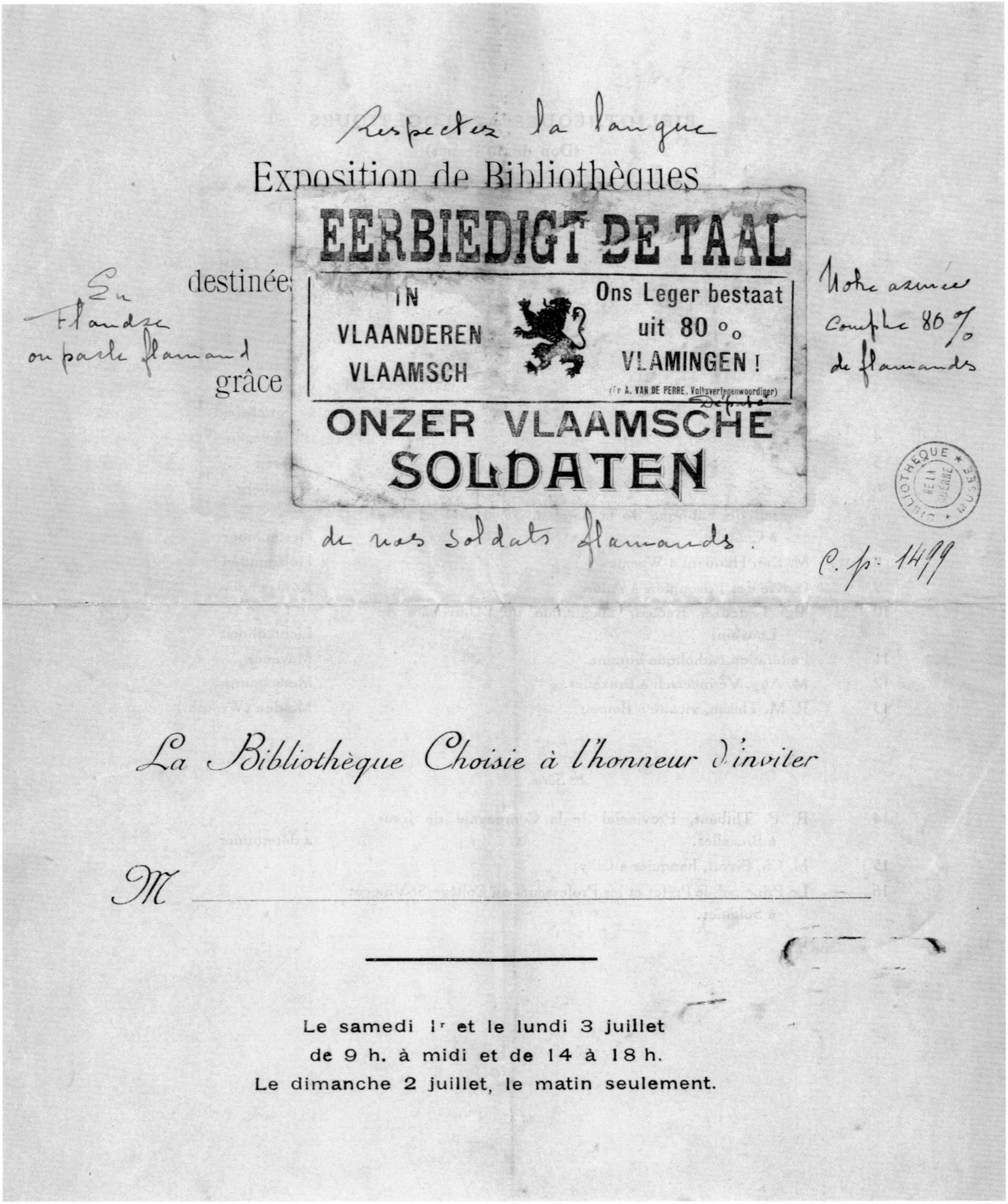

Respectez la langue

Exposition de Bibliothèques

EERBIEDIGT DE TAAL

IN VLAANDEREN VLAAMSCH

Ons Leger bestaat uit 80 o/o VLAMINGEN!

(Fr A. VAN DE PERRE, Volksvertegenwoordiger)

Député

ONZER VLAAMSCHE SOLDATEN

En Flandre on parle flamand

destinées

grâce

Notre armée compte 80 % de flamands

de nos soldats flamands.

C. p. 1499

La Bibliothèque Choisie à l'honneur d'inviter

M

Le samedi 1r et le lundi 3 juillet
de 9 h. à midi et de 14 à 18 h.
Le dimanche 2 juillet, le matin seulement.

Many Flemings in the Belgian army protested against the unilingual use of French. They did so amongst others by sticking protest notes, as shown here, on a document of a soldiers' library. The librarian added the French translation.
(BDIC-Musée de l'Histoire Contemporaine, Paris)

great opposition from army command. It is important to note that Flemish awareness rapidly spread among many Flemish soldiers and officers. Even after the war the Flemish Front Movement would continue to play an important role in Belgian politics. The same applies, albeit to a lesser extent for Wallingantism. Shortly before the war, in 1912, an Assemblée wallonne defined the movement's demands. During the war the magazines La Wallonnie and L'Opinion Walonne had continued to spread Wallingantism among Walloon soldiers and refugees.

In occupied Belgium and in the prisoner of war camps in Germany the language problem also played an important role. The German occupant used this to divide the Flemings and Walloons as much as possible by way of a 'Flamenpolitik'. Thus the University of Ghent became Dutch-speaking in 1916 and a Council of Flanders was founded in 1917, both exclusively populated by collaborators, the so-called activists. There were also some Walloon activists but their numbers were even lower than in Flanders.

As opposed to the French and British Belgium did not deploy any colonial troops, not on the Yser at any rate. The Congolese Force Publique was, however, fairly successfully active in the campaign against German East Africa. Only 27 coloured soldiers, all full blood Congolese barring two, served in the Belgian Army on the Western Front. Most of them were already living in Belgium in 1914 or had worked on the Congo ships.

Flemish soldiers were greatly irritated by the unilingual Belgian army. Whereas a vast majority of soldiers were Flemish-speaking, virtually the entire officers' corps only spoke French. Pro-Flemish intellectuals set up the Front Movement as a reaction to this. They advocated Flemish rights but experienced

Not only the Flemish but also the Walloon national awareness was boosted in the trenches on the Yser. This trench newsletter for soldiers of Namur and surroundings carries the Walloon title 'Nameur por tot'.
(Collection Philippe Oosterlinck)

Belgian troops on their way to the front, 25 October 1914. The Belgian army drew the attention of foreign troops because of their use of dog carts. It is assumed this photo was taken in Poperinge.
(© Imperial War Museum, London)

— Portugal

Portugal, a traditional ally of the British Empire and only a republic since 1910, declared its neutrality at the outbreak of war. In spite of this it entered into conflict with Germany in its African colonies and at sea. Finally, in March 1916 the country declared war on the German Empire. A Corpo Expeditionario Portugues was created and was trained in Portugal as well as in Great Britain. On paper this corps would comprise two divisions, yet it would never reach its full strength. The Portuguese were equipped with French and British material that wasn't always of the best quality: the helmets they wore had previously been rejected by British army command.

The Portuguese troops started arriving in French-Flanders in May 1917, their sector was a strip of some 12 to 18 kilometres near the small village Neuve-Chapelle. This had been the Indian sector two years before. They were also present from time to time on the Belgian side of the border. On 8 August 1917 Father Van Walleghem in Loker met Portuguese soldiers: 'They wear blue like the French, but have another uniform cap'. In Ghent a small plaque on the Korenlei commemorates the deployment of the Portuguese troops in Belgium.

The situation of the Portuguese was not an envi-

A Portuguese soldier, 1917-18.
(© BDIC-Musée de l'Histoire Contemporaine, Paris)

Carrying their flag in front, a Portuguese column passes a farm in the French-Flemish Lys Valley, 1917-18. (© BDIC-Musée de l'Histoire Contemporaine, Paris)

able one: although the 'Sector Portugues da Flandres' in the Valley of the Lys to the South of Armentières was considered to be a peaceful sector, the flat, cold and very damp landscape was not the ideal climate for the Portuguese. The British considered them as second rate soldiers. In addition to having some equipment of inferior quality they never reached full capacity. Moreover, in 1918 Portugal was faced with a major political crisis. President Pais was opposed to the Portuguese participation in the war and prevented the transfer of new troops, equipment and other provisions. He was assassinated later that year. All this contributed to the low morale of some 40,000 Portuguese. The British also realized that the Portuguese divisions were a weak link and in anticipation of the imminent German offensive they scheduled their withdrawal on 9 April 1918. That same day at dawn the well-prepared German troops attacked in force. That day was a complete disaster for the totally surprised Portuguese: 400 were killed and over 6500 were taken prisoner of war, in all about one third of the men in the trenches. The Portuguese Expeditionary Force would not survive this blow. The Portuguese soldiers who remained active in Belgium and France until the Armistice did so behind the front, or as supplementary troops of a British division.

The Portuguese Captain Herreira made this aquarelle of his soldiers in the trenches of the Lys Valley in 1918. It goes without saying that the Portuguese soldiers were not familiar with snow. (© BDIC-Musée de l'Histoire Contemporaine, Paris)

The funeral procession of a Portuguese soldier in Saint-Venant, 1917-18. (© BDIC-Musée de l'Histoire Contemporaine, Paris)

— Italian and Russian prisoners of war

Originally, Italy had been an ally of the German Empire and of Austria-Hungary. When war broke out the country initially declared its neutrality but in May 1915 it declared war on Austria-Hungary and in August 1916 on Germany. The sequence of the war was fairly catastrophic for Italy. Especially after the Battle of Caporetto, the Italian name for present day Kobarid in Slovenia, in October-November 1917 many Italian prisoners of war came into German hands. The Germans saw the prisoners of war as a solution for the lack of manpower behind the Western front, so they 'imported' Italian prisoners of war on a relatively large scale into occupied Belgium and Northern France. The local Belgian population took pity on the miserable Italians. Julie Cattrysse from Aartrijke remembered:

> They were barely clothed. They had holes in the soles of their shoes, and in their socks. You could see their toes. That was all they had to walk in even when it was freezing or snowing. No clothes, no food.

Her fellow-villager Jules Depuydt wrote in his diary that you could give the Italian prisoners food but you could not take an interest in them on penalty of a 100 Mark fine! The Italian prisoners of war in German hands who died in Belgium were subsequently re-buried in Italian military graves, amongst others in

These cardboard badges were worn by Portuguese war veterans of the *Grande Guerra*. (Collection Philippe Oosterlinck)

Together with the Belgian King Albert I, the Italian King Vittorio Emanuele III visited the Belgian field hospital L'Océan II in Vinkem on 29 September 1917. No Italians fought in Flanders during the First World War. However, Italian prisoners of war were deployed by the Germans as workforce behind the font.
(© Royal Army and Military History Museum, Brussel)

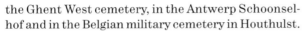

the Ghent West cemetery, in the Antwerp Schoonsel-hof and in the Belgian military cemetery in Houthulst.

The Germans also brought Russian soldiers taken prisoner of war to the Western front to perform hard labour. The Flemings showed concern for them as they had done for the Italians. Amongst others in Geluwe the Ter Stock farm was installed as a camp for the Russians in November 1915. Torn and worn uniforms, dirty, untended long beards, emaciated, sick: that was what they looked like. In spite of a prohibition, the inhabitants of Geluwe occasionally tried to give them food or clothing. In exchange the Russians would often give them a figurine, frequently a bird carved in wood. In addition to performing front work in the Westhoek, the Russians were often used to build railways in the Fourrons Region and in the Ardennes. For the Russian prisoners of war the October Revolution of 1917 and the subsequent Treaty of Brest-Litovsk signed between the new Bolshevik rulers and the Central Powers brought little change. Even after the Armistice the Russians — some sources speak of over 5,000 men — remained in Bel-

gium. The allies had hoped to be able to deploy them in the fight against Bolshevism. That is why as from February 1919 the former Belgian military camps Tabora and King Albert in Houtem (near Veurne) were made available to them. The lack of leadership and control, the uncertainty about their future and the continuous coming and going of soldiers finally led to unrests among the Russians in April 1919. For the Belgian authorities this was the signal to stop the influx of Russian prisoners of war from Germany and to renounce any further militarization. Finally, a small number of genuine volunteers for the White Army — some thirty soldiers — were isolated in a camp in Wulpen, also near Veurne. In December 1919 they left this camp for the vagrants' colony in Wortel in the Northern Campine. Ultimately very few or no former Russian prisoners of war (organised) from Belgium would join the White Army. Graves of Russian prisoners of war or former prisoners of war can be found in the municipal cemeteries of Mons, Tournai and Ghent (West cemetery).

The woodcarvings of Russian prisoners of war were a very popular souvenir, not only among the Flemish population but also among the German soldiers. This stall exhibits Russian woodcarvings from the prisoner of war camp at Zossen-Wünsdorf. (© Bildarchiv Preußischer Kulturbesitz, Berlin)

A group of Russian prisoners of war in Warneton, December 1915. The Germans put Russian prisoners to work behind the front in Flanders virtually throughout the war.
(© In Flanders Fields Museum – Collection Kurt Zehmisch)

— Other European countries

In addition to the above-mentioned nationalities there were representatives of almost all European countries in or close to the front in Flanders, be it as an observer or reporter, as a military attaché or as a war volunteer in the German, Belgian or British army. However, in this instance they were always individuals or small groups at the most. And although the war was mainly a man's business, some women were involved too. The Dutch nurse Rosa 'Roosje' Vecht already offered her services to the Belgian Red Cross in September 1914. During the removal of the Belgian Field Hospital from Veurne to Hoogstade on 23 January 1915 she was hit by 'a bomb dropped from a plane'. She died of her injuries the following day and was buried in the military cemetery of Adinkerke. After the war her remains were reburied in the Dutch-Jewish cemetery in Muiderberg near Amsterdam. Roosje Vecht is just one of a small number of inhabitants of the neutral Netherlands who lost their lives because of the First World War.

— Concise bibliography:

Adriansen, Inge and Hans Schultz Hansen, *Sønderjyderne og den Store Krig 1914-1918*, Aabenraa, 2006.

Antoine-Toussaint, Antona, *Ceux du 173ᵉ. Les Corses au combat, 1914-1918*, Alata, 2005.

Decuypere, Dirk, *Het malheur van de keizer. Geluwe 1914-1918*, Geluwe, 1998.

Elfnovembergroep, *Van den grooten oorlog: volksboek*, Kemmel, 1985.

Filhol, Emmanuel, *Un camp de concentration français. Les Tsiganes alsaciens-lorrains à Crest 1915-1919*, Grenoble, 2004.

Johnstone, Tom, *Orange, green and khaki. The story of the Irish regiments in the Great War, 1914-18*, Dublin, 1992.

Le Mer, Gabriel, *Les régiments bretons dans la Grande Guerre 1914-1918*, Plessala, 2001.

Stiehl, Otto, *Duitschland's Vijanden. 96 karakteristieke koppen uit Duitsche gevangenenkampen*, Amsterdam [1916].

L'Armée de terre Portugaise en France 1918, Lissabon, s.d.

Field Service Pocket Book, London, 1914.

Various files, documentation centre IFFM

With thanks to Bram Libotte for the data on the Congolese soldiers

1. The German cemeteries in Belgium use flat gravestones that make any religious identification impossible.

A group of Russian and German soldiers, probably taken after the signing of the Treaty of Brest-Litovsk between Russia and the Central Powers in March 1918.

FRENCH COLONIAL TROOPS
AT THE FRONT IN FLANDERS

PIET CHIELENS

When Max Deauville saw the first colonial troops of the French army in Lo on 19 October 1914 — a group of Moroccan *Spahis*, colourful desert horsemen on lively small horses — he noticed, as a true writer would, how 'a ray of sunshine had illuminated this new scene in the oldest town of Flanders'[1]. The *Spahis* with their colours and their *fantasies* on the beach and their encampments in the dunes as if they were still in the Sahara, are probably the best documented troops of the French campaign in Flanders, yet probably also the least important. Exoticism took precedence over military or historic relevance. For the cavalry the First World War was already a war too far. The colonial infantrymen, like the Zouaves and the tirailleurs from North and West Africa were all the more important. They made a substantial contribution at difficult moments of the war in Flanders. Groups from other colonies were mobilized and came to Flanders. The historiography in France as well as in Flanders virtually disregarded or forgot this or reduced it to a colourful anecdote.

However, the negation was not complete. Before and during the war so much was said in favour of deploying this large population potential of Africa in the world war that this aspect received considerable attention. General Mangin's argument for a *force noire*[2] that would give France extra troops to absorb its demographic deficit was mainly put into practice during the last two years of war. At the time propagandistic texts also described and praised the *épopée* of the colonial troops. However, all this would soon be forgotten in all subsequent historiography. With the growing interculturality of Europe a number of outstanding studies have recently been published[3], but

this is hardly relevant for Flanders. This is unjustified but probably understandable as the great importance of French colonial troops at the Flemish front occurred in the very early days of the war. However, this was also the case for instance for the *Fusiliers Marins* of (Vice-)Admiral Ronarc'h, who are still renowned. In spite of their exoticism the colonials probably had and have too few advocates that appeal to the imagination, like the Breton mariners who from the outset were supported by the illustrator Charles Fouqueray and historian Charles Le Goffic[4]. This overview does not have this pretention but aims to highlight what has virtually become invisible today in the collective memory of the First World War in Flanders.

Some men of the 4th Regiment Spahis (from Algeria), 1916 (© ECPAD – Médiathèque de la Défense, Paris)

A column of German prisoners of war is accompanied by Spahis near De Moeren. (© Royal Army Museum, Brussels)

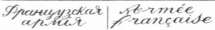

Raoul Dufy (1877-1953): Postcard designs for the Russian troops at the front in France. The postcards represent different soldier types present in the French army. Since 1916 a Russian military force of some 40 000 men was attached to the French army. These cards were intended for them.
(© BDIC-Musée de l'Histoire Contemporaine, Paris)

СПАИСЪ — Spahi

Французская армія | Armée Française

МОРСКОЙ СТРѢЛОКЪ — Fusilier marin

Французская армія | Armée Française

ЗУАВЪ — Zouave

Французская армія | Armée Française

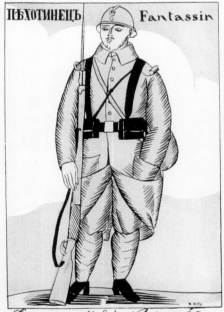

ПѢХОТИНЕЦЪ — Fantassin

Французская армія | Armée Française

СЕНЕГАЛЬСКІЕ СТРѢЛКИ — Tirailleurs sénégalais

Французская армія | Armée Française

АННАМИТСКІЙ СТРѢЛОКЪ — Tirailleur annamite

Французская армія | Armée Française

1. NORTH AFRICA: TIRAILLEURS & ZOUAVES

LES REGIMENTS DE ZOUAVES

This outsider leads the way. Historically the Zouave corps was the first corps to be set up by France in Africa. After the incorporation of Algeria four Zouave regiments were created between 1830 and 1854. Initially the troops were of mixed origin: French and Algerian. The name of the new corps in the French army originated from *Zouaouas*, a Kabylian tribe from the mountains to the east of Algiers that supplied a major part of the new recruits. After the corps of *tirailleurs indigènes* was set up (1840-1841), all the soldiers of Algerian origin transferred to these regiments and from then onwards all Zouaves would be of French origin.

When the First World War broke out it appeared that many of them were born in the North African colonies. Many more were stationed in the active (professional) battalions. Therefore the Zouaves must not be omitted from an overview of non-European French troops in WW1. Furthermore, some names indicate a Spanish and more specifically a Sephardi connection such as Fernandez, Hernandez, Levy, Lopez, Tobaïlem or Ortega. These North African Jews had already acquired the right to French citizenship in 1870 and thus all belonged to the Zouave regiments or to the *bataillons d'Afrique* (see infra) and not to the North African *tirailleurs*. During the First World War the corps of Zouaves and of the (native) tirailleurs became partly intermingled not only as separate battalions and regiments fighting side by side in the North African divisions but also as mixed units, the RMZTs, *régiments mixtes de zouaves et de tirailleurs*. The Zouave regiments mirror the French colonial world of North Africa to the same extent as the tirailleur regiments.

In French military mythology the Zouaves lead the way. They acquired fame through their involvement in battles during the *Second Empire*: Alma (1854), Magenta (1859) and during the Franco-Prussian war (1870). They were also deployed as troops in the colonial oppression in Africa and Asia (Annam, the Boxer Uprising).

At the beginning of the First World War most battalions were established in Morocco and Algeria but

of each regiment a number of battalions were being trained in France (including five *bataillons métropolitains*, from the greater Paris region).

The numbering of the various Zouave units in the First World War is particularly confusing. This was mainly due to the many reorganizations of the French army during the mobilisation and after the first months of the war. Battalions of existing regiments were incorporated in various *régiments de marche*, i.e. regiments ready for action. Others were transferred during reorganizations, others still were absorbed, and new units with other names were created. Meanwhile, the individual registration of many Zouaves continued to mention their original regiment.

Thus on 29 October 1914 a *1er Régiment de Zouaves* (1 Z) in the *38e Division d'Infanterie* (38e DI) arrived in Veurne. But at the same time a regiment by the same name, which played an important part in the Second Battle of Ypres, was present in the *45e Division d'Infanterie*. In December 1914, for no specific reason that regiment became the *7e Régiment*

A member of the 1st regiment Zouaves in Veurne, November 1914, meeting the local population. The dark blue baggy pants are richly embroidered with pre-war braiding. (© Royal Army and Military History Museum, Brussels)

A typical tirailleur of 1914: Chechia headwear, light blue baggy pants and tunic with yellow braiding and light blue tombô as a characteristic of the tirailleur from Tunis. (© Collection Philippe Oosterlinck)

de Marche de Zouaves (7 RMZ) and on 20 June 1915 it merged with the 3rd battalion of the *4ᵉ Régiment de Tirailleurs* that was stationed in Morocco to become the 3rd RMZT. The reason for this last reorganization and change of name was simply the enormous loss of men during the first ten months of war. Confusing? Certainly, but the date of death is usually a good clue. For instance according to the register of the only large French necropolis in the Flanders' Westhoek, *Saint-Charles de Potyze* in Ypres, the Zouaves Emile Maurer, Vincent Fluxia and Victor Dantin all belonged to the *1ᵉʳ Régiment de Zouaves*. Dantin fell on 30 October 1914 near Drie Grachten, Maurer on 23 April 1915 in the first counteroffensive after the gas attack between Boezinge and Pilkem and Fluxia died on 21 June 1915 near Steenstraat. All three had indeed died in the vicinity of the Ypres-Yser Canal, but the first had fought with the 1 Z in the 38th division, the second with the 7th RMZ and the last in the newly created 3rd RMZT. Both last units belonged to the 45th Algerian division, and whereas Dantin came from Béthune in Northern France, Maurer was born in Breisach am Rhein (in Germany) and Fluxia in the Département d'Alger. The last two had indeed been recruited in Algiers.

It only really becomes confusing when the administration clerks subsequently completed or transcribed personal records or *journaux de marches* (regimental diaries) using the current denomination of the unit instead of its original denomination.

The participation of French colonial troops in the war in Flanders therefore only becomes clear when you also explain the date of the facts and the origin of the soldiers concerned.

There is similar confusion about name and origin in the other major North African army group.

Zouaves and tirailleurs in primitive trenches near Ypres, spring 1915.

An NCO of 7 RMZ drinking from a seized German messtin, under the interested eye of a group 1 BILA. Probably a scene of the 45ᵉ DI after the Second Battle of Ypres.
(© Royal Army and Military History Museum, Brussels)

A mixed unit of *zouaves* and *tirailleurs* in the trenches along the Yser before Nieuport, 1915-1916.
(© In Flanders Fields Museum)

— LES REGIMENTS DE TIRAILLEURS 1914-1918

On the eve of the First World War nine regiments of tirailleurs from North Africa were formed, some 40 battalions in all. As from 1840 *Régiments de Tirailleurs indigènes* had been set up with recruits from the indigenous population of Algeria. From the start there were three such regiments and eventually four. The first three were called the *Régiments de tirailleurs algériens* and had recruitment bases in respectively Algiers (town and province) (1e RTA), Oran (2e RTA) and Constantine (3e RTA). In 1884 a regiment of *tirailleurs tunisiens*, (4e RTA of 4e RTT) from Tunisia was also created. In the years of chaos and uprising in the Protectorate of Morocco they were often deployed for so-called pacification assignments. In 1913 the existing regiments were doubled. The new regiment was allocated the original number plus four. This is how the 5e and 9e RTI (*indigènes)* or RTA (*algériens*) were created out of the 1e RTA (i.e. from Algiers), the 6e (from the 2e) from Oran, the 7e from Constantine and the 8e RTT from Tunis. In 1912

various battalions of regiments stationed in Morocco were renamed to become *Régiments de Marche de Tirailleurs*, 2 from Eastern Morocco, a third from Western Morocco. In 1914 no fewer than 19 of the 40 battalions of tirailleurs were established in Morocco. Six of them remained behind, two did not leave Algeria. All other 32 battalions left for the War in 1914. Each battalion comprised four companies of approximately 200 to 250 men. In total an army of almost 30,000 infantrymen supplemented with the necessary staffs. More than three quarters of them were active soldiers, the rest were reserves. All superior officers were French, the Non-Commissioned Officers were both white French and *indigènes*. The three divisions that originally included North African troops (initially the 37e, 38e and 45e DI) all had regiments of tirailleurs. The Moroccan division (*Division de marche d'infanterie coloniale du Maroc*) initially (briefly) only consisted of battalions of tirailleurs. A further two separate (3rd and 4th) Moroccan brigades followed.

A North African *tirailleur* in De Moeren, May 1915.
(© Royal Army Museum, Brussels)

Tunisian *tirailleurs* in front of their camp in Oostduinkerke-Bad,
1 November 1915. (© BDIC-Musée de l'Histoire Contemporaine, Paris)

On the Western Front these tirailleurs were reorganized into ten different marching regiments of tirailleurs and two *régiments mixtes*, mixed with Zouaves. However, further changes would be made to these newly appointed units in 1914 and 1915.

Yet another example from Flanders, read on the few graves of tirailleurs to be found here. AHMED BEN ZIDI BEN ALI Smaïl was one of the many hundreds of North Africans to die during the Battle of the Yser on 11 November 1914 along the Ypres-Yser Canal between Drie Grachten and Steenstraat. He is one of the few to have a known grave. His records state that he belonged to the 8th RTT, whereas you can read on his grave in St. Charles de Potyze in Ypres that he belonged to the '4 T'. His registration refers to his original 'organic' regiment, the 4th RTA (or RTT) from Tunisia, from which the 8th had originated. Another casualty of St. Charles, EL MOULDI ben Othman ben Mabrouk El Bechraoui was a tirailleur 2nd class in the 8th T when he was killed to the North of Ypres on 9 May 1915. He originated from Tunisia and had been active in the Tunisian army since 1909. MOHAMED BEN BRAHIM Ben Nasser, sub-lieutenant in the *8ᵉ Régiment de Marche de Tirailleurs* of Tunisia, who died in the trenches near Nieuwpoort on 20 March 1916, lies buried near the church of Koksijde Dorp (Koksijde Village). All three were Tunisian tirailleurs from the 8th regiment. However, if you take a closer look it becomes more intricate. The dead of 11 November 1914 along the Canal had attacked with the 38th division. A battalion of 8 RTT was virtually wiped out on 10 and 11 November. Consequently, the regiment was temporarily withdrawn from the front in January 1915. The *Régiment de Marche de Tunisie*, 8 RMT, that subsequently fought in the Second Battle of Ypres, belonged to the new 152ᵉ DI, which was immediately dispatched to Steenstraat and Het Sas van Boezinge (Boezinge Lock) as reinforcement after the gas attack. Six weeks later this regiment would partly merge with the new 4 RMZT. The sub-lieutenant of 8 RMT in Koksijde belonged to the new/restored 8 RMT that only returned to its original division (38ᵉ DI) in Nieuwpoort in October 1915. What you see is not always how it was.

For reasons of clarity we have included a short list of the units present in Flanders.

Woesten, 12 July 1916. In the shadow of the ruins of the small church there are some Muslim graves: North African *tirailleurs* who had died the year before near Ypres. Cyriel Buysse wrote about a similar spot near Adinkerke in 1916: ... ...*with emotion and astonishment you reach a small spot where small oddly shaped white gravestones stand on which are painted or engraved letters and epitaphs that strike us here as exotic and movingly strange. These are the graves of the fallen Moroccans and Senegalese.*"
(© BDIC-Musée de l'Histoire Contemporaine, Paris)

—ZOUAVE AND TIRAILLEUR UNITS ON THE FLEMISH FRONT

(abbreviations used: battalion = Bn, regiment = R, company = Cie, Infantry Division = DI; others as indicated in the text)

1 Z, 1 RMZ

1er Régiment de Zouaves (1 Z) in 75th Infantry brigade of the 38ᵉ DI (4, 5, 11ᵉ Bns of the 1st regiment Zouaves). The 38th division was in Flanders from 29 October 1914 and remained there until April 1916. It was mainly deployed on the Yser front but also in the Ypres Salient (mainly in November and December 1914).

In December 1914 their name changed to the *1er Régiment de Marche de Zouaves* (1 RMZ). The regiment then transferred to the 76th Infantry brigade. After the dreadful month of November in Flanders (the Drie Grachten sector, see infra) the 1 RMZ was

King Albert reviewing tirailleurs of the 38e DI. Veurne, 3 November 1914.
(© Royal Army and Military History Museum, Brussels)

Gefangene Turkos,
Araber aus Algier
in ihrer Winterkleidung,
von der Kampffront
Nieuport - Dixmuiden.

allowed to rest and would only return in February 1915, this time near Nieuwpoort. In July 1915 the 1 RMZ transferred to the 25e DI and left Flanders.

7 RMZ, 3 RMZT

Régiment de Marche du 1er Zouaves (1 Z) in the 45e DI. In December this 1 Z (with the 6th and 14th Bns of the 1st regiment and the 6th Bn of the 4th) became the 7 RMZ to distinguish it from the similarly named unit in the 38th division. The 45th division arrived in Flanders on 15 April 1915 and left the Flemish front a first time in March 1916, to return on 8 October 1916 and finally left Belgium for good in early January 1917.

In July 1915 7 RMZ became the *3e Régiment mixte de zouaves et de tirailleurs* (3 RMZT). To this end the battalion of the 4th regiment was replaced with the 3rd Bn of the *4e Régiment de marche de tirailleurs*. As stated above the latter was a Tunisian regiment. We often see on gravestones or in French army[5] records that soldiers who died before July 1915 had already been assigned to the 3 RMZT.

2 bis Z

There was a similar name confusion between the two 2 Z regiments in resp. the 37e DI and the 45e DI. As from January the name *2e Régiment bis de zouaves* was given to the unit in the 45th. In October 1915 2 bis Z left the 45e DI and departed for Macedonia.

3 bis Z

Same name confusion between regiments 3 Z in the 37e DI and the 45e DI. When that regiment arrived in Flanders with the 45e DI it was already called the *3e Régiment bis de zouaves* (3 bis Z). This unit remained in Flanders until the beginning of 1917.

According to the caption on this German propaganda photo from the winter of 1914-1915 these Algerians were taken prisoner of war at the Yser front. Their captors gave them a chunk of bread each.

(© Bildarchiv Preußischer Kulturbesitz, Berlin)

4 Z, 6 RMZ, 4 RMZ

The *Régiment de marche du 4ᵉ zouaves* (4 Z) was the other Zouave regiment of the 38ᵉ DI. This regiment was also present in Flanders from 29 October 1914 and remained there until the end of 1915. It was the first North African unit in the Ypres Salient (as from 2 November near Zillebeke, then near Veldhoek). 4 Z partly comprised battalions of the Paris region (the 5ᵉ and 11ᵉ Bns from Rosny-sous-Bois, one of the Parisian camps, in addition to the 3ᵉ and 4ᵉ Bns from Tunis). In December 1914, the regiment was briefly called the 6 RMZ by analogy with the 7th, but finally it became the *4ᵉ Régiment de marche de zouaves.* (4 RMZ).

There is a similar massive name confusion among the regiments of tirailleurs.

1 RMT, 9 RMT

The *1er Régiment de marche de tirailleurs* (1 RMT) had three battalions (2 of the 1e RTA and one of the 9e RTA). Here also there is confusion with the 1st tirailleur regiment of the 45ᵉ DI. Consequently, in December the 1 RMT briefly became 3 and as from March 1915 9 RMT. 1 or 9 RMT belonged to the 75th Brigade in de 38ᵉ DI. In June 1915 this brigade transferred to the 25ᵉ DI, and departed for France.

The *1er Régiment de tirailleurs de marche* (1 RMT) was the 1st tirailleur regiment of the 45ᵉ DI, with also three battalions, from resp. Algiers, Fez and Rabat. In the records and on the graves in Flanders we usually find a reference to the old pre-war division of the nine, so-called 'organic' regiments. For the victims in Flanders the distinction is usually straightforward: every indication 1 RMT (or 1 T) before 15 April 1915 is for a member of 38ᵉ DI, after that usually of the 45ᵉ DI.

4 RMT

After a short period in the 38ᵉ DI the *4ᵉ Régiment de marche de tirailleurs* transferred with two battalions of the 4th (R)T(T) to the *Division marocaine* in France in December. The unit returned with the *4ᵉ Brigade du Maroc* after the gas attack of 22 April 1915, as a part of 152ᵉ DI.

8 RMT

The *Régiment de marche du 8ᵉ tirailleurs* (8 RMT) belonged to the 38ᵉ DI. It only comprised two battalions of the 8ᵉ RTT. A third battalion would only be assigned to it in August 1915. It was withdrawn from the front from January to July 1915 for recovery due to heavy losses.

8 RMT(I), 4 RMZT

Of the two Tunisian regiments (4 and 8 RTT) one more *régiment de marche* was formed that was officially called the 8ᵉ *Régiment de marche de tirailleurs indigènes*, but which was often simply referred to as the 8 RMT. This regiment belonged to the 4th Moroc-

A group of tirailleurs posing with a Flemish girl in an open polder landscape, 1915.
(© Royal Army and Military History Museum, Brussels)

Two tirailleurs somewhere behind the front in Flanders, around 1915. (© Royal Army and Military History Museum, Brussels)

can Brigade that only joined the 152ᵉ DI in April 1915 for deployment on the front near Ypres. On 21 June 1915 one battalion returned to North Africa and the 8 RMT(I) merged with a battalion of the 4 RMZ to form the *4ᵉ Régiment mixte de zouaves et de tirailleurs* (4 RMZT) in the 45ᵉ DI.

7 RMT

Four battalions of tirailleurs stationed in Morocco were assigned to the Moroccan division that arrived in France at the end of August. Initially organized in two mixed regiments of Zouaves and tirailleurs, the tirailleurs and Zouaves were split after incurring heavy losses in the Ardennes. On 13 November 1914 the 2nd brigade of the division arrived at the front on the Ypres-Yser Canal, where they recaptured the *Bois triangulaire* near Bikschote on 17 November. In December the *Régiment de marche de tirailleurs de la Division marocaine* was given its own name, the *7e Régiment de marche de tirailleurs* (7 RMT). After this they were deployed near Hill 60 and then (around 22 December 1914) on the right bank of the Yser near Lombaardzijde and Nieuwpoort. The division was retired at the end of January 1915 near Dunkerque.

8 RMZ

The battalions of Zouaves of the Moroccan division followed the same route as the battalions of tirailleurs. Initially mixed then separately as the *Régiment de marche de zouaves de la Division marocaine* they finally became the *8ᵉ Régiment de marche de zouaves* (8 RMZ) in December 1914. In May 1915 the Moroccan division left for Artois.

2, 3, 5, 6 R(M)T

On French cemeteries in Flanders, on both sides of the French/Belgian border, there are occasional references to these other tirailleur regiments. They were not present as a unit in the war in Flanders, however, as already stated there are many references to the old 'organic' regiments in North Africa. Some units also belonged to the 37ᵉ DI that was resting nearby.

1, 3 en 4 RMZT

During the mobilisation of the North African troops in August and September it was difficult to quickly transfer to France all the troops stationed in Morocco. After the first two Moroccan brigades

had merged into one division (see under 7 RMT), two other brigades were merged in September 1914. Here also this initially occurred with mixed units of Zouaves and tirailleurs. Later, when some battalions had virtually been wiped out, they proceeded in the same way. This is why there were also mixed regiments at the front in Flanders. The 3rd and 4th have already been introduced to this end, only the 1st remained.

1 RMZT, 9 RMZ

The 3rd and 4th Moroccan Brigades were unable to form a second Moroccan division like the 1st and 2nd before them. Once they had arrived in France it appeared that there was no artillery available. The 3rd Moroccan brigade was first integrated in the 37ᵉ DI and subsequently as from 14 April 1915, in the 153ᵉ DI. Just like the 152nd this division would be called as reinforcement to the front near Ypres as from 23 April 1915 after the first gas attack. The brigade included the mixed regiment 1 RMZT, comprising a battalion of Zouaves and two battalions of tirailleurs. The other regiment was the *9ᵉ régiment de marche de zouaves* (9 RMZ).

The third 'Algerian' division, 37ᵉ DI, was not deployed at the front in Flanders. After having lost almost half its troops in Champagne the division came to rest in the vicinity of Dunkerque and Bergues during the first winter of the war.

Sheep being slaughtered in the yard of
a farm for the benefit of the *tirailleurs marocains*.
(© BDIC-Musée de l'Histoire Contemporaine, Paris)

— BATTLES OF TIRAILLEURS AND ZOUAVES IN FLANDERS

Army reorganizations are always motivated by bad experiences: major losses, poor organization. The multiple changes among the regiments of tirailleurs and Zouaves in the first year of war are indicative of both. The losses incurred during the first year of war were dreadful. Also at the front in Flanders. Even today it is very difficult to obtain an accurate figure of these losses. The repatriation of French bodies as from the end of 1920 and the large numbers of missing soldiers who are not remembered by name by the French war graves agency mean that we only know a fraction (estimated at 20%) of all French dead in Flanders[6]. Via the personal records of the fallen soldiers available via the website of the French Ministry of Defence we can often learn more. However, to date (2008) these data are not yet available in a digital database. There are certainly many hundreds and probably thousands of North African dead. The more than 1250 names of tirailleurs and Zouaves we have been able to gather ourselves from the death records of the French army (see www.inflandersfields.be)[7] also show that an enormous number of victims have no grave, or that these graves were subsequently lost. In our provisional list 75% of the tirailleurs and 47% of the Zouaves have no known grave. Furthermore, it would appear that a number of colonial casualties were never entered in the administrative records. As we do not hold exhaustive figures we are unable to prove the extent of this 'negligence' but there is a prevailing feeling that as in the British Empire, French colonial fatalities were less carefully processed than their European colleagues.

RAMSKAPELLE — DRIE GRACHTEN

38e DI was the first 'Algerian' division to arrive in the Westhoek at the end of October 1914. They were used to strengthen the Belgian army during the Battle of the Yser. From August to 5 November 1914, when the 3rd battalion *d'Infanterie légère d'Afrique* joined it (see below), the division consisted entirely of units from North Africa, Zouaves and tirailleurs, the 1st and the 4th regiment Zouaves and the 1st and 8th regiment tirailleurs. 8 RMT/RTT was the first unit in the 38e DI to suffer major losses in Flanders, near Ramskapelle on 30 October. Cyriel Buysse discovered these graves in 1916 when he wrote:

> *Ramskapelle: rough death and soft prayer! ...with emotion and astonishment you reach a small spot where small oddly shaped white gravestones stand on which are painted or engraved letters and epitaphs that strike us here as exotic and movingly strange. These are the graves of the fallen Moroccans and Senegalese.*[8]

Moroccans were not (yet) present, but the Senegalese were, as we will see below, but the greatest losses were among the Tunisian tirailleurs of the 8e RTT.

During the month of November matters became even worse. To the North and South of Diksmuide French troops tried to stop the German advance. Diksmuide, which had been defended as from 22 Oc-

A caravan of *tirailleurs* and *Spahis* is passing before the inn In de Sportwereld in Roesbrugge-Haringe, in the spring of 1915. The event drew the full attention of the innkeeper and of her neighbour, the hairdresser. (© In Flanders Fields Museum)

tober by the Fusiliers Marins and a Belgian battalion, fell on 10 November 1914. The flooding of the right bank of the Yser (the so-called Inundation of the Blankaert) brought salvation when the town had to be surrendered but until that moment the French commanders had their minds set on the attack. They aimed to push back the Germans to the South of Diksmuide, in the sectors Luigem, Drie Grachten, Pijpegale (*Maison du Passeur* or *Withuis*), Steenstraat, Bikschote (Kortekeer). On 9 November 1914, General Humbert, commander of the 32nd army corps (which included the 38ᵉ DI) claimed that the assaults may not have always proved successful but that *'yet again we have shown that under the leadership of resolute leaders, the French soldier was irresistible in a bayonet attack.'*[9] The French soldier was amongst others also a Zouave stationed in Algeria or a tirailleur of the Tunisian army, hundreds of which 'disappeared in battle' (*disparus au combat*) during assaults that were barely supported by the artillery. The mutual attacks between Germans and French claimed thousands of lives for little more than a status quo along the canal and the line near Bikschote. Whereas the Germans were fairly successful during the first ten days of the month, the French counterattacks in the second half of the month (on 17 November, 2nd Moroccan Brigade in the *Bois triangulaire*) and in December (38ᵉ DI, Fusiliers Marins, 87 DIT along the canal) allowed to recapture the positions lost to the Germans.

A famous anecdote of this chilling period of *assauts à la baïonnette* (bayonet assaults) is the German at-tempt to capture the bridgehead near Drie Grachten on 12 November after the *Maison du Passeur* on 9 November. To this end they used a number of Zouave prisoners of war as a human shield. As the Zouaves of 1 Z saw their mates coming towards them in the first line they did not shoot. Until one of the prisoners shouted out that it was an ambush and that they had to shoot to prevent the Germans from capturing the bridge. The words uttered by the Zouave, who remains unknown and who was obviously killed, can still be read today on a stone in the façade of the former inn Café Drie Grachten: *'Mais tirez donc, n. de D.'* — well shoot damn you.

Much attention was subsequently paid to this heroism that definitely existed. The feat of the *Zouave inconnu* of '*Drie Gratchen*' (sic) soon found its way to the repertoire of the *café-concerts* in Paris, where a programme critical of the authority or humanitarian programme had made way for the *Union sacrée* and great patriotism[10].

CÔTE 60 (HILL 60)

At the front exhaustion caused by the 'irresistible' charges of the tirailleurs and Zouaves had become noticeable. When on 8 December the 15th Cie of 8ᵉ RTT (4th battalion) was allowed to rest in Fintele (Pollinkhove) after weeks of battles along the canal, the tirailleurs were already recalled after half an hour to rush to the South East of the Ypres Salient to launch a counterattack near *Côte 60* (Hill 60) and Verbrande Molen which had just been lost to the enemy. They marched the 25 km to the new front

under protest and some men were left behind because of exhaustion. After successive pointless attacks an order was finally disregarded on 13 December. The diary of the commanding unit, 1 RMT, gives a detailed account of the incident:

At 8.20 a.m. Commandant Amis gave the signal to attack. Capitaine Lasserre stood up and jumped out of the trench raising his kepi and pointing towards the direction. The Zouaves, the 1st half-section of the Engineers and the 5ᵉ Cie [1 RMT] advanced at a run shouting: Let's go.

Once they had advanced 30 m. the Ct ordered the Cie of the 8ᵉ T to follow the movement to form the 2nd wave of the assault, but he was unable to move this Cie whose men demonstrated the most absolute inertia. Meanwhile, the 1ˢᵗ wave was falling in bunches, there were many losses and a small part of the attackers had reached the German trenches. Ahead on the right were Capitaine Lasserre, an NCO, a corporal and some fifteen men, on the left an NCO and 20 men; they jumped into the German trenches and disappeared from the sight of our lines. Some men jumped back and sheltered in a shell hole in a blind angle just a few metres away from the German trenches and would return to our lines during the night. The 9ᵉ Cie then the 12ᵉ took position behind the Cie of the 8ᵉ T but time was running out, the enemy line which the Germans had briefly

been forced to evacuate because of the artillery fire before the attack had had the time to redeploy. Enemy fire, gunfire, machine guns, shellings had intensified. Launching a new assault column in these conditions would be doomed for certain failure. The attack had failed and could only be repeated after a new artillery intervention.[11]

General d'Urbal, commander of the French 8th army in Roesbrugge, was outraged. On 15 December he issued the fatal order to *decimate* the 15th Cie, contrary to every directive, and in spite of the protests of the division general De Bazelaire.

My orders are that one tirailleur in 10 of the company that refused to march be drawn, without prejudice to the instigators of this insubordination, if they become subsequently known, that the tirailleurs be marched before the front carrying a notice with the word 'Coward' in French and Arabic; they shall be shot immediately afterwards.[12]

There is obviously no trace of the shot soldiers. Colonel d'Anselme, commander of 1 RMT, who had led the counterattacks on Hill 60, kept going until 19 December when he decided that without a proper siege the hill would never again fall into French hands. The British would demonstrate the accuracy of this analysis in the following spring.

By Christmas everything had quietened down

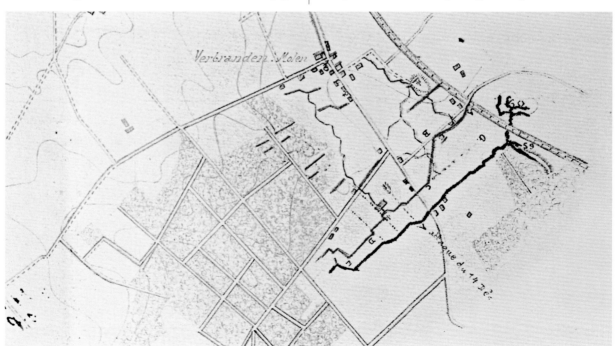

for the tirailleurs near Verbrande Molen. The whole 1 RMT as well as the 4th battalion of 8 RMT were allowed to rest in Poperinge. Between 12 November and 17 December the 4th battalion had incurred 200 dead and missing and at least as many injured soldiers. In Poperinge Capitaine Gendre was buried with great military honours, he was the first fallen officer to have been brought back.[13] In 1 RMT on Boxing Day a *conseil de guerre spécial* (special court martial in the field) was convened to judge tirailleur 2nd class Thiriet, who was accused of self-mutilation. The tirailleur was given the death penalty, which was carried out on the following morning in Poperinge. There is no trace of tirailleur Thiriet either, he was not included in the loss statistics of his unit and there is no known death record of him.

Towards the end of the year 1 RMT also drew up a balance of the campaign in Flanders: between 30 October and 31 December 1914 the regiment suffered 1206 losses: 26 officers (9 dead, 12 wounded and 5 missing) and 1180 men (264 dead, 790 wounded and 126 missing). In our previously mentioned meagre dead register, we find 28 names for 8 RMT and 64 names for 1 RMT, of which only 22 have a known grave, or resp. and at the most (assuming that not a single missing soldier was killed and no injured soldier later died of his injuries) 19.4% and 4.6%. In short in the Flemish front region there is almost *no* trace (and hardly anything is known)[14] of the tragedy that struck the North African troops.

The second and last time tirailleurs and Zouaves would be tested to such an extent on the Flemish front was during the Second Battle of Ypres (22 April — 24 May 1915). The ranks of the *anciens*, the prewar professional soldiers, have meanwhile been supplemented with many new recruits with little training or with soldiers wounded in 1914 who had recovered. In mid-April 1915 the 45th Algerian division arrived in the Ypres Salient with recovered regiments of Zouaves (2 bis, 3 bis, 7 RMZ) and tirailleurs (1 RMT) and with two battalions *d'Infanterie légère d'Afrique* and a squadron of *Spahis*.

2. NORTH AFRICA: BATAILLONS D'AFRIQUE AND SPAHIS

— ESCADRONS DE SPAHIS

The *Spahis* were colonial cavalry, like the *Chasseurs d'Afrique*. Just like the other North African regiments they had originated in the first years of French colonization in the Maghreb. In the First World War four regiments from Algeria and one from Morocco were deployed on the Western Front, but they only played a minor part in trench warfare. By the time the war reached Flanders the cavalry charges were already a thing of the past, or a figment of the imagination of overly optimistic generals, who in spite of everything wanted to keep cavalry units on stand-by for the great moment of the breakthrough (which would never happen). In the meantime... the desert horsemen waited, carried out communication assignments and inspired the *iconographers* of this war to emblematic pictures of the World in the Westhoek. The filmed *Spahis* often belonged to the 10th

Situation map of one of the many French December attacks near Côte 60 (Hill 60). This is where the 15ᵉ Cie 8 RMT refused to attack on 13 December. With fatal consequences.
(© Service Historique de la Défense, Vincennes)

Two Spahis in a camp near Hoogstade, 1914-15.
(© Royal Army and Military History Museum, Brussels)

squadron of 45ᵉ DI. The film, which was made on the beach of De Panne, in the dunes of Koksijde or on farms near Veurne appealed to the imagination, even though the Spahis were incorrectly called *Goumiers*. The painting by Paul Jouve *A Spahi near Ypres, June 1915* is equally impressive. Jouve was an *animalier*, a painter of wild animals, and even before the war he was a renowned specialist of North African scenes. This is probably why the *Musée de l'Armée* sent him along with the 2 bis Z to film the North Africans of 45ᵉ DI. The painted scene, the watch next to the regimental flag, can also be seen in the film. The flag flaps in the Westerly wind, the tents stand at the foot of a Flemish mill, but the colourful saddles of the desert horsemen are left untackled and unused.

The most telling icon of all the foreign presences in the Westhoek is in my opinion the set of photos taken opposite the *Estaminet In de Sportwereld* in

A camp of Spahis near Mardyck (Dunkirk), July 1915.
(© Royal Army Museum, Brussels)

Food supply of the Spahis. West-Vleteren, May 1915.
(© Royal Army and Military History Museum, Brussels)

Paul Jouve (1878-1973): A Spahi near Ypres, June 1915. (© In Flanders Fields Museum)

The tent of the Colonel of a Spahi regiment.
Northern France, 1916.
(© BDIC-Musée de l'Histoire Contemporaine, Paris)

Men of the 2d Regiment Spahis in front of
an improvised café. Northern France, 1916.
(© BDIC-Musée de l'Histoire Contemporaine, Paris)

Roesbrugge-Haringe. A battalion tirailleurs and a squadron *Spahis* are passing by, the innkeeper of the café has heard them first and calls her husband in the hairdressing saloon next door. Soon Flemish women, men and children are watching them absolutely fascinated. The hairdresser shouts something at the foot-soldiers and feigns nonchalant indifference. Meanwhile the horsemen ride past, silent and utterly indifferent to the people staring at them. Maybe they were lost in dark considerations, as Ben Chérif suggested in *Ahmed ben Mostapha, Goumier* (1920), whether they should serve France, the country that had aroused their dormant country or the German Emperor and his ally the Ottoman Emir el Mounimin, Prince of True Believers, and hence one of them...[15]

A walking stick whose knob represents the head of a Spahi. The stick was made by a Spahi, billeted near the Abbey of Saint Sixtus near West-Vleteren, and donated to the Belgian civilian Julien Delplace who lived nearby and worked for the monks.
(In Flanders Fields Museum)

Chef d'escadron Moog between his men of the 4th Regiment Spahis, 1916-1917.
(© ECPAD – Médiathèque de la Défense, Paris)

— BATAILLONS D'INFANTERIE LÉGÈRE D'AFRIQUE

Things were quite different for the *Bataillons d'Infanterie légères d'Afrique* (BILA) or *les Bat'Af's* in short, or maybe not. They were not North Africans but French. These battalions had originated as from 1832 as an occupation force in the North African colonies. As would later become the task of the entire French colonial army in other colonial areas, *l'Infanterie coloniale* (see further). But the *bataillons* maintained their highly specific status. As serving abroad was not always an enjoyable prospect the units of the BILA evolved to become regiments of punished soldiers. They were called *les zéphyrs* and later mainly *les joyeux*. '*Joyous, the lost children who are not punished soldiers, but simply soldiers united in a special corps for civilian reasons,* 'wrote Pierre MacOrlan[16]. Hence they were not punitive companies of the army, but just as in the foreign legion many soldiers joined the *Bat'Af's* because they had misbehaved in civilian life. As from the end of the 19th century recruitment actively focused on this population group or among civilians who had previously shirked the general military service. The lure of the new opportunity in the army.

Once the Zouaves and tirailleurs had left for France the BILAs were the actual occupation army in North Africa. After the catastrophic campaign of the first months in terms of casualties it was decided to send some of them to Europe also. At the beginning of October the order was received to create a 3rd *Bataillon de marche d'infanterie légère d'Afrique* (3 BILA)

in the occupation force of Tunisia, that would consist of four companies of 250 men from the 4th and 5th 'organic' battalions. On 27 October 1914 they embarked in Tunis. On 5 November they already bivouacked in Hoogstade, as reinforcement for the seriously weakened 38ᵉ DI. The first four dead fell the following day along the Ypres-Yser Canal, just to the North of *la Maison du Passeur*. Although the *joyeux* did not enjoy a particularly good reputation in the army, they did the utmost to prove that their reputation was undeserved at the front. Two months later they had participated in three major attacks (two at the *Maison du Passeur* and one near Verbrande Molen (*Hill 60*)) they had received three commendations in the army, army corps and division and suffered major losses. The battalion commander and 12 other officers had been killed together with over 100 men. Of the more than 1100 *batailloneux* who had left Africa at the end of October 1914 only 552 remained standing in the Flemish fields near Busseboom[17] on 10 January 1915.

At the beginning of February 3 BILA was transferred to the 45ᵉ DI, in which 1 BILA had already been incorporated while it was fighting on the Somme. On 15 April 1915 the whole division arrived in the Ypres Salient. The *Bataillons d'Infanterie Légère d'Afrique* had meanwhile been supplemented with fresh *joyeux* and with groups of *chasseurs d'Afrique*.

THE SECOND BATTLE OF YPRES

The last two French divisions still present in the Ypres Salient on 22 April 1915, namely the 87th DIT

from Britanny and the Calvados and the 45ᵉ DI from North Africa (recently arrived), fell victim to the first gas attack. How this occurred is described elsewhere[18]. Here we will try to define the always underestimated participation of the North Africans and mixed French/African troops. In the sector of the 45ᵉ DI, 1 BILA and the 1st and 2nd battalion 1 RMT were in the front line from left to right between the road Bikschote-Langemark and the road Poelkapelle-Ypres. Behind them, as support near *Ferme Morteldje* (later renamed *Turco Farm* by the British in reference to the North Africans), up to the bridges and footbridges over the Ypres-Yser Canal, each time two companies of 2 bis Z and 7 RMZ.

The losses of the first day will probably never be known exactly. Men were overcome by the gas in the first line and died, others managed to escape but died later of their injuries. The front line collapsed, everyone who was able to tried to escape from the gas. Not all regiment diaries were preserved; they were usually incomplete and offered few details as many witnesses had fallen during battle. Almost all reports were written days later. The number of dead was always underestimated as they had no idea at the time how many injured and missing would finally have to be added to the death toll. Total losses for the first day and for the three battalions in the front line were estimated at 60%, the next day the brigade diary reported: *'the units of the Brigade who were in the first line on the 22nd no longer exist.'* In the period from 22 to 28 April the 1 RMT lost 24 officers and 1170 men, 1 BILA did not even give a total death toll. Other North African troops also suffered dreadful losses. The Zouave units in support (7 RMZ, 2 bis and 3 bis) were also hit by the gas cloud. Yet the main losses were incurred during the counterattacks that were launched that same evening and night and continued for a full three weeks. Canadians, British, Indians and Irish held the line from near Morteldje/Turco Farm towards Sint-Juliaan. The three Zouave regiments, occasionally alternating with units of tirailleurs and *chasseurs à pied*, were present from the Canal to Turco Farm. No total figures are available but a unit like the 2nd battalion of 2 bis Z, which quite exceptionally listed all the names of the dead, and which had been in the heat of the battle during the first days, totalled more than 200 dead, i.e. over a quarter of all deployable troops.

Among the divisions sent as reinforcement (amongst others the new 152ᵉ DI and 153ᵉ DI) were also the 4th and 3rd Moroccan brigades. They included 4 RMT and 8 RMT in the 3rd (153ᵉ DI) and 9 RMZ and 1RMZT in the 4th Moroccan Brigade (152ᵉ DI). They helped recapture the area between Lizerne and Het Sas on the left bank of the canal. The 4th Moroccan Brigade also helped during the counterattacks on Pilkem Ridge with the 90th Brigade (45ᵉ DI) led by Colonel Mordacq. At Steenstrate 4 RMZ (of the 38ᵉ DI near Nieuwpoort) also assisted. All these units suffered heavy losses.

At the end of the Second Battle of Ypres thousands of North African troops had fallen victim to the gas attacks and to the heavy battles during allied counterattacks. Insofar as we were able to count more than thousand of them were killed.

For the remainder of the war in Flanders North Africans were only deployed outside the Ypres Salient, which had become entirely British after the Second Battle of Ypres. The tirailleurs and Zouaves of the 45ᵉ DI were positioned in the sector Boezinge — Steenstraat, on the right flank of the Belgian army; the men of the 38ᵉ DI were positioned on the flank of the Belgians near Nieuwpoort. As from October 1915 the 45ᵉ DI also arrived in Nieuwpoort (*Grande Dune* — Lombaardzijde, Nieuwpoort Bad). The division disappeared for an 'intermezzo' near Verdun and the Somme from March through October 1916, but then returned to Nieuwpoort until January 1917, with in its ranks the known and newly mixed regiments.

When Jean Cocteau served as a French Red Cross medical orderly in this sector from December 1915 until June 1916, he was highly fascinated by the world of the fusiliers marins, tirailleurs and Zouaves. They are the real characters of his lyrical war epiphany *Discours du Grand Sommeil*. In other poems (*La Douche, Ballade de l'enfant du Nord*) he draws a picture of black troops. He was probably referring to the dark Maures (Mauritanians) from the regiments of tirailleurs, and not to the West Africans from the *Régiments de tirailleurs Sénégalais*, who had left the Yser front a long time ago.

Probably members of 9 RMZ having arrived with 153ᵉ DI on 23 April 1915, along the road from Lizerne to Boezinge. The following night this unit stormed the German positions on Het Sas.

3.BLACK AFRICA: TIRAILLEURS SÉNÉGALAIS

— THE COLONIAL ARMY

As befitted a colonial world power France had a large colonial army that included a white/French occupation force and native troops. The situation on the eve of the First World War was as follows.

There were three white divisions of the *Infanterie coloniale* in France: 1ᵉ (stationed in Paris), 2ᵉ (Toulon), 3ᵉ (Brest) and there were large detachments (called *Groupements* or *Groupes*) in all colonies. These comprised native troops (*indigènes*) led by French officers (white) and occasionally reinforced/controlled by an extra white battalion. In total there were eight such colonial armies: *Indochine* (Hanoi), *Chine* (occupation force in Tien-tsin — today: Tianjin), *Antilles* (Martinique), *Pacifique* (New Caledonia) and four African detachments: two smaller detachments in *Afrique équatoriale* (Brazzaville, Tchad — Fort Lamy, today N'Djamena) and *Afrique oriëntale* (Madagascar) with its own *Tirailleurs Malgaches*.

The detachments in North and West-Africa were far greater. West Africa consisted of a large group of black troops, supplemented with/led by one battalion of whites. The black troops were *Régiments de Tirailleurs Sénégalais*. Created as from 1857 they were the largest native group after the tirailleurs of Algeria, with 1 RTS (stationed in St.Louis), 2 RTS (Kali), 3 RTS (Ivory Coast), 4 RTS (Dakar) and two more battalions in Mali (Tomboctou, Zinder), with their own cavalry: *les Spahis sénégalais* (St.Louis). *Sénégalais* as such is a misleading term, not all tirailleurs originated from present day Senegal, they also came from Mali, Guinea, Ivory Coast and in fact from the entire former AOF, *l'Afrique occidentale française* which extended from the West Coast

Dia Bagou, *tirailleur sénégalais de la classe* 1912, 11 June 1917.
(© Médiathèque de la Défense, Paris)

Two tirailleurs sénégalais posing with their coupe-coupe, the machete much feared by the Germans. According to the caption these two soldiers belonged to the 'race bambara', i.e. to the Bamana people who today mainly live in Mali, and also in Guinea, Burkina Faso and Senegal.
(© Musée départemental Albert Kahn, Boulogne-Billancourt)

to Benin and Niger. The RTS and BTS were also deployed with other detachments, like in equatorial Africa and Indochina, and also in North Africa. In 1914 some 14,000 *tirailleurs sénégalais* were stationed in West Africa, 15,000 outside this region with the largest part in Morocco. In North Africa, in addition to the well known tirailleurs and Zouaves and *Bat'Af's* of Algeria, Tunisia and Morocco, six more *Régiments de Marche d'Infanterie Coloniale* were stationed. Each regiment had three battalions: one white and two native. These native troops included *Tirailleurs sénégalais du Maroc* and *Tirailleurs Sénégalais d'Algérie*. The left overs of these battalions arrived in Lo on 25 October 1914, to reinforce the French army in Belgium.

— TIRAILLEURS SENEGALAIS D'ALGERIE ET DU MAROC

The 102 battalions of the colonial army, of which 36 battalions were stationed in France (*métropolitains*) and 21 in North Africa, were reorganized at the beginning of the war into *régiments de marche*, which comprised active soldiers and reserves. As a division or marching regiment they would not be involved in trench warfare in Flanders. Senegalese units of that colonial corps were the exception. Ten 'Moroccan' and 'Algerian' Senegalese battalions had come over with the colonial corps and had been deployed in many battles in Rocroi, on the Marne, near Arras in August and September. On 24 October 1914 the remainder was integrated into a mixed

Tirailleurs sénégalais at work in a wood depot near Oost-Vleteren, 5 September 1917.
(© BDIC-Musée de l'Histoire Contemporaine, Paris)

The German Camp Commander Otto Stiehl made this studio portrait of one of his West African prisoners of war in 1915.
(© Bildarchiv Preußischer Kulturbesitz, Berlin)

group of white and black troops allocated to General d'Urbal in Flanders. No later than 26 October 1914 the various units were split to fill up gaps and to relieve exhausted French units at the front. One battalion *(2ᵉ Bn Sénégalais d'Algérie)* under Commandant Debieuvre was sent to the canal banks before Luigem and *la Maison du Passeur*. One white colonial battalion *(Bn Mixte Coloniale du Maroc)* was sent to Sint-Elooi. The two remaining battalions, led by Commandant Pelletier, were the *3ᵉ Bn Sénégalais du Maroc* and the *1ᵉ Bn Sénégalais d'Algérie*. They were placed under the command of Vice-Admiral Ronarc'h of the *fusiliers marins* to help defend Diksmuide.

That same day this group was deployed by Ronarc'h to occupy the Hoge Brug (High Bridge) in Diksmuide and the outposts around the town. Some days later the tall Wolofs were noticed by Max Deauville in Kaaskerke:

> *Long, thin, lanky and smiling Senegalese are on their way stepping like storks. They are exceedingly tall and their long neck protruding from a collar carries a small round head wearing a fez. They wear a short ultramarine jacket and baggy pants. They march barefoot and carry their boots in their hand.*[19]

Ronarc'h had the three 'types' of units under his command (Belgians, Bretons and Senegalese) organize their relief within their own battalions. On 1 November he already noticed that the Senegalese were finding it difficult to acclimatize to the Northern climate:

> *They are already suffering from swollen feet,*

Tirailleurs Sénégalais on the railway embankment between Nieuport and Dixmude, near Pervijze, October 1914. (© Royal Army Museum, Brussels)

and relieving them will be a problem. It is quite obvious that the climate and season have become too harsh for black troops.[20]

Doctor Duwez, alias Max Deauville, also noted that:
In the morning along the destroyed road the Senegalese pass carrying their comrades on their backs. The poor beggars are barefoot. At the end of their thin legs their feet dangle, large like children's heads. Every day dozens of them go past their feet frozen. They suffer dreadfully and thick tears run down their faded cheeks.[21]

On 4 November Ronarc'h ordered the marines to relieve the 3[e] BTS *du Maroc* in the outposts to the North of the town. The previous day both battalions had suffered tremendous losses. In spite of the great

voluntarism the situation was no longer sustainable. One week later Diksmuide was lost. Marines, Belgians and tirailleurs were totally exhausted. In one week's time the Senegalese had lost their main officers: the commander, company captains, lieutenants. On that fatal last day of 10 November, the battalion chief of 1 BTS *d'Algérie*, Ernest Brochot, whom Ronarc'h had appointed deputy commander of the defenders of Diksmuide, was killed at the level crossing on the road to Esen. Somewhat to the South right next to the municipal cemetery almost all the remaining Senegalese of the 2e Cie died. They suffered the same fate as the 3[e] the previous day.[22] Alfred Guignard, one of their French officers, described how they broke into a multilingual rhythmic chant in the assault against the German superior strength, a monotonous chant silenced by German fire.

At fifty metres the hail of bullets mowed down the black flesh. Under the volley, silenced forever, with the dead, this unique hymn grew fainter then stopped, but it should be eternally echoed in history.[23]

In his memoirs Ronarc'h wrote that at the end of the day on which he lost over 2000 men, of the two battalion that had been entrusted to him two weeks earlier only 600 Senegalese soldiers remained, just enough to form one (incomplete) battalion. Other sources report even far fewer survivors. In the 2nd Algerian battalion of Debieuvre along the Ypres-Yser Canal not enough men remained after 10 November 1914 to allow the battalion to continue to exist.[24] Few survivors of the *Bn Mixte coloniale du Maroc* arrived from Sint-Elooi. All of them came together in Hoogstade on 17 November, there were not even

thousand of the three thousand men who had arrived in Lo three weeks earlier. *'Rain, wind, mud... a Belgian band is playing. The Senegalese are dancing, poor beggars.'* was the entry made by the battalion doctor of the *fusiliers marins* in his diary.[25] One week later the remaining men were sent back to France, to Fréjus and Nice, to await new batches that would be arriving from Africa.

In the cemeteries of the Westhoek we barely find fourteen Senegalese graves from this period! It is highly unlikely that they were repatriated (except for their French officers).

Many prejudices against black troops originated in this period: that they were afraid of gunfire and were thus unreliable (white, i.e. French, British and Belgian, criticism), that they crept into the German trenches at night to cut off the enemy's ears and

Three scenes from the camp of *tirailleurs / travailleurs malgaches* and/or *tirailleurs sénégalais* in Roesbrugge-Haringe, July 1917, with respectively the roll call and departure for work and a dance, accompanied by the sound of a drum and clapping.
(© ECPAD – Médiathèque de la Défense, Paris)

noses and wore them as trophies from their belt (German, but also confirmed by stories of Belgian veterans) and that the Senegalese warrior was first and foremost a tiger in bed (everyone reported this). The insights that prevailed at the time with regard to the bestial characteristics of the black race also gave them a status of sexual supremacy. Even if all this had been true it certainly did not apply to the group involved in the Battle of the Yser. This group consisted of professional soldiers with a long service record in Morocco or Algeria, who were familiar with the sound of gunfire, and who (the few that survived or their successors) subsequently had little access to European women.

— LATER RECRUITMENTS

Once the pre-war professionals had virtually been eradicated at the end of 1914, new recruits were called in. This occurred hastily and with great success. The bottomless reservoir of Africa now had to be tapped into. The 30,000 professionals of before the war were now joined by almost as many recruits in 1914 and double that number in 1915. As from 1916 and the large-scale mobilisation, a further 120,000 West Africans were called to arms until the end of the war. 130,000 (or 5000 more than the *Tirailleurs Algériens*) were sent to the war in Europe. The Senegalese tirailleurs never returned to trench warfare in Flanders, they did serve and die at the Chemin des Dames (1917) and the Somme (1918). It was only right at the end that three other black units would participate in the last phase of the Final Offensive.

MARIALOOP — MACHELEN

On 24 September 1918 three battalions (43^e, 45^e and 75^e BTS) joined the 132^e DI that had come to support the Belgian army in the battle for the liberation offensive as from 13 October 1918. The successful initial advance was stopped, the Belgians were exhausted and depleted and the French were (yet again) required to assist. Between 13 and 18 October amongst others Senegalese battalions were deployed to capture Marialoop (Meulebeke) and Dentergem. The division advanced towards the Lys and finally the Scheldt (Markegem, Waregem). Today some 25 graves bear witness to this ultimate Senegalese presence in the war in Flanders in the French military cemeteries of Machelen on the Leie, Roeselare and Potijze.

JOURNÉE DE L'ARMÉE D'AFRIQUE ET DES TROUPES COLONIALES

DEVAMBEZ, PARIS

The French war artist Lucien Jonas made this splendid poster to promote a « Day of the African army and the colonial troops ». The poster shows a victorious *tirailleur sénégalais* of 1914 next to a *tirailleur* in the uniform worn later on in the war.
(Collection Philippe Oosterlinck)

—DIE SCHWARZE SCHANDE

But this was not the end of the campaign for the tirailleurs. During the mobilization of black African volunteers they had been promised a favourable regime and a career in the colonial administration upon their return. This would only start much later than the Armistice. Many coloured troops (tirailleurs Sénégalais, Algériens, Tunisiens, Malgaches and Antillais) were deployed alongside the French (and Belgians) for the occupation of the left bank of the Rhine. Hardly three months later a major racist campaign was launched against the fact that black troops were occupying a white region. Although the French considered the black troops more like big children, naïve but willing, capable of being moulded into excellent soldiers by a hard hand, and who could relieve and offer a solution for the own French soldiers who wanted to rush home after the Armistice, the German nationalistic press did not hesitate to speak of 'vertierte Neger' ("animal-niggers") who abused white women and exercised a barbaric terror on their already heavily afflicted country.[26] Nobody denies there were instances of rape and plundering (name just one occupation army in the world who never experienced this problem), however, it was perfectly obvious that this uprising against the 'Schwarze Schmach' was mainly a violent propaganda war. Back in the August days of 1914 Germany had been portrayed in the allied press as a nation with a barbaric 'Kultur' because of its acts of terror against the civilian population of Belgium and Northern France, for the destruction of old monuments and art treasures (Leuven, Reims, Ypres...). The German Empire countered this with the deployment of colonial troops by France and the British Empire. If you take a look at the colourful catalogue of Germany's enemies, who were the real barbarians, and who were the real defenders of European culture?[27]

After Germany's humiliation in the Treaty of Versailles, the presence of coloured troops was fresh evidence of the allied contempt.

Although all this was to be expected of a society that would soon be focused on revenge, treason and race, today the international response triggered by the protest gives a better insight into racism in that period. The British journalist and left liberal politician Edmund D.Morel, before the war the great assailant of the atrocities committed in Leopold II's Congo, claimed for instance that:

> the militarized African, who has shot and bayoneted white men in Europe, who has had sexual intercourse with white women in Europe, would lose his belief in white superiority.[28]

This pacifist believed that only segregation could eliminate interracial tensions. In 1937 in Nazi-Germany for these same reasons 385 half-blood children (Afro-German) would be sterilized! The Italian Prime Minister Professor Francesco Nitti, a great advocate of a Unites States of Europe, condemned the deployment of colonial troops. The occupation as such was a provocation of one nation state against another, and prevented the harmonious cooperation of all European peoples, cultures and classes. The fact that black troops were (also) involved was the final insult against conquered Germany. Indeed they were 'members of an inferior race that were occupying one of the most developed regions in the world'.[29]

Cultural superiority and racism were the main topic of the international debate. Under this pressure France gradually withdrew its black troops: the Senegalese returned home in 1920, the Malagasies (1921) and all the others followed (1923). In Africa and in France a number of positive ideas were voiced. African leaders, like Blaise Diagne, the first black member of parliament believed that 'the school of the army' would allow many blacks to be better trained for the development in their home country. The future Senegalese president Léopold Senghor would indeed be a tirailleur sénégalais in the next war. In spite of the harsh treatment of the black troops, it became increasingly obvious for France and the army that the commitment of the black troops demonstrated the equality and equal treatment of everyone. It was a start even though the path to equality would still be very long.

In 1921 a smaller, chaste version of the propaganda token by Karl Götz against the black troops in the French occupation force (see page 19). The phallus has now been replaced with a column stating the words 'Zum Hohn der Deutscher Frau' ('The scorn of German women').
(In Flanders Fields Museum)

4. COLONIAL LABOURERS: MADAGASCAR, ANNAM

If the deployment of colonial troops was perfectly justified in colonial thinking, then this applied even more for the deployment of colonial labourers. In 1914 French parliament reasoned that French colonization had brought peace and prosperity to the native population, and that consequently in times of need a favour in return could be expected of these populations.

> *We have brought them prosperity and peace. We have freed them from epidemics and raids, from periodic famines, and civil wars. We have shed our most precious blood to release them from the invaders and slave merchants. Today, we are fighting for them as they are fighting for us.*[30]

The colonial troops that came to Europe comprised French colonial (white) and native (coloured) troops. The first group would amount to a total of 134,000 units, the native to 437,000.[31] In proportion this was very little indeed. Whereas approximately 20% of all French were called to arms (7.8 million) only 1% of the population in the colonies was mobilized. Even in the Maghreb which had been a recruitment base for colonial troops for a long time the number of recruits was no higher than 4%. However, as compared to the situation before the war the effort was ten times greater. In the army the *indigènes* represented 5.3% of the total troops. This share grew as the war went on.

However, the picture is quite different for (militarized) labourers. Over 220,000 men were recruited, 190,000 of which were deployed in Europe. As opposed to this there is a fairly comparable number (225,000) of European labourers (mainly Spaniards, Portuguese and Italians). The colonials represented 4% of the total workforce in France. In the arms sector their share even increased to 8%. Up to 20% in the army. Even though there were fewer of them in absolute figures, as a workforce the colonial population (+ China) made a greater contribution to the French war effort.

If we consider the relationships between troops and labourers we notice that some countries pro-

Tonkinese labourers grow vegetables.
Paris region, March 1917.
(© BDIC-Musée de l'Histoire Contemporaine, Paris)

vided far more labourers whereas others provided far more soldiers. Independent China did not supply any troops but it did provide 36,500 labourers to the French army. The Chinese who worked in Flanders did so on behalf of the British army.

Indochina sent both soldiers and labourers (43,000 soldiers and 49,000 labourers). But the *tirailleurs tonkinois* never reached the front in Flanders. The *Travailleurs Annamites*, Vietnamese labourers, did make it to Flanders and were active amongst others in the port of Dunkerque and in the hinterland along the French-Belgian border. On the road to Quadypre (Nord) the French soldier Frédéric Branche, whose regiment was on the way to relieve the British on Mount Kemmel (99ᵉ RI, 39ᵉ DI), saw a group of Vietnamese pass on 14 April 1918:

> *We are behind Bailleul. On the road we came across a convoy of Annamite labourers, supervised by English soldiers: they are horrible little men, dirty and lousy; on their backs they carry an enormous bag that weighs them down and in which they keep their clothes and the most*

miscellaneous items imaginable. They excite our hilarity...[32]

This denigrating tone was not unusual, even though soldier Branche did not realize what such a labour corps represented for him. Labourers were needed wherever troops were present, but often semi-retired troops or troops on picket were used to do all kinds of jobs. Without special labour corps the infantry soldier would have to do the work himself. Militarized units of labourers were available for many structural works related to transport, road construction, supply of materials and ammunition. In Flanders this permanent workforce for the French army was mainly present in the port of Dunkerque and in the hinterland of the front near Nieuwpoort and of the front along the Ypres-Yser Canal. The headquarters of that hinterland was in Roesbrugge. All kinds of labourers worked there, often French soldiers on semi-rest, sometimes German prisoners of war, Belgian refugees, auxiliary troops from North Africa, and in September 1917 there was also a group of labourers from Madagascar.

A *travailleur annamite* poses in front of a destroyed British tank in Poelkapelle, around 1919. As opposed to the Chinese, labourers from Vietnam were never present in large numbers in Flanders.
(Collection Philippe Oosterlinck)

A tirailleur indochinois. Northern France, June 1917.
(© Musée départemental Albert Kahn, Boulogne-Billancourt)

At the beginning of September 1917 a large number of French soldiers were quartered near Roesbrugge Station. They were negroes from the island of Madagascar... After having made all the necessary arrangements with their superiors, French officers, I was allowed to visit them regularly outside working hours in order to instruct them in European civilization. I went to instruct them in the Christian Religion three or four times a week. The French officers were exceedingly satisfied with the boys who had followed the lessons in European civilization: they were zealous and very obedient.

This was reported by Jos Brutsaert, acting parish priest of Roesbrugge, to the Bishop of Bruges, after the war. The shepherd proudly added that he was eventually successful in baptizing some of them. There is even a photo of these *Travailleurs Malgaches* cooking their meal in the field along a hedge. This picture is quite exceptional as no more than 5,500 labourers from Madagascar would be deployed in Europe. Some 34,000 *Tirailleurs Malgaches* arrived at the front in Europe but were only deployed in France.

Cooking *tirailleurs* or *travailleurs malgaches* in Roesbrugge-Haringe, July 1917.
(© ECPAD – Médiathèque de la Défense, Paris)

1. Max Deauville, *Jusqu'à l'Yser* (Paris, 1917), Ed. Pierre De Meyere, Brussels, 1964, p.89.

2. Mangin (Lieutenant-Colonel), *La Force noire*, Paris, 1910. See also chapter 2 by Christian Koller.

3. E.g.: Chantal Valensky: *Le Soldat Occulté. Les Malgaches de l'Armée française, 1884-1920*, Paris, 1995; Jean-Yves Le Naour: *La honte noire. L'Allemagne et les troupes coloniales françaises, 1914-1915*, Paris, 2003; Jacques Frémeaux, *Les colonies dans la Grande Guerre. Combats et Épreuves des peuples d'Outre-mer*, Paris, 2006; Eric Deroo & Antoine Champeau, *La Force noire, Gloire et infortunes d'une légende coloniale*, Paris, 2006.

4. Charles Le Goffic, *Dixmude, un chapitre de l'histoire des Fusiliers Marins*, Paris, Librairie Plon, 1915 and *Steenstraete, un deuxième chapitre de l'histoire des Fusiliers Marins*, Paris, Librairie Plon, 1917. Charles Fouqueray had already been appointed the official artist of the French navy before the war and extensively illustrated the campaign of the Fusiliers Marins in Flanders in 1914 and 1915.

5. In November 2003 the French Ministry of Defence opened a site with scanned records of dead French soldiers from the First World War. They can only be selected by name and not in a correlated database. Records with personal data (usually clinical pictures) are not public. To date almost 1.5 million records can be accessed. (www.memoiredeshommes.sga.defense.gouv.fr)

6. Here the front in Flanders must be taken literally. North African dead fell in great numbers in the first weeks of the war (22-25 August 1914) in Wallonia (Charleroi, along the border).

7. In February 2003 a dual database of French dead at the front in Flanders was opened on the museum website. The *Gabriel* database includes all the names of French soldiers who today lie buried in 41 different cemeteries in the Westhoek, on both sides of the French/Belgian border. There are only 11 669 names. The *Pierre Martin* database is growing constantly and includes the names of French soldiers who fell at the front in Flanders but whose current last resting place is not known. The two databases were created and are updated by Ghislain Kepanowski from Loker (www.inflandersfields.be).

8. Cyriel Buysse, *Van een verloren zomer* (Amsterdam, 1917), Collected Works, Volume 6, Brussels, A.Manteau, 1979, p.457.

9. SHAT,Vincennes, D.A.B., 32ᵉ CA, Military Staff, General Order No.113, signed Humbert, in: JMO 3ᵉ BILA, 1st of August – 31 December 1914, 26 N 860 – dossier No3.

10. See amongst others 'Le Zouave' in *La Cantine militaire*, poems by Paul Ferrier. In August 1914 critical chansonniers like the pacifist 'humanitarian chansonnier' Montéhus would openly endorse the *Union sacrée* and the war: 'we will sing *la Marseillaise*, and will keep *l'Internationale* for the final victory. We will sing it when we return!' (Montéhus: Letter of a Socialist)

11. SHAT, Vincennes, JMO 1ᵉ RMTA, 1August – 31 December 1914, 26 N 844 – dossier No1.

12. SHAT, Vincennes, VIIIe Armée, Special Orders, 16 N 194 – dossier No.3, and 38ᵉ DI Operation Orders, 24 N 841- dossier No.1.

13. see Commandant R. Drevet, *l'Armée Tunésienne*, Paris, 1922. After the war the grave of Capitaine Gendre was transferred from the French cemetery near Château Elisabeth (today Poperinghe Old Military Cemetery) to the French field of honour at the municipal cemetery of Roeselare.

14. It is noteworthy that in many classical published French sources on the first war year in Flanders, like Charles Le Goffic, Louis Madelin, Generals Palas or d'Urbal, and also in more personal testimonies like those of Docteur Nel or Vice-Admiral Ronarc'h, although Zouaves and tirailleurs are mentioned their unit name is very seldom accurate.

15. Mohamed ben si Ahmed Bencherif (1879-1921) was the first Algerian author to be published in French. The strongly autobiographical novel *Ahmed ben Mostapha, Goumier* tells the story of an officer of the Spahis during the pacification of Morocco and at the beginning of WW1. He was taken prisoner near Lille in October 1914 and in the prisoner of war camps of Zossen and Krefeld he was faced with the question of whether he had indeed chosen the right side.

16. Piere MacOrlan, *Le bataillon de la mauvaise chance* (*Un civil chez les Joyeux*), 1933.

17. SHAT Vincennes, JMO 3 BILA, October 1914-March 1915, 26 N 860 – dossier No.3. In addition to the 100 listed dead there are more than 250 missing. A random check for 9 November 1914, the first assault on *Maison du Passeur*, indicates that at least one third of all the missing also died. The actual death toll was probably twice as high as indicated in the regimental diary.

18. See papers of the colloquium *Gas 1915. Innocence Slaughtered*, held in the In Flanders Fields Museum in Ypres from 17 to 19 November 2005.

19. Max Deauville, *op.cit.*, p.131.

20. Vice-amiral Ronarc'h: *Les Fusiliers-Marins au Combat. Souvenirs de la Guerre*, Paris, 1920.

21. Max Deauville, *op.cit.*, p.146.

22. Léon Bocquet & Ernest Hosten, *Un fragment de l'Épopée sénégalaise, Les Tirailleurs noirs sur l'Yser.* Brussels and Paris 1918.

23. Commandant Alfred Guignard in *Revue des Deux Mondes*, Paris, 15 June 1919, p.856.

24. A.Guignard, *op.cit.*, p. 855.

25. quoted by Charles Le Goffic, op.cit. 1917, p. 50

26. See Jean-Yves le Naour: *op.cit.* and Iris Wegger: *Die 'Schwarze Schmach am Rhein'. Rassistische Diskriminierung zwischen Geschelcht, Klasse, Nation und Rasse*, Münster, 2007.

27. See Otto Stiehl: *Duitschland's vijanden*, Amsterdam, 1916. And below Chapter 10: Britta Lange: research into exotic prisoners of war.

28. Quoted in Dick van Galen Last: *Black Shame*, in History Today, Vol.56 (10), London, October 2006.

29. Iris Wegger: *op.cit.*, p.51.

30. French Parliament, Document No.1246, 11e legislature.

31. For these and the following figures please refer to the research performed by Jacques Frémeaux, *op.cit.*

32. The carnets de route of Frédéric Branche were published by his grand-nephew Bertrand Channac, on his personal site: http://pagesperso-orange.fr/bertrand.channac.

Two Australian soldiers in front of
the old town gate in Bergues, 2 September 1917.
(© ECPAD – Médiathèque de la Défense, Paris)

THE BRITISH DOMINIONS AND COLONIES
AT THE FRONT IN FLANDERS

DOMINIEK DENDOOVEN

At the beginning of the twentieth century the extent and power of the British Empire was unequalled. In 1921 it comprised a quarter of the land mass on the surface of the earth and totalled some 458 million subjects, also about one fourth of the total world population. Great Britain was the world's policeman and imposed its Pax Britannica. In addition to the mother country, the United Kingdom of Great Britain and Ireland, the British Empire comprised (crown) colonies, dominions and protectorates. The British mother country and its largest crown colony India are discussed in separate contributions in this book.

To a large extent dominions enjoyed self-rule, including certain privileges with regard to foreign affairs and defence. The British Empire had five such dominions in 1914: Canada (1867), Australia (1901), New Zealand (1907), Newfoundland (1907) and the Union of South Africa (1910). In theory within the

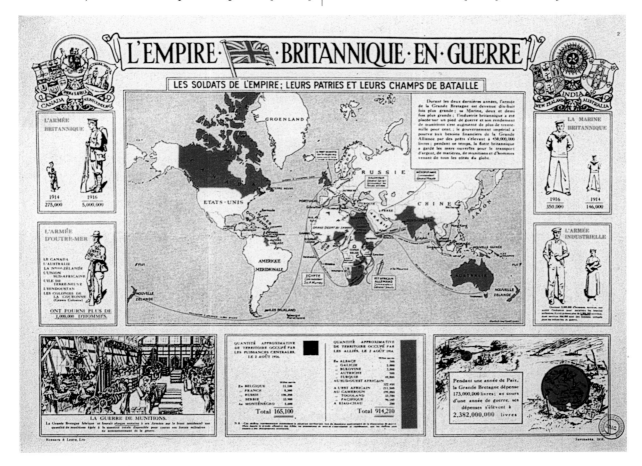

This informative propaganda poster for the French public was intended to show how the war efforts of the British Empire had expanded massively in just a few years' time. (© BDIC-Musée de l'Histoire Contemporaine, Paris)

Empire the dominions were equivalent to the United Kingdom. Because of their far-reaching autonomy they had their own army troops during the First World War, which, although they belonged to the British armed forces and were under British command, still had their own specific characteristics and statutes. For each dominion the First World War was a major step in the creation of their nation. Whereas in 1914 their image and self-image was that of a glorified colony, after the war the dominions started being considered as young nations. Consequently, in 1919 they all signed the Peace Treaty of Versailles individually. In virtually all dominions self-rule mainly applied to white immigrants and their descendants whereas the native population groups held a subordinate position. This was also the case in the colonies.

— The Canadian Expeditionary Force (C.E.F.)

Before the First World War, Canada with its 7.5 million inhabitants only had an extremely small army. However, within a few weeks after war was declared over 30,000 men volunteered to fight in Europe. Father Van Walleghem of Dikkebus saw the first Canadians, belonging to the Princess Patricia's Light Infantry, in February 1915:

You can see that they are of a different type than the English. Their uniform is slightly greener. Many of them speak French.

On 22 April 1915, the 1st Canadian Division occupied the front line to the right of the French 45th Algerian Division when the Germans opened the gas cylinders for the first time. These Canadians launched the first counteroffensive after the gas attack and suffered heavy losses. Later the Canadians would participate in the Battle of Mount Sorrel near Ypres in June 1916, and in the last phase of the Battle of Passchendaele in

A somewhat improvised *Devil's Circus* offered Canadian soldiers behind the front some relaxation, May 1918. The wagon with the band was drawn by no fewer than eight mules.
(© Imperial War Museum, London)

October-November 1917. Impressive monuments were subsequently erected in Flanders to commemorate each of these battles. The main Canadian First World War site is Vimy Ridge between Lens and Arras, where the Canadian Expeditionary Force gained its most memorable victory. In the end some 620,000 Canadians would serve during the First World War. One tenth of them did not survive the war, and over

14,000 are remembered in cemeteries and on monuments in Belgian Flanders.

The Canadian soldiers were partly kitted out with their own Canadian equipment that had often been ordered from friends of the particularly controversial Minister of Defence Sam Hughes. The most renowned item of equipment is probably the Ross Rifle, manufactured in Canada. This was a highly accurate yet vulnerable rifle with numerous shortcomings. For instance, it would lock as soon as it came into contact with mud and its bayonet frequently dropped off during firing, which was a major inconvenience in the trenches of Flanders. The weapon was soon hated by the troops. After countless other blunders that included ordering shoes with cardboard soles, Minister Hughes was dismissed in November 1916.

In line with the majority of the population of this young country the Canadian Expeditionary Force mainly comprised immigrants. The latter usually originated from the mother country: it is estimated

The funeral of a Canadian soldier at Poperinghe New Military Cemetery, 1917. (© Imperial War Museum, London)

Lieutenant James Moses was a native Canadian from the Delaware band, Six Nations of the Grand River Reserve, Brantford, Ontario. Moses first served in France and Belgium with the 107th Battalion Canadian Pioneers. Transferred to the Royal Flying Corps in September 1917, he was reported missing while serving as an observer and air gunner on 1 April 1918 (© John C. Moses)

that two thirds of the men in the first Canadian contingent of 1915 were born in the United Kingdom and in 1918 this still applied for almost half the C.E.F. The largest Canadian minority was the French-speaking Canadians and most of them originated from the Province of Quebec. The Canadian divisions also included fairly large groups of Ukrainians, Russians, Scandinavians, Belgians, Dutch, French, Americans, Swiss, Chinese and Japanese, in addition to African-Canadians and natives.

After the bloody Battle of Vimy Ridge in 1917, the Canadian Expeditionary Force needed new men; the Canadian government introduced conscription. Almost all French-speaking Canadians were opposed to it, whereas the English-speaking Canadians were in favour of the measure. The opposition against conscription was so great that violent unrests broke out in Quebec City during Easter 1918. The rounded up soldiers started firing into the crowds killing a number of protesters. The commemoration of this 'Crise de la conscription' (Conscription crisis) would cast an additional shadow on the already difficult relationship between these two population groups right until the Second World War. Canadian conscription would have little effect on the actual course of the war: ultimately 'barely' a few tens of thousands of Canadian conscripts would join the army in Europe before the end of the war.

The French-speaking Canadians were far less enthusiastic about the war than the English-speaking Canadians as French-speaking Canadians had less strong ties with Europe. Furthermore, the military establishment was strongly pro-English and little inclined either to set up French-speaking units or promote French-speaking officers. On the contrary, Minister of Defence Sam Hughes had greatly irritated the French-speaking community by sending protestant, English-speaking chaplains to Quebec to lead the recruitment campaigns and by obliging the French-speaking war volunteers to speak English during their training.

French-speaking Canadians could be found in many units. Because of the policy adopted by Sam Hughes French-speaking soldiers were initially intentionally split up and integrated into English-speaking units. Only the 13th battalion and 14th battalion of the first contingent of the C.E.F. respectively included one and two French-speaking companies. Following political pressure from Quebec and public protest actions an exclusively French-speaking battalion was created, i.e. the 22nd (French Canadian) Infantry Battalion. Because of its number it was given the nick name 'Van Doos', a corruption of the French *vingt-deux* (twenty-two). In September 1915 it reinforced the *Corps Expéditionnaire Canadien* on the Western Front. The Quebecois spent the first year in the trenches near Ypres, amongst others near Kemmel, Sint-Elooi and Zillebeke (Mount Sorrel). Later the 22nd saw action in Passchendaele during the last days of the Third Battle of Ypres, before being virtually decimated near Arras on 27-28 August 1918. The 22nd would be the only French-Canadian battalion to remain at the front throughout the war. The *Van Doos* acquired a cast-iron reputation, in spite of (or because of?) the fact that as the sole French-speaking battalion within the British armed forces they were distrusted or at least were greatly exposed to criticism whenever anything went wrong. During the First World War it totalled over 4000 fatalities and injured soldiers, approximately 67 % of its men! Even though 85 % of the men originated from Quebec and more specifically from Montreal, all the Canadian provinces were represented in the 22nd. A surprising number of soldiers in the French Canadian Battalion, some 5 %, originated from abroad, especially from the United States.

Next to a large minority of French-speaking Canadians, the Canadian Expeditionary Force included many smaller minority groups and thousands of individual soldiers of 'foreign' origin. They also included some recently emigrated Flemings, like Ostend born Richard Verhaeghe who fell on 30/31 October 1917 and who lies buried at Tyne Cot Cemetery in Passchendaele, or William Vangheluwe from Roeselare who died on the same day and is commemorated on the Menin Gate in Ypres. The irony of fate is not only that both these Canadian Flemings died in their former homeland but also that the original purpose of the Third Battle of Ypres was to liberate the Belgian ports, including Verhaeghe's native Ostend. It is all the more cynical that William Van Gheluwe died in Passchendaele, less than ten kilometres from the place where his parents lived. These are but two of at least 17 Flemings who died as Canadian soldiers in Flanders during World War One.

In certain battalions of the C.E.F. more volunteers

of a specific origin were found than in others due to the adopted geographically-based recruitment policy. The 102nd (North British Columbian) Infantry Battalion originated from the Canadian West Coast and consequently included many Russians who had migrated to Canada via the Pacific Ocean. Some of them had served under the Tsar during the Russo-Japanese war, like George Pavluchuk who now lies buried in Reninghelst New Military Cemetery.

Black Canadians who volunteered to fight in the war were often turned down. Under pressure the army finally agreed to set up a black battalion even though it was a non-fighting labour battalion, i.e. the No. 2 Construction Battalion. In the spring of 1917 the battalion arrived in France where its task was to chop wood for use in the trenches and behind the front. One of their officers was the Reverend William White, at the time, probably together with Tottenham-Hotspur football star Walter Tull[1], the only black officer in the British armed forces. In spite of considerable resistance and racism individual black soldiers could sporadically be found in other Canadian units. However, their numbers remained limited.

The most multicultural battalion of the C.E.F. was quite probably the fiftieth from Alberta. The high level of cultural mix in the unit is already apparent in the names of its missing soldiers on the Menin Gate in Ypres: the probably French-speaking Louis Beauchène is mentioned next to the Swedish Canadian R.O. Björkblad, the Japanese Canadian Hikotaro Koyanagi and Mike Foxhead, 'son of the late Fox Head and his wife, Mary Many Shots, of Blackfoot Indian Reservation'. Koyanagi was just one of the 200 Japanese who served in the Canadian army. Fifty-three of them would not survive the war. Most Japanese came from British Columbia on the Canadian West Coast and that is why the monument dedicated to them stands in Vancouver. The Japanese Canadian war veterans have an eventful history: they were the only members of their community to be given the right to vote in 1931. During the Second World War, however, like all other 22,000 Japanese Canadians, they were imprisoned in an internment camp as 'hostile aliens'. Masumi Mitsui for instance, who had fought in the Third Battle of Ypres with the 10th Battalion C.E.F., had ended the Great War with the rank of sergeant and had been awarded the Military Medal. During the Second World War his successful poultry farm was confiscated. He was separated from his family and lost all his possessions. When they came to take him to the internment camp an irate Mitsui threw his medals to the ground saying: 'What good are these!'. Mitsui would remain bitter about his Second World War experience until his death in 1987. In addition to the Japanese Canadians there were also the Chinese Canadians. They were faced with even greater racism and discrimination and the number of Chinese Canadian soldiers does not appear to have been very high during the First World War.

The situation was quite different for the native inhabitants of Canada, the First Nations (Indians, Inuit and Metis). At least 4000 Canadian aboriginals, approximately one in three native young men, served in the C.E.F. Not every band supported the war effort in the same way, yet some First Nations saw virtually all their young men leave. The tribal council of the Six Nations (Iroquois) opposed young men joining up yet some 300 band members served in the army, more than from any other Indian band in history. War volunteers also joined up from remote areas like the Yukon or the Northwest Territories. Others still had to go to a great deal of trouble to serve: William Semia of the Cat Lake Band was 18 years old and a trapper for the Hudson Bay Company when he joined up in September 1916. He did not speak a word of English or French and was unable to write. It was a great culture shock for him and many others to be suddenly confronted with discipline and uniformity, let alone with 'modern life' with steam boats, trucks, etc. Semia finally joined the 52nd Battalion and was seriously injured near Passchendaele at the end of October, beginning of November 1917. When he was finally dismissed from the army he made the long trek home on foot and by canoe.

The first Canadian native to have been killed on the battlefield was probably Angus La-Force, a Mohawk of the Caughnawaga Band in Quebec. He was killed during the first gas attack near Ypres on 22 April 1915 and is remembered today on the Menin Gate. This is also where the Mohawk Cameron Brant, who died two days later, is remembered. Brant had followed an old family tradition when he volunteered: his great-grandfather had already assisted the British in the 18th century during the Seven Years' War and the American Revolution. Joseph Standing Buffalo also continued a family tradition: he was the

The *war deed* of Mike Mountain Horse. Mike Mountain Horse depicted his experiences as a Canadian soldier on the Western front on this piece of cow hide. He wrote a statement under each section. The main war deed can be found top left: 'August 21st, 1917. The 50th battalion of Calgary attacked the German trenches. Corporal Mountain Horse led his machine gun section on an old building behind the German defence. On obtaining their objective, Mountain Horse heard noises in an old cellar. He called upon the enemy to surrender but received no answer. Then he descended the stair. Looking down, he saw a German officer kneeling and aiming to shoot... [damaged page]... tain quickly fired at the officer, killing... [damaged page] he himself was wounded'. The scene at the bottom on the right shows how Mike Mountain Horse and three other Canadians raid a German machine-gun outpost near Amiens on 12 May 1918.
(© Esplanade Museum, Medicine Hat, Canada)

Recruits of File Hills Colony in Saskatchewan pose with their parents, chieftains and a Government representative before their departure for Europe. Remarkably, a variant of this photo fell into German hands and was used in their anti-ally propaganda.
(© Library and Archives Canada)

son of the Sioux chief of Fort Qu'Appelle in Saskatchewan, and the grandson of the legendary Sitting Bull. He was killed in September 1918. The tradition of warrior and/or ally of the British was indeed one of the many reasons for which Canadian Indians joined up. Thanks to their traditional skills they were outstanding scouts and snipers. Although this confirmed the accepted stereotypes, many Canadian natives were quite pleased to be given such assignments.

The best known among them is Francis Pehgamagabow, an Ojibwa of the Parry Island Band who became the most decorated native Canadian. Pehgamagabow was injured during the Second Battle of Ypres in April 1915, but later rejoined his unit to fight in the Third Battle of Ypres in 1917. He survived the war and died in 1952.

The fact that the warrior tradition played a major role is also demonstrated by the 'War Deed' of Mike Mountain Horse. This Canadian Indian, born in 1888, originated from a family of warriors from the Blood reserve in Alberta. His brother Albert Mountain Horse had suffered major gas injuries during the Second Battle of Ypres, which he later died of during his repatriation. Driven by the example of his forefathers and to avenge the death of his brother Mike also joined up. In 1917 he joined the 50th battalion at the front in Europe and was actively involved in the Battle of Vimy Ridge. In October 1917 he suffered shell shock near Cambrai: during a bombardment the shelter in which he had taken cover was buried under rubble. He was only freed four days later. In his memoirs Mike Mountain Horse bears witness to how the Canadian natives continued to cherish their traditions in Europe. For instance in 1917, he joined some other Bloods on a small clearing in the woods to pray. His fellow tribesman and battalion comrade George Strangling Wolf decided to make a sacrifice to the Sun Spirit to obtain its protection during the forthcoming battle. Strangling Wolf inserted a needle in the skin under his knee and cut off a piece of skin with a knife. He pointed this bloody piece of skin to the Sun while praying: 'Help me, Sun, to survive this terrible war, that I may meet my relatives again. With this request I offer you my body as food'. He then buried the offering in the ground. Strangling Wolf would survive the war and return to the reserve. Mike Mountain Horse also returned. In the reserve he decided to follow the tradition of the Indians of the Great Plains by painting his pictorial war memories on a cow hide. He did not dictate the events in chronological order but in a sequence of interest to the painter Ambrose Two Chiefs. He did not work in a traditional manner: thus Mountain Horse's war painting is not multicoloured, but monochrome, which may be due to the poverty that prevailed at the time, and some scenes are represented in a more realistic than symbolic manner. Once the cloth was completed Mountain Horse wrote the necessary explanations for all the depicted events under the title 'The Great War Deed of Mike Mountain Horse'. After the war Mike Mountain Horse joined the mounted police and worked for the railways. He became a respected member of the Bloods tribal council and a celebrated author. A school was named after him in Alberta.

Two other famous Canadian Indian soldiers were long distance runners Tom Longboat, marathon world champion in 1909, and Olympic athlete Alexander Decoteau, who died near Passchendaele on 30 October 1917 and lies buried in Passchendaele New British Cemetery.

Half the men in two Canadian battalions, the 114th and 107th, were native war volunteers (400 out of 800). The fact that, similarly to the American army, the Indians were rated higher than their black fellow countrymen, is also demonstrated by the fact that various officers were of indigenous origin. However, not everything was quite so positive: depending on the unit and recruitment area, e.g. the Yukon, the Indians experienced considerable discrimination, Indian war veterans would wait a long time before they would enjoy the same privileges as their former white comrades and the veterans brought back diseases from Europe to which the native population was more sensitive. These were but a few of the negative effects of the war on the indigenous population. The involvement of native Canadians in the First World War ultimately had few beneficial effects at a political, economic or social level.

At least 300 native Canadians fell on the battlefield and many more died of diseases or injuries incurred in Europe. It was only in 2005 that their spirits would be 'called back home' at a private Calling Home ceremony on Mount Kemmel organized by the Canadian government.

The Newfoundland Regiment marching through Berneville, 9 May 1917. Newfoundland was the smallest British dominion. The regiment was present in Flanders at different moments.
(© Imperial War Museum)

The Newfoundland Regiment

From 1907 to 1949 Newfoundland was a separate British dominion, after which it became the tenth Canadian province. In spite of its scarce population, about one quarter of a million in 1914, it was a fairly prosperous country. Newfoundland did not have an army, merely a cadet corps which can best be described as a military youth movement. When war broke out a Newfoundland Regiment was set up that would soon be swamped with war volunteers. In total some 6500 men joined this Newfoundland Regiment. Two thousand other Newfoundlanders served in the Royal Navy or in the lumberjack battalions, the so-called 'forestry battalions'.

The Newfoundland Regiment is mainly known/notorious for the enormous losses it suffered on 1 July 1916, the first day of the Battle of the Somme. Of the 800 Newfoundlanders who went into attack on that morning only 70 remained at the end of the day. The others were dead, missing or injured. The unit would take quite some time to recover. Barely a month after the infamous 1 July what remained of the Newfoundland Regiment was deployed near Ypres to perform chores. Their barracks were located in the casemates under the ramparts of Ypres. After major actions in France, the Newfoundlanders once more returned to Ypres in the summer and autumn of 1917, when they were deployed near Langemark during the Third Battle of Ypres, and in September 1918 when they participated in the great final offensive from the Ypres region as a part of the 29th Division. For a whole month they helped push back German troops through Dadizele, Ledegem, Bavikhove and Deerlijk to Ingooigem, where their active involvement in the First World War stopped on 27 October 1918. After a short participation in the occupation of the Rhineland the men returned home and the regiment was disbanded. Newfoundland again returned to being a country without an army.

From an ethnic point of view Newfoundland was and is fairly homogeneously Anglo Saxon. The ethnic minorities found in Canada were also present in Newfoundland, albeit in smaller numbers. This was also reflected in the composition of the Newfoundland Regiment. At least 15 Inuit ('Eskimos') from Labrador served in the Newfoundland Regiment. Amongst them were John Shiwak and Fred Frieda. Both joined the regiment after the blood bath of 1 July 1916.

John Shiwak, the best sniper in the regiment, died on 20 November 1917. Fred Frieda, a hunter and trapper before and after the war, remained with the regiment until the war ended and thus participated in the Third Battle of Ypres and in the Final Offensive from Ypres to Ingooigem. He was plagued by nightmares about his war experience until his death in 1970.

The Newfoundland Regiment suffered tremendous losses during the First World War. The Commonwealth War Graves Commission commemorates some 1200 dead of the unit, over 150 of which are buried in Belgium. A further 70 went missing and are commemorated on the Newfoundland Memorial to the Missing in Beaumont-Hamel (Somme), although they actually fell near Langemark and Poelkappelle in August-October 1917.

The monuments commemorating the Newfoundlanders all consist of a monumental bronze Caribou. Only one of them is located in Belgium along the busy Gentsesteenweg between Kortrijk and Harelbeke, close to the spot where the Newfoundland Regiment crossed the Lys in 1918.

The Australian Imperial Force (A.I.F.)

In 1914 Australia had almost 5 million white inhabitants who had mainly settled along the coasts, and some 80,000 aboriginal Australians who mainly lived inland. Australia had a small professional army that could be supplemented with some 45,000 part-time reserves. Every adult Australian male of a certain age was indeed obliged to follow minimum military training at regular intervals. As soon as war broke out the Australian government decided to provide Great Britain with an Australian Imperial Force of 20,000 men at first but that figure would soon increase.

As opposed to Canada or South Africa almost all white inhabitants originated from Britain and they shared the initial British enthusiasm for the war. This in combination with some fierce recruitment campaigns ensured there was no shortage of volunteers, especially in the first stages of the war. In November and December 1914, the first two Australian and New Zealand convoys left for Europe. After the failed landing in Gallipoli and with the rising number of Australian war fatalities the Australian enthusiasm for the war soon faded. To main-

John Shiwak was an Inuit ('Eskimo') from Labrador who served in the Newfoundland Regiment. He fell on 20 November 1917. On this pre-war photo he posed in a Scottish uniform.

tain the recruitment levels the new, pro-British Prime Minister William Hughes promised to introduce conscription. However, his proposal was twice rejected in a referendum and Australia continued to have voluntary soldiers.

Until the end of 1917 the five Australian divisions together with the New Zealand troops and some British units formed two Australian and New Zealand Army Corps, or ANZAC. After having trained in Egypt the ANZACs were deployed on the Turkish peninsula

Gallipoli. The day of the landing, 25 April (1915), is deemed so important for the creation of the nations of Australia and New Zealand that it is still a major public holiday and commemoration day in both countries. In spite of the catastrophic outcome of the Gallipoli campaign, the Australian soldiers acquired a solid reputation as fighters. In the spring of 1916 they were transferred to Northern France, where one division fought in the Battle of Fromelles and four in the Battle of the Somme, all suffering heavy losses. From August to October 1916 Australian troops were present for the first time at the front near Ypres. From a military point of view their presence during the Battle of Messines in June 1917 and during the Third Battle of Ypres a few months later was more important. Whereas the first battle was a success, at 'Passchendaele' the Australians suffered some 38,000 dead and injured soldiers. The blood bath resulted in a shortage of men from which the A.I.F. recovered with great difficulty.

Although the Australian soldiers were reputed to be outstanding soldiers, the British officers were horrified by their disregard for etiquette. This in combination with the fact that they were better paid brought them to the attention of the Belgian population. Furthermore, the Australian troops were the only national army not to enforce the death penalty, even though there is at least one testimony about a summary execution. The prevailing opinion about Australian soldiers was well formulated by Father Achiel Van Walleghem on 11 October 1917:

> They are courageous fighters, who know no fear. This is one of the reasons they are usually posted in the worst sector, which they are quite proud of. However, when they are tipsy and quarrel with the English, they often rile them that they always have to creep into the hole whereas the English choose the best side. However, they are somewhat wild. Their main vice is drink and this is mainly due to the fact they are paid so much... That is why when they come and relax in our village after having spent a couple of weeks in a region without any houses or inns, and with their pockets full of cash, they want to celebrate and drink, and so the beer, wine and champagne flow. Inn keepers and wine sellers make a lot of money....

A 1916 studio portrait of William Joseph Punch, an aboriginal who served in the 1st Battalion Australian Imperial Force. William Punch died of pneumonia in a British hospital on 29 August 1917, aged 37.
(© Australian War Memorial, Canberra)

The Australian Imperial Force was composed of men of British origin and was therefore ethnically fairly homogeneous. The heavily discriminated aboriginals were not allowed to serve or at the very least were discouraged from serving in the A.I.F. As the war progressed the rules were slackened. According to recent estimates between 400 and 500 aboriginals served overseas, and about 160 of them came from New South Wales. Most were probably of mixed European-aboriginal origin. It is hard to trace aboriginal soldiers because military papers did not mention their ethnic origin and the names do not usually allow to classify someone as aboriginal. Moreover, some pretended to be Pacific Islanders, Maori or Indians. Aboriginal recruits were probably driven by the pay and by the hope for more respect and a better life. Even though in the army they were on an equal footing with their white comrades, the First World War brought them little or no improvement at a political, economic or social level. Whereas white ex-volunteers were allocated plots of land by the government, they were not even entitled to own the land on which they had settled. Some aboriginal veterans were not even allowed to join the local war veterans' association. They would only be granted civil rights in 1967 and they have only recently been included in the commemoration ceremonies. Yet there is no shortage of remarkable stories, like that of the Lovett family from Lake Condah in Victoria. Five of the six sons of this aboriginal family served during the First World War, amongst others in Ypres: Alfred, Edward, Leonard, Frederick and Herbert. In the Second World War they joined up again, except for Alfred who was too old but he was replaced by the youngest brother Samuel. All would survive both world wars. In 2000, the tallest building in Canberra was named after them. Some aboriginals in the A.I.F. came from relatively prominent families. For instance Daniel Cooper who died on 20 September 1917 near Ypres and lies buried in Perth Cemetery (China Wall) in Zillebeke.

A group portrait with men of the 57th and 60th Battalion, Australian Imperial Force following a snowball fight in a camp in England, February 1916. An unidentified aboriginal soldier is kneeling in the middle. (© Australian War Memorial, Canberra)

His father William Cooper was a well-known aboriginal rights campaigner who kept reminding the politicians of the sacrifices the aboriginals had also made during the First World War.

In total almost 417,000 Australians enlisted voluntarily in the AIF, over 13 per cent of the white male population and about half of those eligible. Over 330,000 of them embarked overseas and 65 per cent of them (about 215,000) became battle casualties (dead, injured, missing, sick, prisoner of war) — of whom 60,000 died. This was the highest rate of casualties of all the forces of the British Empire. Almost 12,750 Australians are buried or commemorated in Belgium.

— The New Zealand Division

New Zealand, with a total population of approximately 1 million inhabitants in 1914 contributed no fewer than 124,000 soldiers during the First World War, of which 100,000 were deployed overseas. Approximately 18,000 did not survive and 50,000 others were injured. More than 4,700 of them lie buried or are commemorated in the Belgian Westhoek.

All young New Zealand men had received military training. Since 1911, there had also been a national militia of some 25,000 part-time soldiers. They were among the first New Zealanders to join the New Zealand Expeditionary Force. On 1 August 1916, conscription was introduced initially for whites only. Earlier that year the New Zealand Expeditionary Force had been organized into a division: the New Zealand Division. The New Zealand forces comprised

Drawn by Lieut. G. P. Hanna

four regiments; each one was named after a military district: Auckland, Wellington, Canterbury and Otago. The division was almost always deployed with Australian divisions, with which it formed the (2nd) ANZAC and was therefore present in Flanders and Northern France at the same time as the Australians. In Flanders triumph and blood bath were intermingled for the New Zealanders. On 4 October 1917, during the so-called Battle of Broodseinde, the New Zealand division took over 1,000 German soldiers prisoners of war and together with the Australian units, it successfully pushed the frontline back by more than one and a half kilometres. However, they paid a heavy price for this victory with 450 New Zealand fatalities including David Gallaher, the for-

mer captain of the 'All Blacks' national rugby team. One week after this relative victory the Anzac troops had to repeat their daring exploit. This time, however, they were faced with a complete disaster: they failed to reach a single target, in just a few hours 846 New Zealanders were killed and 2000 more were injured. Never in history have more New Zealanders met with a violent death than on 12 October 1917, the 'First Battle of Passchendaele'. The black day also had a highly detrimental effect on morale back in New Zealand. The division would remain in the Ypres area until February 1918.

Possibly even more so than for the Australians, the First World War played an important role in develop-

In this drawing of 1918, New Zealand Lieutenant G.P. Hanna portrayed the German as an eagle, the New Zealander as a kiwi and the Australian as a koala bear, each with his typical headgear.
(© In Flanders Fields Museum)

New Zealand (left) and Australian soldiers (right) examining the seized German armaments in Bailleul after the Mine Battle of Messines, June 1917.
(© Kippenberger Military Archive, Waioru, New Zealand)

THE ISLAND OF OUR LONGING

Far beyond the dim horizon
  Lapped by cool Pacific's waves
Lies the island of our longing
  Bush clad hills and mossy caves
Jewel of the dying sunset
  Land of heroes, brave and free
Purest gem in lovliest setting
  God will send us back to thee

Far from strife and sound of tumult
  Free from every scar of war
Yet thy heart is filled with longing
  Thoughts of days that are no more.
Darkest night brings fairest morrow
  Wait a while, and thou shalt see
Joyous end to all our sorrow
  When God sends us back to thee.

J.D.A.

G. J. Calman
N Z Ent Group
Hdqrs
France

Drawn by G. J. Calman

ing the national spirit of the New Zealanders. Far from home the New Zealand soldiers became conscious of who they were and where they came from. In battle they compared themselves to the other armed forces and from this they gradually derived their own identity. Many soldiers started referring to themselves as 'Kiwis', the remarkable, typical New Zealand flightless bird.

Generally speaking there were two population groups in New Zealand: the native Maori and the Europeans, also referred to as Pakeha, who were mainly of British origin. At the beginning of the war New Zealand had also deemed the joining up of the indigenous population undesirable, however, no later than February 1915 a Maori contingent was formed. Indeed, even though they were not treated as equals the discrimination of the Maori was less intense than that of the Australian aboriginals. Thus the Maori were recruited at the instigation of the four Maori members of parliament of that day. One of them, Peter Buck (Te Rangi Hiroa), also joined up. These members of parliament were convinced that the involvement in the war would support the Maori demand that they should be treated as equals by the Pakeha and would help eliminate the negative aspects of tribalism, which they believed was a handicap for the future development of the Maori. It would indeed appear that many Pakeha and Maori first got to know one another better during the war. Yet many Maori opposed this involvement in the war, especially as conscription also applied for them as from 1917. Mainly the Taranaki, Ngati Maniapoto and Tainui-Waikato tribes, who had lost their land to the British during the 19th century revolts, resolutely refused to serve. In addition to which, Maori King Te Rata declared that military service was a matter of individual choice and no one could be forced to serve.

The first Maori contingent was integrated in the fighting troops and was involved in the battles of Gallipoli. During the formation of the New Zealand Division at the beginning of 1916, it was decided to incorporate the Maori in an engineering unit: the Maori Pioneer Battalion. Many Maori soldiers rejected this option and remained in their infantry battalion, arguing amongst others that they were essentially a martial people. However, all new Maori recruits were incorporated in the Maori Pioneer Battalion. They were supplemented with Polynesians from Niue (at least 140), the Cook Islands (at least 156 soldiers from Roratonga, Atiu Areora, ...), Fiji (at least 14), Tonga (idem) and other islands. As German Samoa had been occupied by New Zealand troops since 29 August 1914, a number of volunteers also originated from that island. No soldiers came from further afield to the trenches of Flanders than these inhabitants of the Pacific Ocean!

The battalion was active near Ypres during the whole second half of 1917 where they made new communication trenches and shelters amongst others. The year 1917 ended on a minor note for the Maori Pioneer Battalion. In the early morning of 31 December a shell hit Lieutenant Paku's platoon that was working at the intersection of the Zonnebeke Road and Saville Road (the present day Jan Ypermanstraat) in Ypres. Six Maori were killed outright. They were buried in the splendid Ramparts Cemetery on the Ypres ramparts. In total 36 members of the Maori battalion were buried in Belgium. In total, between 2200 and 2700 Maori and between 340 and 460 Pacific Islanders served overseas. 336 died.

The book *New Zealand at the Front* of 1918 bundled all kinds of contributions of New Zealand soldiers in Europe. This drawing by G.J. Calman makes specific reference to the Maori heritage, whereas the poem talks about the great longing for Ao Tea Roa.
(In Flanders Fields Museum)

— Troops from the Union of South Africa in the First World War

It was only in 1910 that the former Boer Republics Transvaal and Orange Free State and the two British colonies Natal and the Cape united to form the Union of South Africa, a self-rule dominion within the British Empire. The South African war, better known as the Boer War, had ended merely eight years before, in 1902. During this war some 22,000 Boer women, children and senior citizens and an equal number of blacks had died in British concentration camps. Needless to say that there was still considerable animosity in the very young Union of South Africa between the English-speaking and Dutch-speaking colonists. The majority of the population was black, had no civil rights and was disregarded by the State.

Although the majority of the (white) population had little reason to help Great Britain in the battle, General Botha, the Prime Minister of South Africa and a former Boer Commander, had indeed promised assistance. Botha kept his promise and in 1914-1915 the South African Defence Force conquered all German South-West Africa (Namibia). The campaign was interrupted to settle a revolt of pro-German or rather anti-British — Boers. In April 1915 the British government asked the South African government to supply troops for deployment outside Southern Africa. Three South African Infantry Brigades were formed. The second and third brigade would fight in German

East Africa, whereas the First South African Brigade left for England in November 1915. Obviously, the majority of these soldiers, who had volunteered to be deployed outside Africa, were of British origin and hence spoke English. Without exception blacks and coloured people were not allowed to join up.

Although the men of the First South African Brigade trained in England for deployment on the Western Front, they were initially sent to Egypt and Libya. They first reached France in April 1916. There they were integrated into the 9th Scottish Division, probably because the 4th regiment (4 SAI) comprised the 'South-African Scottish', who wore a kilt with the tartan of Atholl in the Scottish Highlands. The other regiments were: Cape Province (1 SAI), Natal and Orange Free State (2 SAI) and Transvaal and Rhodesia (3 SAI). Their 'trench acclimatisation' took place at the end of April and beginning of May 1916 in the then relatively quiet trenches near Ploegsteert. Shortly later, in mid-July 1916, in Delville Wood on the Somme, the South Africans were butchered with unparalleled violence. That is the reason why the great national monument of South Africa is located there. After the catastrophe of Delville Wood the South Africans remained in Northern France for another year, where they were deployed amongst others during the Battle of Arras. On 14 September 1917, they arrived in Brandhoek, half-way between Ypres and Poperinge to fight in the Third Battle of Ypres. A few days later, on 20 September 1917, they

launched an attack near Zonnebeke. In spite of the enormous losses, this was one of the better prepared and more successful phases of the great British offensive. One of the many South Africans wounded that day was thirteen year old David Ross from Durban. Six months later he would die as one of the youngest casualties of the First World War near Heudecourt. Also in mid-October 1917 — in between two phases of the Third Battle of Ypres — the South African Brigade occupied the front line near Ypres for a few days. It then moved back to France for six months, where it was crushed by the German Spring Offensive at the end of March 1918. A large section of the brigade eventually had to surrender. What remained of the South African troops was again deployed in Belgium in April 1918 to stop the German Spring Offensive near Messines and Kemmel. Even though the South African infantry had only been deployed

twice in Belgium (September-October 1917 and April 1918), outside their 'trench acclimatisation', they had always been present during fierce battles. This explains why one fifth of the South Africans who fell on the Western front are buried or commemorated here.

As from October 1916 South African blacks could join the South African Native Labour Corps (SANLC). Various prominent black activists of the South African Native National Congress, the precursor of the ANC, were delighted with the creation of this labour unit. One of their respected leaders, Sol Plaatje, was actively involved in the recruitment campaign. The prominent blacks not only saw the SANLC as an opportunity to demonstrate their loyalty towards the British, but they considered overseas service as an educational opportunity during which France would

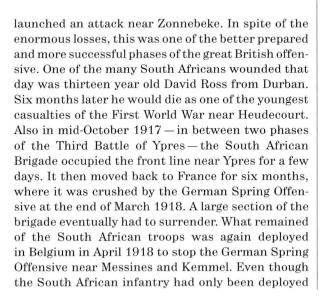

Springbok Nancy was the mascot of the South African Scottish (4 SAI). Together with her appointed keeper A. Petersen she spent the entire First World War near the front, albeit not unscathed. After an explosion in Armentières her left horn was damaged and dangled at an angle. Nancy ultimately survived the war, died on 26 November 1918 and was buried in Hermeton in the Belgian Ardennes.

The springbok (antelope) was and is the national symbol of South Africa. The mascot was also depicted on tobacco bags for South African (and other) soldiers.
(Collection Philippe Oosterlinck)

offer the men a 'university of experience'. And last but not least, it would no longer be possible to ignore black South Africans once they had contributed to the war effort. The South African government was fearful of this. It insisted that the labourers in the SANLC could only be given a one-year contract after which they would immediately be repatriated to South Africa. In January 1918 the South African government decided to stop recruiting men for the SANLC, in spite of the British demand for more manpower, and by May 1918 most 'native labourers' had returned home. In Northern France the South African labourers worked on the supply lines to the front, and even more frequently at the docks in the French Channel Ports. Of all the allied black auxiliary troops they were the least well treated: at the explicit request of their government they were not allowed to have any contact with the local population, they were only allowed to leave their camp if they were accompanied by a white non-commissioned officer and lived in a virtual prison, surrounded by a high barbed wire fence.

One event concerning the SANLC aroused some commotion. On 21 February 1917 the Mendi, a ship transporting a contingent of black labourers from Plymouth to Le Havre collided with another vessel and sank. More than 600 members of the South African Native Labour Corps died. This was not only a human tragedy, the ship also carried a number of prominent blacks like Father Isaac Wauchope and some chiefs. For many blacks this event symbolized their position in South Africa, as black lives were being sacrificed for white interests. The commemoration of the sinking of the Mendi would remain a silent political protest for many years.

After the war the South African government decided that its black labourers who had served in Europe should not be awarded the (Interallied) Victory Medal. They were probably the only allies not to receive this decoration. Indeed, their involvement was even kept silent: for instance the official history *The Union of South Africa and the Great War 1914-1918* published in 1924, does not make any reference whatsoever to the SANLC although some 25,000 men had belonged to it.

In addition to the SANLC there were also the Cape Auxiliary Horse Transport Companies, with a total of some 4200 mainly black men. Such a company was established in Dunkirk and Calais. The smaller group of 'coloured people' from the Cape could join the Cape Coloured Labour Regiment, which comprised some 1900 men.

The official languages of the Union of South Africa were English and Dutch, Afrikaans would only replace Dutch later. Consequently, the South African war graves are the only ones to always display a Dutch text. Indeed, in addition to the national Springbok (antelope) emblem you can read: 'Union is strength — Eendracht maakt macht'. The very rare graves of 'Dutch-speaking' South African soldiers are even entirely in Dutch. Some such examples are the grave of Johannes Niekerk in Perth Cemetery (China Wall) in Zillebeke or of Thomas Engela on Nine Elms Cemetery in Poperinge.

It is estimated that some 30,000 (white) men served in South African units in Europe. A further 10,000 South Africans were active in British units. More than 4,300 South African soldiers died on the Western front including 850 in Belgium. No fewer than 560 missing South African soldiers are remembered on the Menin Gate in Ypres, this is quite revealing for the circumstances in which they died.

Approximately 350 of the black labourers and coloured soldiers have a known grave in Northern France, especially at the cemetery of Arques-la-Bataille. In Belgium you can only find two graves of members of the Cape Coloured Labour Battalion at the old municipal cemetery of Kortrijk.

Another South African symbol was the *ossewa*, the ox-wagon with which the Dutch-speaking Boers had moved eastwards and northwards around 1840 to escape British Colonial authority, i.e. during the so-called Great Trek. During the First World War the *ossewa* adorned the boxes of a British tobacco brand. (Collection Philippe Oosterlinck)

— The British West Indies Regiment

British West India comprised countless islands in the Caribbean region with Jamaica as its largest, as well as British Honduras and British Guiana on respectively the Central and South American continent. As a British *colony* the region was more closely connected to Great Britain than the dominions.

Like elsewhere in the British Empire black men who volunteered for military service were initially turned down. After many discussions between the Colonial Office and the War Office and after the personal intervention of King George V a British West Indies Regiment, which included black war volunteers from the Caribbean, was created at the end of 1915. White colonists from the West Indies served in British units. The first black soldiers arrived in Great Britain at the end of 1915 to receive fighting training. The British West Indies Regiment (BWIR) ultimately comprised twelve battalions and some 15,000 men. Two thirds originated from Jamaica and contingents of 200 to 1000 men originated from Trinidad & Tobago, Barbados, British Guiana (present day state of Guyana), British Honduras (Belize), Grenada, the Bahamas, St-Lucia, St-Vincent and the Leeward Islands (today the island states Dominica, Antigua, Barbuda, St.Kitts & Nevis and the British Overseas Territories Anguilla, Montserrat and the Virgin Islands). Eight battalions of the BWIR served on the Western Front, including at Ypres.

Although the BWIR included trained soldiers, they never actually fought, with the exception of the battalions in Palestine and Jordan. The British government's official policy was that blacks should never fight whites. They also feared that any battle experience the colonial troops might acquire would subsequently be used against the colonizer. The West Indian soldiers were frustrated to be used as workforce, albeit usually quite close to the front. Moreover, they were discriminated against in respect of housing, promotion opportunities, demobilization and pay. When at the end of the war all British troops except the BWIR were given a pay rise, a rebellion broke out among the 9th battalion which was in Taranto (Italy) at the time after a previous passage near Ypres. It was only under pressure of the Colonial Office, which was concerned about possible unrests in the Caribbean, that they were finally also granted a rise.

At least 7 battalions of the BWIR (the 3rd, 4th, 6th, 7th, 8th, 9th and 10th) were active near Ypres between May 1917 and January 1918. One of the West Indian camps was located near the Drie Goên, a borough in the vicinity of Reningelst. This is where they were spotted for the first time by Father Van Walleghem on 26 May 1917:

> *Niggers (from West India and Jamaica) have arrived for work at the farm of Alouis Adriaen and "3 Goên". They are dressed like English soldiers, they are courteous and speak softly, but they are not much liked because of their sticky fingers and on the whole the civilians prefer to see the back of them, because when they enter a place for a cup of coffee they can stay anything from five minutes to a couple of hours. (P.S.: I have found a letter written by the mother of one of those blacks. What sincere, Christian and motherly feelings! None of our mothers could write better).'*

Later he also commented 'that they smoked many cigars whereas the other soldiers preferred to smoke cigarettes.

Similarly to the other colonial troops, the active involvement in the war raised the national awareness of the West Indians. At the end of December 1918, a group of some sixty non-commissioned officers of the BWIR formed a secret 'Caribbean League' stating as one of their demands: '*the black man should have freedom to govern himself*'. The group was betrayed at the beginning of 1919 and its members were harshly punished, including one execution. This event led the British government to decide to

Twice the badge of the British West Indies Regiment: a caravel (of Columbus) at sea. (In Flanders Fields Museum)

disarm the men and disband the BWIR as soon as possible and to repatriate its members. It is remarkable that many veterans of the BWIR played an important role in the politics of a number of islands. Back in Jamaica Norman Manley founded the People's National Party. He later became Prime Minister and led the country to independence in 1962. Another such leading figure was Captain Arthur Andrew Cipriani, a plantation owner from Trinidad with Corsican roots. During his service with the BWIR Cipriani was impressed by how the West Indians handled the circumstances of war. This helped him decide that the

Caribbean people were ready for self-rule. Having returned to Trinidad and Tobago he founded the Trinidad Labour Party and became a respected and leading politician.

185 men of the BWIR were killed or died of their injuries, more than thousand died of illness. However, no fewer than four West Indians were executed by firing squad. One of them was 17 year old Jamaican Herbert Morris who was shot on 20 September 1917 in the courtyard of the town hall of Poperinge. He is one of the 181 men of the British West Indies Regiment who are buried or commemorated in Belgium.

Three soldiers of the British West Indies Regiment sitting in the yard of a large farm somewhere in Flanders or Northern France. Even though they were trained soldiers the Caribbeans were frustrated never to have been deployed as such in Europe.
(© Imperial War Museum, London)

— Other British colonial units and colonials

Once war had broken out in August 1914 white British colonists throughout the world organized contingents of war volunteers like the Trinidad Merchant's and Planter's Contingent and the Barbados Citizens Contingent. These contingents often joined the regular British regiments in batch, like the London Regiment or the Devonshire Regiment. Other colonists travelled individually or in small groups to the mother country or to the nearest dominion to join up. Thus Britishers from all over the world arrived in Flanders and Northern France. They were not exclu-

sively 'colonists'. In neutral Argentina for instance there was a fairly large British community of 28,300 persons, more than in many colonies. At least 4850 Argentinean British joined up and at least 530 of them did not survive the Great War. Many fell in the Ypres Salient. The Argentinean British war volunteers were present in virtually all units and this made it difficult to identify them as a group. British war volunteers from Chile, Peru, Bolivia and Paraguay also travelled to the mother country via Buenos Aires. As from the end of 1918 the British armed forces introduced a special badge for war volunteers from Latin

Ypres, 1919. Some early British war tourists including a decorated war widow pose with a black British soldier, possibly of the British West Indies Regiment.
(© Provincial Library and Documentation Centre, Bruges)

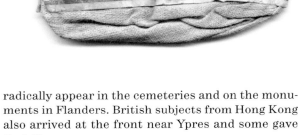

America. The diamond-shaped insignia bore the letters BVLA: British Volunteer Latin America.

In pocket-sized minute Bermuda that did not belong to British West India, there were two military units in 1914: the white Bermuda Volunteer Rifle Corps and the black Bermuda Militia Artillery. Both units sent troops to Europe. The Bermuda Volunteer Rifle Corps was integrated in the first battalion of the Royal Lincolnshire Regiment and thus fought in the Third Battle of Ypres. The Artillery Militia was integrated in the Royal Garrison Artillery, where it was renamed the Bermuda Garrison Artillery. They were also posted at least once near Ypres. It has not (yet) been possible to determine how many men belonged to these two units. The Royal Garrison Artillery seems to have been very welcoming for war volunteers from the colonies as it also included inhabitants of Gibraltar and Malta. Both colonies had ports in the Mediterranean that were of great importance to the British and their inhabitants had previously served in the Navy or in the case of Malta also in labour units in the Dardanelles and Salonika. Yet their names spo-

radically appear in the cemeteries and on the monuments in Flanders. British subjects from Hong Kong also arrived at the front near Ypres and some gave their lives.

Rhodesia, present day Zimbabwe, was a British colony in Southern Africa inhabited by a considerable group of white farmers. Most (white) Rhodesians served in the South African army, amongst others in the Third Battalion (Transvaal and Rhodesia) of the South African Infantry Brigade that fought in Flanders and France and was already mentioned above. However, it is striking that Rhodesians can be found in almost all British regiments. One of the underlying reasons being that the Rhodesian government put off sending Rhodesian contingents to Europe. Many Rhodesians left for the mother country under their own steam. Rhodesians were already involved in the First Battle of Ypres (October-November 1914) as a part of the 2nd battalion of the King's Royal Rifle Corps (KRRC). The very severe winter of 1914-1915 greatly challenged the colonists from Southern Africa. One Rhodesian wrote home: 'The

The dominions and colonies not only supported the combat of the British Empire with manpower. Rhodesia supplied the troops of King George V with cigarettes.
(Collection Philippe Oosterlinck)

cold is frightfully trying. It is snowing and freezing hard tonight, and it makes me yearn to be back on my farm on the Hunyani'. In the 2nd battalion of the KRRC there were soon enough Rhodesians for them to form their own platoon. The Rhodesian soldiers were reputed to be outstanding soldiers, but that did not protect them from disaster. In July 1917 the Rhodesian platoon of 2/KRRC was surprised and encircled during a German raid on their positions in the dunes near Nieuwpoort. Almost the entire unit was killed or taken prisoner.

More than 5700 white Rhodesians served during the First World War and 700 did not survive. Black Rhodesians were unable to serve in the British army and consequently were never present in Europe. The Rhodesian Native Regiment, set up in 1916, was only active in East Africa. The contribution made by white Rhodesians to the British war effort during the First World War would subsequently play an important political role: it was explicitly mentioned when the white minority government of Ian Smith unilaterally declared the independence of Rhodesia in 1965 ...

on 11 November at 11 a.m.

The First World War also played a significant political role in Fiji. Lala Sukuna was an important statesman who paved the way for Fiji's independence. In 1914 he was probably the first native Fijian ever to study in Oxford. He reported for service in the British armed forces but was turned down because of the colour of his skin, after which he joined the French Foreign Legion. There Lala Sukuna proved to be an outstanding soldier and was awarded various medals for bravery. In September 1915 he was injured and repatriated. He received a hero's reception in Fiji. In May 1917 Lala Sukuna returned to Western Europe, this time to serve with the British, i.e. in the Fijian Labour Corps. This was a small labour unit with barely 100 members who worked at the docks of Calais. Sukuna's status as a war hero and his European experience stood him in good stead during his subsequent political career. Other native Fijians served in Europe with the New Zealand Maori Pioneer Battalion.

As had also been the case in other colonies, the

A group photo with a section of the Fijian Labour Corps, 1917. The photo was taken before the Big Tree in Stanley Park in Vancouver, during the trip from Fiji to Europe.
(© Nanaimo Community Archives, Nanaimo BC, Canada)

white inhabitants of Fiji sent various contingents to join British army units. Of the first contingent from Fiji, 43 men formed their own platoon within the 4th battalion of the King's Royal Rifle Corps in April 1915. One month after their arrival, on 8 May 1915, they were slaughtered near Bellewaerde, to the East of Ypres: 9 were killed outright, 31 were injured and only three were uninjured. In July 1915 a second contingent arrived from Fiji. The 9 Fijian dead of 8 May 1915 are remembered on the Menin Gate in Ypres, as are 19 other white Fijians who served in the Australian Imperial Force. Various others are buried in cemeteries in Flanders and France. Some natives of the Fijian Labour Corps lie buried in France.

Not all British colonies displayed the same enthusiasm for getting involved in the great battle. In Ceylon, present day Sri Lanka, only 1800 native inhabitants joined up (of a total population of 4.2 million) in spite of the major recruitment efforts of the colonial government. Some 1600 white colonists joined or had already joined all kinds of militias like the Ceylon Planters' Rifle Corps and the Ceylon Light Infantry. The first unit was deployed in Gallipoli and Egypt, but at least one member subsequently joined the Grenadier Guards, was killed in Flanders and is now remembered on the Memorial to the Missing in Ploegsteert. Some members of the Ceylon Light Infantry also joined the British units in Flanders and Northern France.

Egypt was a special case. Officially, the country was an autonomous province of the Ottoman Empire, but had been occupied by the British since 1880. In December 1914 it became a British protectorate. As from January 1916 Egyptians were drafted into the Egyptian Labour Corps that would ultimately total between 100,000 and 185,000 members. The majority of them was deployed in Palestine but a few companies were transferred to the French Channel Ports. Very little is known or has been written about them.

As in some other Labour Companies, the Egyptians were occasionally treated quite harshly. On 4 September 1917, companies 73 and 74 of the Egyptian Labour Corps went on strike following an air raid on Boulogne-sur-Mer. Their contract stipulated that they would be put to work outside the danger zone.

When the Egyptians threatened to break out of their camp two days later, troops were rounded up to encircle them and they promptly opened fire on these unarmed labourers. 23 were killed and many others were injured. A few days later on 11 September 1917, a new strike of company 74 was reported, this time in Calais. On this occasion seven Egyptian labourers were killed and about ten were injured. Twenty-five others were put in prison. Of the total number of 82 Egyptians who died in Belgium and France in 1917 more than one third was killed by British bullets, a sad record. Only one Egyptian labourer lies buried in Belgium: Sabit Harun Mohamed at the British military cemetery in Adinkerke.

It should be noted that many other territories of the British Empire sent manpower for the war effort but they were not always deployed in Western Europe, instead they were sent to e.g. Mesopotamia or East Africa. From Mauritius, which remained a British Crown Colony until 1968, between 540 and 1000 men served in the Mauritius Labour Battalion, one source claims they were posted amongst others to the Western front. However, I was unable to find any trace of them. The same applies for some 800 inhabitants of the Seychelles who apparently served in 'France & Flanders'. I have therefore only written about those whose presence in Belgium or Northern France can be substantiated with material evidence.

— Black and white in the British Empire

For many colonial or semi-colonial communities within the British Empire the First World War was an important step towards the creation of their nation. More specifically, the war experience helped the Canadians, Australians and New Zealanders realize that they had their own specificity and individual community spirit. Many others like the West Indians became convinced that they were quite capable of becoming (more) independent and that they deserved this independence because of their war efforts. Some communities, especially many minorities, became divided by the choice of whether or not to support the British war effort with manpower. Those who responded positively to the British request for manpower almost always did so in the hope of a fair reward for the loyalty they had shown, e.g. in the form of more rights or (more) self-rule.

As a rule the white subjects of the dominions and colonies had their own fighting units, which belonged to a British fighting unit as a separate contingent or were individually recruited into the regular British units. Barring a few exceptions subjects with a different skin colour were never allowed to join the (regular) British units.

With the exception of the Indian Army Corps in 1914-1915 none of the 'coloured' troops in Europe were ever allowed to use weapons, even though they were fully trained soldiers, as was the case for the British West Indies regiment. Barring few exceptions coloured recruits were used as labourers. The discrimination according to skin colour and the European experience of the indigenous populations would often be mentioned during the decolonisation and/or emancipation processes in the course of the 20th century.

Three soldiers of the British West Indies Regiment. Poperinge, 1917. (In Flanders Fields Museum)

— **Selective bibliography:**

Activities of the British Community in Argentina during the Great War 1914-1919, Buenos Aires, 1920.

Bean, C.E.W., *The official history of Australia in the war of 1914-1918*, 12 vols, Sydney, 1938.

Chabatle, Joseph, *Histoire du 22e Bataillon canadien-français. Tome 1. 1914-1919*, Montreal, 1952.

Cowan, James, *The Maoris in the Great War*, Auckland, 1926.

Dancocks, Daniel, *Gallant Canadians*, Calgary, 1990.

Dempsey, L. James, 'A Warrior's Robe', in *Alberta History. Autumn 2003*, vol. 31, nr. 4, pp. 18-22.

Gaffen, Fred, *Forgotten Soldiers*, Penticton, 1985.

Grundlingh, Albert, *Fighting their own war. South African blacks and the First World War*, Johannesburg, 1987.

http://www.freewebs.com/fiji/index.htm: website Fiji in World War 1.

Joseph, C., 'The British West Indies Regiment 1914-1918', in *The Journal of Caribbean History*, vol. 2, May 1971, pp. 94-124.

McLaughlin, Peter, *Ragtime Soldiers. The Rhodesian experience in the First World War*, Bulawayo, 1980.

Mountain Horse, Mike, *My people the bloods*, Calgary, 1979.

Nasson, Bill, *Springboks on the Somme. South Africa in the Great War 1914-1918*, Johannesburg, 2007.

Nicholson, G.W.L., *The fighting Newfoundlander. A history of the Royal Newfoundland Regiment*, St. John's, 1964.

Pugsley, Christopher, *Te Hokowhitu a tu. The Maori Pioneer Battalion in the First World War*, Auckland, 1995.

Ruck, Calvin W., *The Black battalion 1916-1920. Canada's best kept military secret*, Halifax, 1987.

Smith, Richard, *Jamaican volunteers in the First World War*, Manchester, 2004.

Summerby, Janice, *Native Soldiers — Foreign Battlefields*, Ottawa, 2005.

Van Walleghem, Achiel, *De oorlog te Dickebusch en omstreken*, 3 vol., Bruges, 1964-1967.

1. Walter Tull (1888-1918), who had played professional football for Tottenham Hotspur before the war, was promoted to lieutenant in May 1917. He was the first British born black officer and the first black officer to lead white men into battle.

TROOPS OF
BRITISH INDIA
IN FLANDERS, 1914-1919

DOMINIEK DENDOOVEN

When we speak of Indians in this text we refer to the inhabitants of the Crown Colony of India that belonged to the British Empire. The official name was the British Indian Empire, or also occasionally the British Raj. It was ruled by its own government under the leadership of a Viceroy, representing the British monarch, who used the title of 'Emperor' in this context. In practice the British governed with the help of the Indian aristocracy: tens of princes, maharajahs and other monarchs. British India comprised the present day states Pakistan, India, Bangladesh and Burma (Myanmar). The kingdoms of Nepal and Bhutan were independent, but treaties allowed the British to be very influential. The Indian national leaders supported the British with money and manpower.

About 1.5 million soldiers of the Indian subcontinent served during the First World War, 850,000 of them overseas. About 72,000 would not survive the war. Some 7,000 British Indians were killed on the Western Front, virtually all of them during the first year of war. They are remembered in various cemeteries in Flanders, as well as on the Menin Gate.

The people who lived in the Indian subcontinent had been divided into martial and non-martial ethnic groups by the British in compliance with the racist 'martial races theory'. A 'martial race' was considered brave and well built for fighting but also less intelligent. According to the British a non-martial race was unsuitable as a soldier because of his sedentary lifestyle, build or attitude. Soldiers in the British Indian army were recruited among the martial races. The theory offered numerous advantages for the British rulers: it created a competitive spirit among the various ethnic groups that suited their divide-and-rule policy. Moreover, this theory made the intellectuals and those with a higher education look like cowards, whereas the uneducated and less developed were presented as being brave. Ethnic groups from the plains and from East India were generally considered as 'non-martial'. The Sikhs from Punjab (Northern India/Pakistan) were considered to be the prime 'martial race'. The Gurkhas from Nepal and Northern India are also a famous 'fighting race' and still have an elite unit within the British army. Other martial races were the Baloch (from South West Pakistan), the Dogra (from Jammu, Northern India), Garhwalis (from Uttarakhand, in the Himalaya), Jats (from Rajasthan and Punjab), Pathans or Pashtuns (from the border region between Pakistan-Afghanistan: North West Frontier Province), Rajputs (a community of Hindu fighters in Northern India).

The Indian army reported to the British-Indian government, but on the Western Front the Indian Army Corps and the Indian Labour Corps de facto came under British military authority. The Indian army was organized in a similar way as the British, although there were some significant differences. For instance, it had its own military law. With the exception of a few regiments, each Indian regiment only comprised 1 battalion of some 750 men. An Indian infantry division was composed of three brigades with four battalions, one of which was always British. Ethnically mixed battalions, like the 57th Wilde's Rifles (with Sikhs, Dogras, Pathans and Punjabi Muslims) fought alongside ethnically homogenous battalions, like the 47th Sikhs (Sikhs only).

With this token of 1914 German medallist Karl Götz denounced the deployment of Indian troops by the British. Götz drew his inspiration from the highly mediatized arrival of the first Indians in Marseille at the end of September 1914. However, in reality, no elephant was involved. (In Flanders Fields Museum)

There were two types of officers: British and Indian. The British ranked higher than the Indian. The highest ranks had the same name as the British, but they also had a few specific ranks like subadar (similar to a captain) or jemadar (similar to a British lieutenant). The non-commissioned officers (N.C.O.s) always used Indian denominations like havildar (sergeant) or naik (corporal). A private was a sepoy (cf. British private). The cavalry had other specific ranks like rissaldar, woordie-major, kot-daffadar, daffadar, etc. A cavalry soldier was a sowar, equivalent to a British 'trooper'.

Although the Indian army of 1914 did not reflect the colourful ethnic mix of the subcontinent, it was a melting pot of cultures, peoples and communities, each with its own characteristics and customs.

The story of the Indian army on the Western Front started on 6 August 1914. That day the War Council asked the Indian government to dispatch two infantry divisions and one cavalry brigade to Egypt. The two selected infantry divisions were the Lahore Division and the Meerut Division. Together they constituted the Indian Army Corps. They were later reinforced with the Secunderabad Cavalry Brigade. On 27 August 1914, the British government decided to send the Indian divisions straight to France to back up the British Expeditionary Force that had suffered heavy losses near Mons. At the end of September 1914 the Lahore Division arrived in Marseille under loud cheers of the local population, a fact that was ridiculed by the Germans in their propaganda. Only one brigade, the Ferozepore Brigade, was at full strength because the other units had not yet left India or had been delayed near Suez. Marseille must have offered a very colourful sight as the French colonial troops also usually disembarked in this port. Marseille would remain the Indian 'base port' throughout the 14 months during which the Indian army corps was in Europe.

For the Indians Europe was a totally new and very strange experience. They did not understand the language and the culture was totally different. Indians and French (or Belgians) cast odd looks at one another. Yet in general the Indians were treated kindly by the local population. From Marseille they travelled North via Orleans. When the 47th Sikhs left for the front the battalion spent the night of 20 October in a large convent near St.-Omer, probably Wisques Abbey. The Sikhs were puzzled by the statues of the twelve apostles in the main entrance to the convent. An officer satisfied their curiosity by explaining that these statues represented the gurus of the Christians.

On 22 October 1914 the Ferozepore Brigade already had to go down into the freshly dug trenches between Hollebeke and Messines. The first Indian battalion to be thrown into battle was the 57th Wilde's Rifles in the vicinity of Wijtschate-Oosttaverne. Soldiers belonging to that unit are shown on a photo in front of 't Nieuw Staenyzer inn in Wijtschate. That day the first Indian war casualty fell on the Western Front: naik Laturia, son of Phehu from Hamirpur in the present day North Indian province Himachal Pradesh. His name is mentioned on the Menin Gate.

The following day the 129th Baluchis and the 9th Bhopal Infantry also arrived near Ypres. What was left of the Lahore Division, minus two of the three brigades, was deployed on the other side of the French-Belgian border.

— Sikhs in Flanders'mud

On 26 October, a grey and misty day, troops of the Indian army launched an attack on the German trenches near Gapaard, a hamlet near Messines. It had been raining all night and the trenches were full of mud and water. At the time the trenches were still considered as a temporary measure and were frequently little more than shallow ditches. Furthermore, there was no continuous line of defence. Here and there you could still find large gaps between the various positions through which the enemy could easily infiltrate the line. It was also very difficult to distinguish between an enemy trench and an old trench abandoned by the own troops.

During the attack of 26 October 1914 a few hundreds of meters of ground were won. However, as all aspects of the starting position were far better than the new line, the troops were withdrawn to their initial positions. The Indian soldiers could not understand the reason for this and were disappointed.

After heavy shelling the Germans attacked the Indian troops on 30 October 1914 from Zandvoorde. The Indians and British were outnumbered, did not have enough ammunition and had little artillery sup-

In the yard of a typical Flemish farm Sikhs of
the Indian Army Corps are singing or praying.
In the background others are washing themselves, 1914-15.

port. Needless to say they found it extremely difficult to hold their ground.

The battle continued into the next day. After a whole night's shelling Messines was stormed. The Germans swamped the trenches of the 57th Wilde's Rifles and various units of the battalion were totally wiped out: jemadar Ram Singh was the sole survivor in his group. Another Sikh, jemadar Kapur Singh continued to fight until everyone had been eliminated, with the exception of a single injured soldier. As he did not intend to surrender, he committed suicide with his last bullet. No fewer than 300 of the 750 men in the battalion were killed, injured or taken prisoner and all the British officers of the 57th Wilde's Rifles present in this section of the front were killed.

It was on that same 31 October 1914 that the action took place in the vicinity of Hollebeke for which a few months later Khudadad Khan of the 129th Baluchis would be the first Indian to be awarded the Victoria Cross, the highest and most prestigious British military decoration. The sole survivor of his unit, Khudadad had kept firing his machine gun for as long as possible in spite of his serious injuries. Just before being captured he put his machine gun out of order and pretended to be dead. It is a miracle that shortly later he managed to crawl back from the German lines and rejoin his unit.

During the above-described events the Jullundur Brigade of the Lahore Division was just across the border in the French-Flemish valley of the Lys near Neuve-Chapelle, which would soon become the prime

In front of the inn 't Nieuw Staenyzer in Wijtschate a few soldiers of the 57th Wilde's Rifles have taken up position behind a rudimentary parapet, 30 October 1914. (© Imperial War Museum, London)

Indian sector. Here also the Indian troops were almost immediately thrown into battle. As from 29 October the entire Meerut Division would also arrive on site.

It was a mistake not to deploy the entire Lahore Division. Battalions, half-battalions and even companies were split and deployed separately to support various British divisions, in spite of the fact that the Indian troops had at least expected to remain together. On 29 October 1914 General Willcocks wrote in his diary:

> *Where is my Lahore Division? Sirhind Brigade: Detained in Egypt, Ferozepore Brigade: somewhere in the North, split up into three or four lots, Jullundur Brigade: Manchesters gone south to the 5th Division, 47th Sikhs: half fighting with some British division, half somewhere else, 59th and 15th Sikhs: in trenches,...*

Obviously, all this did little to improve the morale of the Indian troops. Thousands of kilometres from home, in a foreign environment and totally unaccustomed to the dreadful weather conditions the Indians were fighting for a cause they hardly understood. It is quite understandable that the nature of the relationship between the Indian men and their British officers was very specific indeed. The officer understood them: not only did he speak their language, he also knew their customs, habits and culture, and there was a certain amount of mutual trust, a relationship that can best be described as paternalistic. When a large number of these officers were killed during the initial battles, the Indian soldiers felt abandoned. Indian companies that lost their commanding officer were reassigned to British units where no one understood them. The Indians also found new technologies hard to grasp. In the beginning they fired at every aircraft they spotted in the air, irrespectively of whether it was a German or an allied plane. They simply could not understand that such a flying monster might not have destructful intentions. Once the novelty had worn off they hardly raised their eyes when a plane flew past.

At the beginning of November 1914 the Ferozepore Brigade was also transferred from Ypres to the Indian sector between Givenchy and Neuve-Chapelle. On 7 December 1914 the Sirhind Brigade joined them from Egypt, together with reinforcements from India. By mid-November the Indian 1st Cavalry Division had also arrived, they were followed one month later by the Indian 2nd Cavalry Division. These two cavalry divisions would in fact remain on the Western Front after the rest of the Indian Corps had left for Mesopotamia in the autumn of 1915. In December 1914 very heavy fighting took place in the sector of the Indian Corps and on 10 March 1915 the so-called Battle of Neuve-Chapelle was fought and resulted in the unprecedented slaughter of the Indian troops. This explains why the splendid Indian Memorial is located in that French municipality. The losses incurred during the Battle of Neuve-Chapelle were so great that the Indian Corps had to be reorganized. From then onwards each brigade consisted of two British and three Indian battalions.

On the whole, the British paid special attention to the customs, habits and religious practice of their Indian soldiers. For instance, they ensured the Sikhs could continue to wear their articles of faith, the five 'Ks': the round, metal armband (kara), the dagger (kirpan), the combat underwear (kaccha), the small comb (kangha) and the long, uncut hair (kesh). When Sikhs and Hindus died they would be cremated whenever possible. The Indian fatalities were buried and/or commemorated in their own cemeteries or in separate plots of British cemeteries, occasionally even further subdivided according to their religion (Sikh, Hindu, Muslim). In Brighton the Royal Pavilion, a 19th century palace in a pseudo-Oriental style was converted into the main Indian hospital, with amongst others separate kitchens for each religion.

This photo, published in a French magazine at the end of 1915, shows a British Indian trench in the summer or autumn of 1915. The men are wearing the British gas mask of the day: the hypo-helmet. Turbans were a problem: some wore their turban on top of the hypo-helmet, yet most wore it underneath.

— 'We have arrived in hell'

At 5 pm on 22 April 1915 the Second Battle of Ypres began with the first chemical attack in history. Once again the Indian Army Corps was called on to fill a gap in the line. On 24 April the Lahore Division marched towards the North and on the morning of 25 April the division reached Ouderdom, a hamlet between Reningelst and Vlamertinge. Father Van Walleghem of Dikkebus wrote: '*The Indians were quartered in the farmsteads of Maerten, Lievens and Desmarets.*' The men arrived exhausted. They had been marching for twenty-four hours through a landscape that was hilly and on cobblestones that had become slippery through the rain. They had had one single

short break. The Indian troops had been warned that if gas was used they should place a handkerchief or a piece of flannel over their mouths. It was recommended they should drench the handkerchief in urine.

After the gas attack the Germans had conquered a great deal of ground near Langemark and Sint-Juliaan. The British together with the French intended to launch a counterattack and drive the Germans away from their new positions. On the morning of 26 April the Lahore Division gathered near the hamlet of Wieltje, to the North East of Ypres. There they were bombarded with tear gas shells. German planes were doing reconnaissance flights above the heads of the Indian troops without any countermeasures being taken. To the left of the Indian troops were French colonial troops with essentially North Africans, to the right of the Indians were the British. The Jullundur Brigade of the division had previously suffered heavy shelling outside the Ypres ramparts. Most shells fell into the water of the moat or hit the broad ramparts. The men had cheered from time to time whenever a shell fell into the water. However, one heavy shell struck the middle of a company of the 40th Pathans, killing 23 men outright.

After a preliminary bombardment that barely lasted 40 minutes, the signal to attack was given at five past two in the afternoon of that 26th of April. Two officers per unit were sent into No Man's Land to reconnoitre the terrain, but none of them had

Lieutenant General Bhupinder Singh, Maharaja of Patiala, visiting the Belgian trenches on the Yser, 5 July 1918. (© Koninklijk Royal Army and Military History Museum, Brussels)

returned. No information was available on the exact position of the German trenches or at which distance they were located. The men of the Lahore Division were tired after the exhausting march and their position had been accurately located by the enemy as the German aircraft had been allowed to perform their reconnaissance unhindered. Furthermore, the troops first had to cover a distance ranging from a few hundreds of meters to over one kilometre over open terrain before reaching the first German line and launch the actual attack. The relief was unfavourable also as the ground was first slightly raised over a couple of hundred metres then sloped down to finally rise again towards the German front line. The British-Indian artillery was light and ineffective, and it too was unaware of the exact position of the Germans. Once they had left the trench the attacking troops

soon lost any sense: French, Algerians, British and Indians became intermingled. After the first inclination they became trapped in an inferno of gunfire, machine-gun fire and shelling, including tear gas shells. Men were killed by the dozen and the attack was soon stopped. No reinforcements arrived.

One can well imagine the extremely high number of casualties. The 47th Sikhs, in the first wave of the attack lost 348 men out of 444, or approximately 78 % of the regiment. It had virtually been eradicated. In total the attack made 2 000 casualties in the two attacking British-Indian brigades.

None of the attacking troops had even managed to reach the first enemy line. Moreover, every attempt to consolidate the positions reached had failed when the Germans again opened the gas cylinders around 2.30 pm. When the gas reached the Indian troops an

Sikhs of the Indian Army Corps are washing and drying their clothes near the Grote Beek at Ouderdom (Reningelst), 1 May 1915. This spot, where their camp was located, is today Grootebeek Cemetery, where amongst others some Indian headstones are to be found. (© Imperial War Museum, London)

Indian soldiers on the way from Marseille to the front in Flanders, 1914-15. Some are strikingly young.
(© BDIC-Musée de l'Histoire Contemporaine, Paris)

Indian havildar was heard shouting '*Khabardar, Jehannam pahunche*' ('Watch out, we have arrived in hell'). Soon the ground was covered in men being tortured in the most atrocious manner. Although all the attacking troops were hit by the gas, the Ferozepore Brigade and the French colonial troops to the left of them were worst hit. They withdrew in great confusion leaving the dead and the dying behind in No Man's Land.

Hero of the day was jemadar Mir Dast Afridi, who originated from the Pashtoon tribal region on the North Pakistan-Afghan border region. Mir Dast had remained in the chaos of No Man's Land after all officers around him had been injured or killed. He gathered all the men he could find including many who had been slightly gassed and kept going with them until nightfall, when they could safely return. Mir

Dast subsequently helped pick up other wounded Indians and British even though he himself had been wounded. He was awarded the Victoria Cross for this act of bravery. The story of Mir Dast is all the more remarkable because the month before his brother Mir Mast had deserted and defected to the Germans with 14 other Afridis. In 1916 defector Mir Mast would accompany a German-Turkish delegation to Tirah to gain the support of the 'North-West Frontier' tribes for the Turkish sultan's conflict against the British.

The following day, on 27 April 1915, shortly after one in the afternoon the French colonial troops and the Indian troops again launched an attack, but this time they had the back-up of the Canadian artillery. Amongst others two Gurkha battalions and the 9th Bhopals who headed the attack received the heaviest blows. The action was stopped when it was noticed that the barbed wire in front of the German trenches had remained intact. The Indian troops remained in the first line during the following days also. On the morning of 30 April 1915 the Jullundur and Ferozepore Brigade were withdrawn to their camps near Ouderdom. However, as they were still being regularly shelled, the men continued to sleep outdoors instead of seeking the shelter of their tents. Shelling early in the morning on the 1st of May made the beasts of burden of the 47th Sikhs run away. Finally, after a last desperate attempt to reach the enemy lines the Sirhind Brigade was also withdrawn from the front. On 2 May this brigade rejoined the rest of the division in Ouderdom. The following day the division started its return march to the rest of the Indian Corps near Neuve-Chapelle. Between 24 April and 1 May the Lahore Division had lost 3889 men, about 30 % of the deployed soldiers.

— 'Various Indian troops...'

This was the last time Indian troops were massively deployed in Belgian Flanders. However, this does not mean that Indians were not regularly spotted near Ypres. Father Van Walleghem of Dikkebus reported in June 1915 that 'Indian troops' had remained in the region for a number of weeks. His diary notes of 6 June 1915 deserve to be included. It is a splendid illustration of the local population's attitude towards the Indians, an attitude that was not devoid of xenophobic traits:

A Sikh of the British Indian cavalry.
West-Vleteren, April 1915 (© Royal Army and Military History Museum, Brussels)

Alberto Fabio Lorenzi (1880-1969): Attacking Sikhs in a fir wood dug up by the British artillery in 1915. During the First World War French Italian graphic artist Lorenzi created a number of fan-shaped battle scenes in Japanese style. He situated this tableau near Hill 60 in May 1915. Even though British Indian troops were indeed present near Ypres in that period, neither the place nor the landscape is accurate.
(© BDIC-Musée de l'Histoire Contemporaine, Paris)

Sikhs chargeant dans un bois de sapins raviné par l'artillerie anglaise

Cote 60. — SUD-OUEST D'YPRES

Mai 1915.

Brillante attaque des Indiens
à NEUVE-CHAPELLE.

Mars 1915.

Various Indian troops are present in the parish, mostly near Vlamertinghe. They have a dark skin, are dressed like English soldiers except for their head which is skilfully wrapped in a turban. They speak English and some also speak French, they are very curious, ask many questions and are very interested. They will walk for half an hour to find milk, they observe everything while they are being served, are very distrustful yet cannot be trusted themselves and if they can somehow manage to run away without paying they will do so. They tender their Indian money, the rupee (2.80) and are angry when people will not accept it. They don't (or pretend not to) understand the value of our money, and when they exchange it they want to receive more in return than what they gave. Consequently, people don't want to deal with them. On the whole they are friendly and polite, yet they can't repress their curiosity and will inspect you from head to toe and are particularly fond of looking through windows. They bake a kind of pancake and also eat a kind of seed with a very strong taste.

After May 1915 the Indian Corps saw action in the so-called Battles of Aubers Ridge, Festubert and Loos. When at the end of September 1915, the situation deteriorated even further it was decided to transfer the Indian troops to Mesopotamia. Earlier that month the popular commander of the Indian Army Corps, General Willcocks had resigned after his umpteenth conflict with the British commander-in-chief Douglas Haig. Willcocks had been constantly concerned about the morale of the troops, had often protested against the incorrect deployment of the corps and was concerned about the great number of victims and the difficulties to replace them. The general was also indignant about the fact that the Indian public was not informed of the achievements of the corps due to the severe and often irrational censorship and about the impossibility of sending the Indians on leave. All this had irritated his superiors, particularly Douglas Haig, who had lost all patience and sympathy for the Indian Corps a long time ago.

By the end of 1915 almost the entire Indian Army Corps had left Europe. In over fourteen months it had lost more than 34,000 men (dead, wounded and pris-

oners of war), one third of which originated from the British units in the corps and two thirds from the Indian battalions.

In addition to the dreadful circumstances in which the Indian troops had to fight the two major problems they had faced were the lack of reinforcements (from India) and the great number of victims among British officers. The corps had arrived in France with 10 per cent reserves for the Indian units. These reserves had already been used to replace the sick and incapacitated before the corps had even reached the front. The reserve system in India was totally inadequate and a large number of Indians disembarking in Marseille as reinforcements, were unfit for service because they were too old, in poor health or untrained. The problem became increasingly acute because of the many casualties. Replacing the British officers in the Indian army was also a problem. The arrival of new officers with no understanding of the Indians or their background and who had problems communicating with them, was highly detrimental for the morale of the Indian troops.

After the departure of the Indian Corps, Indian soldiers were no longer present in large numbers on the Western Front. However, this does not mean that there were no Indian units, as a few cavalry units and other small groups remained in Europe, including Flanders, until the end of the war. At the end of the war and in the first years after the war units of the Indian Labour Corps were also active in our regions. They arrived in the Ypres area in September 1919 to replace the Chinese coolies to the great relief of the returning population among which the Chinese labourers had acquired a bad reputation. The members of the Indian Labour Corps were not soldiers but civilians who performed tasks such as repairing roads, clearing rubble, etc. for the army behind the front. The corps comprised some 10 different ethnic groups, usually members of the 'non-martial races'. Hardly any research has been done into the Indian Labour Corps or into any of the many other labour corps.

Alberto Fabio Lorenzi (1880-1969): Glorious attack of the Indians, 1915. The artist managed to give an expressive impression of the Battle of Neuve-Chapelle (10-13 March 1915). Here also fantasy took precedence over reality: Neuve-Chapelle is located in the extremely flat Valley of the Lys.
(© BDIC – Musée de l'Histoire Contemporaine, Paris)

OFFICIAL PHOTOGRAPH. (COPYRIGHT).
ISSUED BY THE CORPORATION OF BRIGHTON
WITH THE ASSISTANCE OF THE MILITARY AUTHORITIES.

17. CONVALESCENT SIKHS.

A. H. FRY. PHOTO,
BRIGHTON.

— 'I want to leave this country.'

For the Indian labourers and soldiers Europe was a totally new experience. In their letters home the sepoys wrote all kinds of things about the country in which they were fighting, about the dreadful circumstances but also about the strange customs of the local population. Lance Dafadar Chanda Singh wrote in a letter to his wife:

This is a very nice country. The father and mother invite a visitor to kiss them. If he refuses they feel insulted. Then the whole family, both men and women start telling dirty jokes, and they all enjoy this. This is indeed a free country. Nothing is prohibited, you can do anything you like. In the presence of the father and brothers a man may take a girl's arm and lead her outdoors. They will not say anything. They are quite at ease.

The censor added to this letter that it gave an odd image of life in quarters and we can only hope that this was an isolated case. The writer was inspired by his fantasy or he may accidentally have been quartered with a family with loose morals. The passage was cut out of the letter because it might have given the wrong idea and could have discredited our allies in India.

Obviously, their stay in Europe also had a cultural impact that was even felt back in India. Dafadar Ranji Lal of the 20th Deccan Horse wrote to his father:

… When I look at Europe, I bemoan the fate of India. In Europe everyone is educated, whether man or woman, boy or girl. The men are now at war and the women do the work. They can write to their husbands and read their

During the war the Royal Pavilion in Brighton was used a hospital for the British Indian troops. This is a group of convalescing Sikhs in 1915.
(© The Royal Pavilion and Museums, Brighton & Hove)

answers. You should educate the girls as well as the boys to ensure a better future for us.

Other letters express (veiled) criticism of the British and/of the war. And almost every Indian was homesick for his beloved homeland, this was possibly even more prevalent among the hundreds of Indian prisoners of war in Germany. On 6 June 1916 Gurkha Jasbahadur sang into the recording device of the Prussian phonographic commission:

> *... I do not want to stay in Europe, please take me home to India. The Gurkha eats lamb, but does not eat duck. Alive we serve no purpose yet we cannot die... That is why I want to return to my village. Back in my village I want to cut the grass in the fields. I want to leave this country.*

Jasbahadur Rai from Gantok in the Himalaya state Sikkim was buried at Zehrensdorf Indian Cemetery near Berlin. He died on 3 January 1917, six months after his sad voice had been recorded.

— Selective bibliography

Berlin, Berliner Lautarchiv, Sound Recording PK 307.

Dendooven, Dominiek, *Het Indische Leger in de Ieper Salient 1914-1918*, Ieper, 1999.

Merewether, J. en Smith, F., *The Indian Corps in France*, London, 1917.

National Archives, Kew. WO107/37 'Notes on Indian Labour', 1918.

Omissi, David, *Indian voices of the Great War. Soldier's letters, 1914-18*, London, 1999.

Scheffner, Philip, *The Halfmoon Files* (A documentary film on Indian prisoners-of-war in Germany), Berlin, 2007.

Bhupinder Singh Holland, *How Europe is indebted to the Sikhs?*, Waremme, 2005.

Streets, Heather, *Martial Races. The military, race and masculinity in British Imperial Culture, 1857-1914*, Manchester, 2005.

Van Walleghem, Achiel, *De oorlog te Dickebusch en omstreken 1914-1918*, Brugge, 1963-1967, 3 vols.

Willcocks, James, *With the Indians in France*, London, 1920.

SEPOY KHUDADAD.

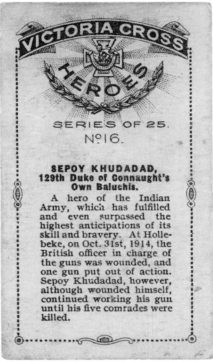

VICTORIA CROSS HEROES

SERIES OF 25.
Nº 16.

**SEPOY KHUDADAD,
129th Duke of Connaught's
Own Baluchis.**

A hero of the Indian Army, which has fulfilled and even surpassed the highest anticipations of its skill and bravery. At Hollebeke, on Oct. 31st, 1914, the British officer in charge of the guns was wounded, and one gun put out of action. Sepoy Khudadad, however, although wounded himself, continued working his gun until his five comrades were killed.

Khudadad Khan was a Muslim Rajput from the present day Pakistan province Punjab. In 1914 he was the first British Indian soldier ever to be awarded the Victoria Cross, the highest British military decoration. An imaginary portrait of hero Khudadad was depicted on popular cigarette cards. Khudadad Khan survived the war and died in March 1971. (In Flanders Fields Museum)

A P. 74. A SEMAILLE BY BALLOON.
Durch Luftballon. Le 29-9-1918.

Die erste Million.

THE UNITED STATES

IN OUR REGIONS DURING THE FIRST WORLD WAR

DOMINIEK DENDOOVEN

After the German Empire had announced an unrestricted submarine warfare, the United States declared war against the Central Powers on 6 April 1917. However, the United States had played an important role in the war effort even before this date both internationally, more specifically in the field of diplomacy, and closer to the front line. As it was the major neutral power both the allies and the central powers tried to get the Americans 'on their side'. For the Germans it was more a matter of trying not to offend the US. The report drafted by James Bryce, former British Ambassador in Washington, on the German atrocities perpetrated in Belgium, and the repeated protests against the brutal occupation uttered by

Brand Whitlock, the American Ambassador in Brussels, had generated considerable sympathy for invaded Belgium in the United States public opinion. This was demonstrated amongst others in the emergency aid which the Americans shipped to Belgium in bulk. The *Commission for Relief in Belgium* effectively ensured that the Belgians living in the occupied region did not starve. Until April 1917 many Americans: journalists, relief workers and diplomats, resided in the occupied country. Americans had also been active on the other side of the front line before 1917. The *American Field Service* was created in 1914, as a voluntary ambulance service that provided services to the allied forces. After the war the organization

Allied pamphlets strewn above German positions in September 1918. The message that already 1 million American soldiers were present in Europe was intended to dishearten the German soldiers. (In Flanders Fields Museum)

Stereo photo with American soldiers, 1917. Stereo photos were very popular during the First World War. The photo could be viewed in 3D by means of a stereoscope. (In Flanders Fields Museum)

evolved to become the well-known cultural exchange programme AFS. The American Red Cross was active in providing aid to refugees and civilians behind the front. Many individual Americans crossed the Northern border to serve in the Canadian army: some were looking for adventure, others were genuinely committed and indignant. For instance, you can read on the grave of Leland Wingate Fernald, buried as a Canadian soldier in Lijssenthoek British Military Cemetery in Poperinge, that this subject of the United States volunteered because he was outraged by the sinking of the Lusitania, the ocean liner torpedoed by a German submarine on 7 May 1915, causing the death of 1200 mainly civilian passengers.

The famous neurosurgeon of Harvard University, Harvey Cushing, also came to Europe in 1915 to work in an American hospital near Paris. After a lengthy stay in the US, he arrived at the British field hospitals in the vicinity of Poperinge in May 1917. There he witnessed the whole Third Battle of Ypres, and ultimately joined the *American Expeditionary Force* in June 1918. His outstanding diary 'From a Surgeon's

American soldiers, including some black soldiers, parade during the funeral procession for resistance heroes Oscar Verschuere and René Sabbe from Waregem who died in German captivity, 15 June 1919. (© Municipal Archive Waregem)

Journal' is a compendium of excellent observations, comments and medical dilemmas.

— Americans in Flanders

It was the arrival of the American Expeditionary Force as from June 1917 that tipped the balance in favour of the allied forces towards the middle of 1918. The main American sector was, however, the Meuse-Argonne region in the North East of France. American troops were only present on Belgian territory during the last months of the war. The four American divisions, 40,000 men in all, who fought in Flanders, had only arrived in Europe in June and July 1918. The 27th and 30th division had already experienced their baptism of fire in July at the front to the South of Ypres, between the Ypres-Comines railway line and Dikkebus Lake for the 30th and from Dikkebus Lake to Kemmel for the 27th. The soldiers of the latter division mainly originated from New York State in the East of the United States. The 30th division was made up of Southerners from North Carolina, South Carolina and Tennessee. Both divisions

remained near Ypres until 4 September 1918. They only faced heavier fighting in the last days when the front line had shifted slightly to the East.

The 37th and 91st division reinforced a French army division on 30 October 1918 between the rivers Lys and Scheldt. One of the last phases of the Final Offensive was launched the following day and the Americans were used as 'shock troops'. They attacked in the direction of the Scheldt between Waregem and Kruishoutem. As fighting took place in a virtually undisturbed landscape between hedges and (inhabited) farms, the defending Germans had many advantages and the Americans suffered heavy losses, particularly in the Spitaalsbossen (Spitaals Woods), not far from the present day American military cemetery *Flanders Field* in Waregem. After the initial shock German resistance waned and the 91st division was able to liberate Oudenaarde without too many problems on 2 November. The next phase of the offensive was scheduled for 10 November, when they crossed the Scheldt and took up position on the hills on the other side of the river. There, in the 'Flemish

The exhumation of Americans fallen in Olsene to transfer them to the cemetery in Waregem that would later become Flanders Field American Cemetery, 1918. This was done amongst others by black American soldiers. (© Flanders Field American Cemetery, Waregem)

A group of American soldiers visiting the British front in Flanders, 17 July 1917. (© ECPAD – Médiathèque de la Défense, Paris)

Ardennes', the American 37th and 91st Division experienced their Armistice the next day just as they were preparing for the next 'push'. The 37th division originated from Ohio, the 91st division was also called the Wild West Division as it included men from the Western states California, Idaho, Montana, Nevada, Oregon, Utah, Washington and Wyoming. In Kemmel and Oudenaarde there are monuments for the American divisions, whereas the Flanders Field American Cemetery in Waregem, the smallest American military cemetery in Europe, commemorates their 368 dead and 43 missing soldiers on Belgian territory.

Although everyone was delighted with the arrival of the Americans, their customs and habits were not equally appreciated by everyone. Eric Hiscock, a young Brit in the Royal Fusilliers remembers them as follows:

> *'They marched through our village in columns*
> *of three, held their rifles like Boy Scouts*
> *presenting arms with their broomsticks, and*
> *spoke what sounded like a foreign language.*
> *"When we get at those cocksucking mother-*
> *fuckers", boasted many of them, and no one*
> *in the 26th Battalion of the Royal Fusiliers had*
> *heard such expressions before, nor knew what*
> *they meant. Their discipline seemed just as*
> *odd, with officers and rankers clapping each*
> *other on the back, and drinking together in*
> *the local estaminets. They fraternised with*
> *local girls in a way we could never have*

> *achieved nor have imagined, mainly with the*
> *help of their wallets. The Yank exuded francs,*
> *and were paid more for one day's soldiering*
> *than we got in a week, and no one in our*
> *village believed for a moment that they would*
> *be fit to fight if they were asked to do so.'*

The American divisions who fought in Flanders were almost exclusively white. The *American Expeditionary Force* had a strict segregation policy with separate units for whites and blacks. The more than 200,000 black soldiers, one tenth of the total AEF, were not considered able by their superiors: only one fifth of them was actually deployed at the front (as opposed to two thirds of the white soldiers), the others worked behind the front or in the inland ports. The Afro-Americans who were deployed at the front, mainly served in the 92nd division that remained in France. Another black unit, however, the 370th Infantry Regiment from Illinois, belonged to a French Brigade that fought near the French-Belgian border in November 1918. Thus the small village of Petite Chapelle in the South of the Province Namur is the only Belgian place to have been liberated by black Americans on 10-11 November 1918. It is quite likely that after the Armistice a number of Afro-American units were temporarily present in Belgium.

— American Indians on the Western Front

Another important group is the American Indians: over 13,000 Native Americans served in the

Like many other heads of state, American President Woodrow Wilson visited destroyed Ypres. Here we see him (with cap) in the company of Ypres Burgomaster Colaert (with a white beard) before the ruins of Saint Martin's Church. Behind them the Belgian sovereigns accompany Mrs Wilson. The photo is dated June 1919.
(© Royal Army and Military History Museum, Brussels)

American army during the First World War, almost one third of all adult male American Indians. Between two thousand and four thousand left for Europe with the A.E.F. The hope for the settlement of ancient claims and full civil rights appears to have been one of the reasons why so many Indians joined up; this hope was fulfilled in the post-war years in respect of civil rights. Virtually all tribes were represented but their involvement varied considerably. The largest group came from the state Oklahoma. As opposed to the Afro-Americans the American natives were not segregated but where barracked with the white units. Because of the prevailing stereotypes about his assumed combativeness, the Indian was rated higher as a soldier than the Afro-American, and therefore he experienced less discrimination. Some smaller units were exclusively made up of American Indians. Remarkably moccasins were a part of their uniform. The First World War had a certain influence on the life of the native people in the US. Not only were they subsequently granted civil rights but the war was and is still occasionally referred to in their ceremonies and dances. For instance, since 1917 the Lakota Indians ('Sioux'), have referred to the Germans in their traditional battle songs, by calling them 'iya sica' (the 'bad speakers' or 'those who speak in an odd way'). On the negative side some tribes lost even more grounds to the state during the war.

There is little doubt that American Indians also fought in Belgium, more specifically in the 91st Division that originated from the (Mid-)West of the United States.

— Flemings in the American Army

As had been the case in Canada emigrated Flemings also joined the American army. One such remarkable example is the Van den Broeck family from Sint-Niklaas. Of the nine children in the family of clog maker Jan Van den Broeck five boys and two girls emigrated to the United states shortly before the First World War. When war broke out the two boys who had stayed in Belgium, Leon and Frans, were mobilized. Shortly later, probably in September 1914, the brothers Emiel and Jozef left Chicago to return to Europe and become Belgian volunteers. When the United States declared war on the Central Powers on 6 April 1917, the brothers Henri, Charles and August and sister Henriette joined the American army. The latter as a multilingual telephone operator. Thus eight children of a single family from Sint-Niklaas served on the Western Front: four as Belgians and four as Americans. And all eight of them survived the war.

— **Selective Bibliography:**

Applegate Krouse, Susan, *North American Indians in the Great War*, Lincoln, 2007.

Camurat, Diane, *The American Indian in the Great War. Real and Imagined.* Master's thesis at Paris VII, 1993.

Clarke, William, *Over there with O'Ryan's Roughnecks*, Seattle, 1969.Cushing, Harvey, *From a Surgeon's Journal 1915-1918*, London, 1936.

Hiscock, Eric, *The bells of hell go ting-aling-aling*, London, 1976.

A. Murphy, Elmer en Robert S. Thomas, *The Thirtieth Division in the World War*, Lepanto, 1936.

Van Den Broeck, Lutgart, 'We hebben zeven ridders voorbij zien gaan', in: *Archivaria* 1998, nr. 8, pp. 68-73.

Portrait of the seven Van den Broeck brothers in military uniform: three as American soldiers and four as Belgian soldiers, February 1919. From left to right: Jozef, Emiel, August, Frans, Charles, Leon and Henri. The photo was also printed in the Chicago Sunday Tribune of 11 November 1919.
(© Hugo Van den Broeck, Ostend)

An American helmet with the badge of the 27th US Division from New York. This unit was posted near Ypres in the summer of 1918.
(In Flanders Fields Museum)

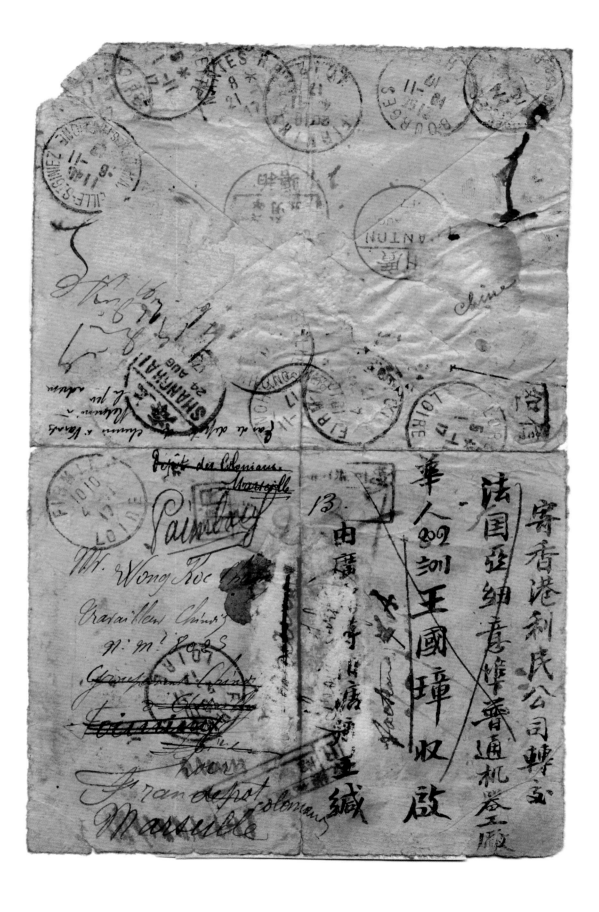

THE CHINESE LABOUR CORPS

GWYNNIE HAGEN

Chinese and British interests

The Chinese Republic, which had been just formed in 1911, had a double agenda when it decided to send labourers to the Western Front. By becoming involved in the war effort the Chinese Republic aimed to convince European powers that the country was definitely on its way to become a modern nation, and that in future it would respect the international playing rules and would be a reliable partner for the Western powers. Furthermore, the Chinese authorities aimed to secure their seat at the post-war peace conference. Indeed, this is where the future of the German concessions in China would be decided. This issue was very urgent as China's rival Japan had immediately invoked its military alliance with the United Kingdom as soon as war broke out in order to occupy the strategically important German concessions on the Northern Chinese peninsula Shandong. In spite of Chinese protest the region firmly remained in Japanese hands until the end of the war. During the further course of the war China would contribute to the allied war effort in order to have enough clout at the peace conference to obtain a favourable decision on the Shandong issue.

Back in June 1915, the Chinese government proposed to the allies to deploy Chinese labourers in Europe. Although the British government immediately dispelled the proposal as not feasible, it would reconsider its decision in the autumn of 1916. Due to the heavy losses incurred near the Somme there was a dire shortage of workforce. The enormous reservoir of manpower in China had now become an appealing option. All the more so, since the French government had started recruiting labourers, to the greatest satisfaction of French army command.

— Recruitment and life in the CLC

Practical considerations led the British to concentrate their recruitment for the *Chinese Labour Corps* (CLC) in Weihaiwei (now Weihai) and later Qingdao, two concessions located in the Northern peninsula Shandong. Because of its very dense population and milder climate Shandong offered the best opportunities to find the most suitable candidates for shipment to Europe. To attract future recruits announcements were posted in tea houses and other public places. When a labourer registered he signed a three-year contract and was allocated an identification number. From then onwards his name would be unimportant. Conditions were sufficiently appealing to encourage many tens of thousands of mainly poor farmers to embark for a continent most hardly even knew existed. Although the pay the labourers received was modest according to Western standards, it was four times as much as they would have received as labourers in Shandong. In addition to their pay the labourers were given food, clothing, housing and medical care. Part of their pay was sent to their families in China. The standard clothing for a labourer during the winter was a quilted linen outfit and for the summer two blue cotton outfits. They also received a felt hood.

The first batch of some 1,000 labourers arrived in Europe in April 1917. Under British command their numbers would increase to just under 95,000 between 1917 and 1920. The French army employed 44,000 labourers. The labourers were organized in companies of 300 or 500 men under the command of a British officer, and each company was divided into platoons commanded by British and Chinese non-commissioned officers. In 1917 a correspondent of *The Times* visited the Chinese camps in Northern

This envelope of 1917, addressed to *travailleur chinois* Wang Guozhang, is full of Chinese and French stamps. The Chinese text means: 'To be delivered via the Li Min firm in Hong Kong, (in) France, the port of 'Yaxiyi', ordinary machine factory, for the attention of Chinese 802 Wang Guozhang, sent by Wang Jian from the commune of Botang in the province of Guandong'. The letter never reached its destination as the French postal service probably failed to understand what 'Yaxiyi' meant. (Collection Philippe Oosterlinck)

Badge of the Chinese Labour Corps. This simple insignia was virtually the only badge worn by the Chinese labourers. (Collection Philippe Oosterlinck)

France where he found the Chinese working zealously like and '*always with that inscrutable smile of the Far East upon their smooth yellow faces*'. In practice they worked eight hours a day, excluding the marching time to and from work and meal times. Through the mediation of the Chinese Ambassador in London the men were entitled to half a day's rest per week or a whole day per fortnight. The British officers also allowed the labourers to celebrate the Chinese feast days and holidays, even though this was not always observed due to misunderstandings.

The labourers were mainly used for construction and demolition work, road construction, digging trenches and clearing battlefields, working on the railways, loading and unloading ships and trains. After the armistice in 1918 their contract continued to run and labourers would be deployed until early 1920 for clearance work in Belgium and France as well as for the construction of war cemeteries. The CLC labourer was generally considered to be a quality worker who could adapt to any type of work. '*The Chinaman is versatile and adaptable. He can handle stores and do other things for which a certain intelligence and initiative are required. But he makes a very good coolie also, and can pile or unload timber all day without feeling the strain*', claimed the correspondent of *The Times*. In spite of this the British failed to repress their obvious feelings of superiority. British reports frequently adopted the view that the labourer should be kept in his place, just like a child. This may be the reason why the labourers insisted on being given their orders directly by a Chinese foreman and not by a British soldier.

They spent their free time in their own camps playing music, singing songs, breeding dogs, chickens and cats. However, the main leisure activities were drinking tea and gambling. The labourers gambled a lot even though the stakes were rather modest. The amounts gambled were small and the number of participants was limited.

— Risks

His contract clearly stated that the Chinese labourer is not to be considered as a combatant and is not be put to work in the vicinity of hazardous locations. Yet the labourers were exposed to some major risks. After August 1917, when China declared war on Germany, the labourers were deployed closer to

A group of coolies of the Chinese Labour Corps in Oudezeele,
3 June 1918. The letters CLC can be clearly distinguished
on the straw hat of the man on the right at the front.
(© BDIC-Musée de l'Histoire Contemporaine, Paris)

M. M. 6 MONT KEMMEL — de la Guerre 1914-18. Camp Chinois (Annamites britanniques)
Br, Souvenir Van den Oorlog Kamp van Chinoezen (Engelsche annamiten)
Of the War Chinese (Pekin) Camp British

the front line to repair trenches and supply ammunition. Their camps behind the front line offered no guarantee of safety, as was demonstrated by the German shells that killed respectively thirteen and four labourers near Reningelst on 15 November 1917 and 12 April 1918. Today some 2,000 Chinese labourers are buried in Northern France and in Belgian Flanders, most of them between British, French and occasionally German soldiers.

Even though the Chinese were recruited as labourers and initially China was still neutral, the CLC belonged to the British army and its members were governed by military law. In the event of problems they would also be court-martialled. It is highly unlikely that the labourers were fully aware of this when they signed their contract. Between 1917 and 1920 ten labourers of the CLC would experience the harshness of martial law. They were charged with murder by the British army command and were executed. Nine of the ten executions were carried out for murdering a fellow countryman. The story of labourer

Wang Junzhi shows that gambling debts were often the underlying reason for these dramas. In 1919 before a court martial Wang Junzhi testified that co-labourer Liu Huaiyu owed him 80 francs for quite some time. After repeatedly begging, demanding and threatening the victim he finally lost patience in the night of 2 February 1919. Wang Junzhi found a rifle and shot the sleeping Liu Huaiyu through the head. He shot another labourer as he fled outside. Yet another labourer who crossed his path was knocked down. On 8 May 1919, at 4.24 a.m. Wang Junzhi was executed in the courtyard of the town hall of Poperinge. He would be the last person to be executed there under British orders.

— A social experiment

The shipping of thousands of labourers was seen in China and Europe as a unique opportunity to bring poor Chinese in contact with education and modern social ideas. The most successful organization in this field was the *Young Men's Christian Association*.

Contrary to the caption on the postcard Peking Camp of the 101st Chinese Labour Company was not located near Kemmel Hill but in Reningelst. It had a beautiful Chinese style entrance gate.

A shell artistically decorated by a Chinese labourer. Above the peony rose and next to the butterfly you can read: 'This represents the luxuriant splendour of the peony roses'. On the other side of the shell a poem by Wang Zhihuan of the Tang dynasty (688-742 A.D.) is engraved. (Collection Philippe Oosterlinck)

The *YMCA* sent 150 British, American and Chinese workers, who had previously done Christian missionary work in China, to France and Flanders. They provided recreation and helped the labourers write letters home; they taught them national awareness, civil rights and the principles of modern management. During special evening classes the labourers were taught to write using a phonetic system and Chinese characters. They were also instructed in basic French, history, hygiene and singing. This soon produced results; when they arrived in France only 20% of the labourers were literate. By the end of 1921, after two years of evening classes their number had increased to 38 %.

The programmes of the *YMCA* also allowed Chinese students of the upper classes to come into contact for the first time with fellow countrymen of the poorer layers of the population. In China their worlds

were quite distinct but behind the front line people like Yan Yangchu, who had recently graduated from Yale University, worked on reading out, translating and summarizing foreign newspapers for the labourers. In January 1919 he launched his own newspaper for all the Chinese in France, *The Chinese Laborers' Weekly (Huagong Zhoubao)*, in which the labourers were given the opportunity to write their own articles. People like Yan had high expectations of the labourers. They hoped that because of their foreign contacts the labourers would become aware of their national identity and would contribute to the future of modern China. The fact that this was not a vain hope was demonstrated in an article in *The Chinese Laborers' Weekly*, written by labourer Fu Shengsan in March 1919. He wrote that before coming to Europe the labourers had not clearly understood the relationship between an individual and his country. Yet seeing European populations fight one another for years on end in defence of their country had sparked off their own nationalism. He also believed that the Chinese were a match for the Europeans and that China would soon be as powerful as the European countries. This national pride was also demonstrated during an incident that occurred after the armistice. To celebrate the end of the war British army command organized a major sports event in Belgium. Six thousand Chinese labourers attended the event, but turned back as soon as they realised that there was not a single Chinese flag among the allied flags.

This enamelled serviette ring, probably a product of Chinese labourers during or shortly after the First World War, has a Christian connotation. Not only does it mention the Western words 'Vive Labeur', but it also carries the Chinese inscription: 'Lord give me peace in this life' and a representation of a cross (Collectie Philippe Oosterlinck)

— Two worlds

The fact that the British government boasted that labourers at the service of the British were subjected to far stricter discipline and were more restricted in their movements than their colleagues serving the French, did not prevent the labourers from seeking contacts with the local population. The Chinese labourers occupy a special place in the testimonies of Flemish civilians. Usually people in Flanders speak of 'Tsings', which is derived from the very disparaging English word *Chinks*. On 6 August 1917, the parish priest of Dikkebus, Father Van Walleghem, described the Chinese labourers as:

Yellow in colour, with flat noses and slanting eyes and they always seem to have a foolish smile on their faces and are continuously looking around, to such an extent that it is

quite surprising that they have not yet met with a fatal accident on our busy roads.

The local tradespeople were delighted with the labourers. According to Van Walleghem they always looked for the best and most beautiful items and there was no point in trying to sell them rubbish. He did not know what they earned but commented that some carried large amounts of cash on them. They were particularly keen on watches and rings:

Lately I came across a Chinaman who wore a watch on each arm, he was very proud when he saw me looking at his watches.

However, some people exploited the labourers. Jeanne Battheu from Poperinge was seven years old when the first Chinese labourers arrived in 1917. In an

Members of the Chinese Labour Corps celebrating the beginning of the Year of the Horse, 11 February 1918. Two men are playing the Erhu, the traditional two-string bowed string instrument, whereas the cymbals seem to have been made from British helmets.
(© Imperial War Museum, London)

interview in 1995 she explained how the labourers preferred champagne:

> ... *on the corner someone had a beer store and of course he also sold lemonade as 'champie, champie' to the Chinese ... and it fizzed and sprayed and went 'psssht' when they uncapped the bottle.*

The Armistice on 11 November 1918 marked a clear turning point in the civilian population's perception of the Chinese labourers. Testimonies no longer spoke of laughing and hard working men but of dangerous individuals who erred through the region murdering and plundering. In 1978 Gaston Boudry spoke of 'a young girl of approximately sixteen years of age. She was followed on the street by the Tsjings. She ran indoors, locked the door and propped it up.

They fired shots through the door and killed her'. Most of these assault and murder stories were hearsay, offered very superficial descriptions and can no longer be verified. However, there are reasons to assume that the relationship between the civilians and labourers turned sour as from 1919. The withdrawal of the British troops led to growing laxness in maintaining discipline in the CLC, allowing the labourers to wander about aimlessly. The labourers were also given less pleasant tasks like the hazardous retrieval of ammunition and the reburying of hundreds of thousands of fallen soldiers. All this in combination with a strong feeling of homesickness made it obvious that the European experience had run its course for many labourers.

The returning citizens found a destroyed and desolate region. The long standing enemy may have dis-

Two Chinese coolies worshipping in front of an ancestors' shrine, 11 February 1918. (© Imperial War Museum, London)

appeared but the region was full of foreign people: released German prisoners of war, marauding civilians and '*odd blokes, strikingly dressed, with strange eating habits and a peculiar language*'. This caused suspicion, and unsolved murders and other crimes were soon blamed on these foreigners. The fact that the labourers helped to clear the region after the war is a reality that was omitted in most testimonies

— **Selective Bibliography:**

Hagen, Gwynnie. *Eenen dwazen glimlach aan het front*. Leuven 1996, unpublished dissertation

Jones, Arthur Phillip, *Britain's Search for Chinese Cooperation in the First World War*, Garland Publishing, 1986.

Xu Guoqi, *China and the Great War. China's Pursuit of a New National Identity and Internationalization*, Cambridge, Cambridge University Press, 2005.

Bailey, Paul, 'From Shandong tot the Somme; Chinese Indentured Labour in France During World War I' in: Kershen, Anne J. (ed.), *Language, Labour and Migration*, Ashgate, 2000.

In a Chinese Labour Corps camp: the hairdresser at work, 1918.
(© Imperial War Museum, London)

EXCERPTS FROM THE REPORTS OF AN
AGENT POUR LES AFFAIRES DES OUVRIERS CHINOIS
AND A MANUAL ON
HOW TO TREAT CHINESE COOLIES

PHILIP VANHAELEMEERSCH

An interesting source of our knowledge about Chinese labourers in Europe during the First World War, are the regular reports sent to Peking by the Chinese representation in Paris. These reports were written for the Chinese government and are therefore customized for this purpose. In the eyes of the Chinese, the Labour Corps enterprise was officially a commercial venture. China had reached an agreement with the warring parties to supply a scarce commodity, i.e. manpower. It was the task of its representatives in Europe to ensure the terms of this agreement were observed. Where necessary they had to intervene with the French (or British) Ministry of Defence to remind them of the details of the contract they had signed with the Chinese government. Thus, they mediated between two governments and very frequently between two cultures too, more specifically regarding the practicalities of daily life. One Chinese who appears to have excelled in this was Li Jun.

Li Jun had a so-called fast-track career. In 1912, barely twenty years old, he was appointed secretary at the presidential palace of the young Chinese Republic. Shortly later he left for Liverpool, where he obtained a university degree. He left England for Paris to continue his studies. In 1922, he was appointed consul and this heralded the start of a diplomatic career that would culminate in an ambassadorship in Copenhagen, where he would die in 1948.

— A young inspector

For Li Jun the story of the Chinese Labour Corps started in Paris. In a letter to his Minister, Chinese Ambassador Hu complained about the many problems caused by the coolies and about the lack of personnel to intervene. Li Jun was known to the ambassador as an ordinary student in France. However, his talents had not escaped the ambassador and at his request on 19 April 1917 Peking agreed that Li Jun should henceforth visit the coolies on site as *agent pour les affaires des ouvriers chinois, attaché à la Légation* (403). The situation in France was becoming increasingly tense. On 12 June 1917 the ambassador telegraphed Peking that Li Jun should urgently return (from England?) (410). Peking could only answer that Li Jun was underway (411). Li Jun's task was to highlight the abuses of the employers to his ambassador, but he was also expected to keep the coolies under control (402). He fulfilled this last assignment successfully where even French colonels, generals and prefects had failed: *'Everything calms down as soon as he arrives, and it will be white, if he says white, black if he says black'* (Auguste Dupouy, p. 156).

Li Jun was kept fully occupied with his inspections in France (474). Before scheduling the inspection of a workplace Li Jun informed the French ministry of his intention. Usually the news of his inspection reached the bosses before Li appeared, but Li cleverly found a way round this. First, he made accurate notes of

In July 1919 near Ypres the battlefield grave of the young Belgian officer Louis de Mahieu (+ 31 August 1918) was exposed to exhume his body and transfer it to his final resting place in Oost-Vleteren. This gruesome task was carried out by a Chinese labourer amongst others, standing on the extreme left on this photo.
(© In Flanders Fields Museum – Collection de Mahieu)

The Chinese Labour Corps on its way to work.
Oudezeele, 3 June 1918.

what the boss had to say. Then he went into the workplace to check whether this reflected the actual situation. Complaints were recorded and where necessary Li Jun proposed remedial measures. The coolies were instructed to adapt to the local habits and to comply with the laws of their host countries. These were the 'standard inspections'. However, at times this routine had to be broken. A succession of minor frictions occurred between the Chinese and the local population. A minor misunderstanding often resulted in an open conflict. Li Jun would then be called in by the French Ministry of Defence, abandoning his ongoing inspection, he would hasten to the scene of the incident to mediate. Occasionally, the problems were simply caused by the labourers' ignorance of the Western judicial procedure. It was then up to Li Jun to alleviate their distrust and convince them that the 'law' was not merely repressive but that it also made all citizens 'equal'.

Li Jun's prime concern was the every day needs of the labourers. For instance, the coolies complained about their daily rations. The contract stipulated to the gram what the coolies had to be served. This quota was frequently disregarded and Li Jun was expected to submit a complaint. Occasionally, Li Jun simply had to bridge cultural sensitivities. When the French tried to feed the Chinese far 'healthier' horse meat it was Li Jun who told them about the Chinese aversion to that kind of meat. The contract also stipulated provisions with regard to the clothing and footwear of the coolies. At times the French army would give them used clothes to wear. Here also Li Jun intervened. Moreover, even though the bedding provided for the Chinese met French army standards it failed to protect their Chinese constitution against the cold European climate.

In time Li Jun was faced with far more complex problems. There was the problem of mixed Chinese-French relations. During the last months of the war Li Jun was inundated with this type of issue. The Chinese had acquired some experience with mixed marriages in France. The usual procedure was for the future groom to present himself with a letter from his parents at the Chinese Embassy in Paris, where it would be stamped, and then the future groom would take this document to the town hall for the marriage ceremony. This procedure had now become inadequate.

First, the Chinese in the Labour Corps in France were under contract and hence were not free. They were continuously at risk of being punished, transferred or even of being sent home to China. Some Chinese first started a family with a French woman, and subsequently wanted to regularize their situation with a certificate stating they were single when they married in France, but this was impossible due to the lack of a proper registry office back home in China. Initially, Li Jun had no objections to this type of mixed marriages. On the contrary, according to Li Jun all modern biologists claimed that it was good to mix 'races'. He also wrote to his Minister of Foreign Affairs in China that the coolies could acquire many minor and major skills through their marriage with a Western woman, which will allow them to lead a full life when they return to China.

An even more delicate question was posed by the deceased labourers. In the summer of 1917, Li Jun counted a total of 281 dead. The same problem as for mixed marriages arose in this situation namely that of false identities. Many Chinese labourers were not afraid to adopt another Chinaman's identity, depending on how it suited them. This occurred when they boarded the ship in China in order to avoid the medical examination, and continued to be a detrimental practice in Europe, e.g. when money was to be drawn. The result was that the identity of a fairly large number of bodies was uncertain. There was a real risk that a family would be notified of the death of a relative, who in fact did not belong to the family, while another family would be left in doubt. Luckily the French provided a solution. Upon arrival each labourer was asked to complete a statement with the name of an heir back home in China, including the address and his degree of kinship to that person. Furthermore, the French introduced procedures stating the exact steps to be followed in the event of the death of a labourer. Li Jun admired such efficiency, and set them as an example for China that had no experience whatsoever with the registration of deaths. In this respect France could be a model for China.

— Discipline

Another issue was the question of discipline. At times discipline was sadly lacking among the coolies. Li Jun also had to look into this. The coolies were obliged to submit to an authority structure they had not agreed to. They had travelled to Europe as civilian personnel, but were later subjected to all aspects of military discipline. Li Jun would also delve deeper into the causes of their dissatisfaction. For instance there were many missionaries who had travelled along from China. Many of these missionaries were used to dealing with their Chinese converts, who were often poor devils from the lower layers of Chinese society. The Chinese labourers they had to deal with in Europe were quite different. They were proud Chinese with a profound belief in the young Chinese Republic. Li Jun excelled at conveying the feelings of these Chinese:

For many years they [= the missionaries] have been used to dealing with Catholics at home in

Chinese coolie 18693 Song Xiufeng posing together with Maurice, the son of photographer René Matton, in Proven. The central board also displays the date '1917 in the Republican era'. The text on the other board: 'Che Pupe Now Goedze' remains unexplainable to the present day.
(© Heirs René Matton, Proven)

*China. They know nothing of our Chinese civili-
sation but they are familiar with all our bad
habits. Therefore they approach our labourers
as famished rickshaw drivers working in all
weathers, the type of people intended to carry
loads and other people in their sedan chairs.
Just look at them here in our civilized France,
they say! Ten times better nourished, better
dressed, better housed and paid than in China!*

Matters came to a head with the Americans in France.
At the beginning of 1918 they asked the French government for Chinese manpower. The French willingly
lent them Chinese labourers but the latter rebelled
and some fled. The crisis was so urgent that on 29
July Li Jun went on site to assess the situation. Li Jun
found a number of reasons for the incompatibility between the Chinese and Americans. First, the Americans had also acquired an image of the Chinese back
home in America and, just like the missionaries, they
now projected that image onto the labourers in
France. There was the 'arrogance' of the Americans
and there was the whole body language of the Americans: Li Jun wrote:

*They are incredibly temperamental and
conceited. If they do not like something they
wave their arms about and stamp their feet,
much to the dislike of the Chinese (p. 398b).*

The Americans did not appear to understand that
they had only been lent the Chinese and that ultimately they were under French command. The Chinese felt they had fallen between two chairs: the
Americans had come to help their French friends, so
if you wanted to remain friendly with the French you
had to get on with the Americans. The resentment
experienced by the Chinese towards this ambiguous
situation only ended when photos appeared of American instruments of torture and the French wisely
decided to withdraw their Chinese labourers.

How should the French treat their Chinese coolies?
Confrontation was the least indicated manner of getting things done by the Chinese. Very few Western
persons in authority seemed to grasp this. One exception to this rule was a certain Commandant Defontaine.
Defontaine had been put in charge of the Chinese
labourers in the north of the country by the French
Ministry of Defence, as such he was the French coun-

terpart of Li Jun: whenever problems arose with the
Chinese labourers, Defontaine was dispatched on
site. The man had been a (vice) military attaché with
the French legation in Peking. It would appear that
he had become quite familiar with the customs and
sensitivities of the Chinese. In 1916, Defontaine had
been commissioned to write a manual on how to handle Chinese coolies by General Famin, who had also
acquired some experience in the Far East. Li Jun
translated this manual into Chinese and quoted
extensively from it in his report to the Minister of
Foreign Affairs in Peking.

Defontaine's manual starts by stating the obvious:
There are Chinese and there are Chinese. The Chinese
my colleagues are having to deal with, wrote Defontaine,

Three Chinese labourers and their British officer
pose willingly with an early war tourist before
a ruin in the G. de Stuersstraat in Ypres, 1919.
(© In Flanders Fields Museum)

are Chinese from Northern China and display their typical national character: *docile* - which makes it relatively easy to keep them under control — *yet they have a solid constitution and can withstand bitterly cold temperatures*. The French climate does not differ much from the climate they are used to in China. Therefore, with a little good will you can quite easily make the Chinese feel at home in other areas as well.

This good will can be shown with little things: food and drink for instance. Obviously, there are the terms of the contract. They take precedence and must be complied with, but where this is not possible, a good alternative must be provided. Chinese people love *salty fish and vegetables with soy oil*, these are relatively easy to find in France. The cooks, who are mainly French, should open their kitchens to the Chinese and learn from them. As concerns beverages, Defontaine stresses the Chinese custom of providing hot tea everywhere and at all times, a custom the French would be well-advised not to oppose. It is preferable not to get the Chinese used to wine. However, if a Chinese manages to bring *samshoo* (a kind of Chinese liqueur) from China, then there would be no harm in letting the labourers enjoy a drink from time to time: *they will do the work all the more joyously and zealously.*

Some small tricks will allow you to win their sympathy: Chinese can best be encouraged with an occasional small present. In the best Chinese tradition the present need not be large or expensive. You should

also ensure the Chinese are not housed at too great a distance from their workplace, so they don't have to walk in the rain.

Obviously, Chinese work ethics are not those of Westerners. Providing a little information will help avoid many misunderstandings. When the Chinese arrive in the workplace the first sight of the work will make them panic and they will feel disorientated. The only adequate response to this is *soothing words*. Defontaine claimed that you should never assume that Chinese people reason clearly and *precisely* in all situations. The expression *chabuduo*, 'more or less' is often uttered by the Chinese and illustrates their manner of thinking. Furthermore, the Chinese need a clear timetable that tells them when to get up, when to eat, when to follow lessons and when to go to bed. This timetable must be clearly displayed in the Chinese language.

— Interpreters and conflicts

This brings us to the interpreters. They fulfil a crucial role. The French would do well to pamper the interpreters as they can raise the work enthusiasm of the labourers. Indeed, they do far more than just translate: they are also responsible for conveying and explaining the official work instructions. However, some of these interpreters also abuse their position in order to deceive and mislead. They must be filtered out.

What about conflicts? Conflicts must be handled correctly or better still, should be nipped in the bud. For instance, be very weary of any Chinaman who does not belong to the own camp. If such a person approaches the camp then it can only be someone who wants to settle a score with another Chinaman or who wants to create an uproar. If a disagreement originates among Chinese labourers within the camp, you must intervene immediately and sanction the culprits to prevent the situation from deteriorating. Labourers who fail to submit to authority must be removed from the camp. However, even in such a situation you must consider the sensitivities of the Chinese. For instance, reprimanding Chinese labourers in the presence of their fellow countrymen is extremely counterproductive:

> *Do not make rash or tactless comments; do not mock them; do not take out your anger on them; do not insult them; and never use violence against them. They will not accept it*

For reasons of clarity it was also stated in Chinese that the village of Formerie (in Northern France) was out of bounds for all troops under British command.

and will be out to take revenge. If their work is unsatisfactory or if they accidentally make a mistake, take them to a place where no one can see you. Show them the error of their ways but remain flexible. The Chinese labourer will repent. However, if you call him to order in the presence of all his fellow labourers and if you violate his dignity, remember that you will not be able to read his anger on his face.

Here ends Li Jun's presentation of Defontaine's instructions on how to deal with Chinese labourers. The instructions are dated 26 September 1916, the period of the first contact of the French with the Chinese labourers. According to Li Jun they bear witness to the good will present in France in the early days of the Chinese Labour Corps saga. There was probably some degree of mutual idealization, this became evident in what Li Jun wrote about mixed marriages or the registration of births, deaths and marriages in France. However, the report in which Li Jun men-

tions Defontaine's instructions is dated almost two years later. At that time little remained of the initial good will of the French. The Chinese continued to admire the French for a little longer, but eventually this admiration would also come under pressure. In 1918, strikes of the Chinese labourers succeeded one another at an incredible rate. Li Jun was probably disheartened when he reported to this Minister in Peking that he too had had enough...

— **Bibliography:**

Dupouy, Auguste, 'Un Camp de Chinois', in: *Revue de Paris*, 26 (1919) No. 21 (1st of November) pp. 146-162.

Chen Sanjing, *Huagong yu Ouzhan* (= 'The Chinese Labor Force in the First World War') (Monograph Series, 52), Taipei: Institute of Modern History at the Academia Sinica, 2005 (In Chinese; second edition, the first edition was published in 1986).

Chen Sanjing (e.a.), *Ouzhan Huagong Shiliao 1912-1921* (= 'Historic Documents on the Chinese Labour Corps in Europe during the First World War, 1912-1921'), Taipei: Institute of Modern History at the Academia Sinica, 1996. The references in our text refer to the number of the document in this collection.

Chinese coolies at work in an ammunition depot near Proven, 1917
(© Imperial War Museum, London)

Farbige Engländer

ACADEMIC RESEARCH ON
(COLOURED) PRISONERS OF WAR
IN GERMANY, 1915-1918

BRITTA LANGE

During World War I non-European and especially coloured peoples in the allied armies — French and British colonial soldiers from Africa, Asia, India, and the South Seas — became a big issue in the war propaganda of the so-called 'Central Powers'. The German press wondered whether their presence on the European battlefields violated international laws. Moreover, an important tenet of German war propaganda held that their morally and militarily weak European enemies had recruited shamefully large numbers of soldiers from 'primitive peoples' who were obliged to fight in the war as 'coloured auxiliaries.' This challenged the old 19th century imperial and colonial order of the world, according to which the civilized 'cultural peoples' ruled legitimately over the 'natural peoples'. Because of the political alliances this hierarchy changed in the constellations of the First World War: 'Natural peoples' fought together with 'cultural peoples' against the 'cultural people' of Germany.

At the same time, the Ottoman Empire, which in November 1914 had declared a Jihad, i.e. a holy war against the armies of the Entente powers, was one of Germany's allies. The German government therefore adopted the political strategy of making all the Muslims among their prisoners join in the Jihad and fight against their own colonial masters. The best way to make captured colonial soldiers defect seemed to be by using offensive propaganda. Soon after the outbreak of war, two special camps were installed in Wünsdorf, a little town near Berlin, for Muslim and coloured POWs. Approximately 12,000 Muslims from Russia and about 4,000 POWs from the French and British colonies were detained in the camps 'Weinberge' and 'Halbmondlager', the so-called 'Halfmoon camp'. However, during the year 1917 the German government recognized that the Jihad propaganda had failed, yet coloured and Russian soldiers continued to be interned in these camps until the end of the war.

Besides propagandistic, political and popular[1] interests, academic research was also inspired by the ethnic situation on the battlefields and consequently in the prison camps. In 1915 Rudolf Martin, a professor of physical anthropology from Munich, stated:

The practices of our enemies, to pull in auxiliaries from everywhere, has resulted in representatives of the most varied peoples coming to Germany, who under normal circumstances would never have set foot on German soil in such numbers.[2]

German anthropologists, linguists, and musicologists recognized the opportunity this presented for their disciplines: They were interested not only in the quantity of 'study objects', but also in their ethnic identity and diversity. To study many different 'foreigners' in the camps would save them the trouble and expense of embarking on expeditions to their native countries. Instead, with comparatively little logistical effort and expense, they could conduct comparative studies of a multitude of different ethnic subjects on their own soil.

German academics were successful in procuring funds and visitors' permits from the government itself. This indicates a close relationship between scholarship and politics. The scholarly interest in many different and as 'exotic' as possible peoples equalled the propagandistic interests on the part of the government. The access to the prisoner of war camps that the researchers secured for themselves

Camp Commander Otto Stiehl made a number of albums with photos and souvenirs of the temporary guests in the camps of Zossen-Wünsdorf. He devoted this page to the 'coloured English'. (© Bildarchiv Preußischer Kulturbesitz, Berlin)

from 1915 onwards is thus comparable to the access western researchers had to the colonies. If one understands the colonies around 1900 as 'laboratories of modernity'[3], that is, as a place where western knowledge could be created and tested, then the German POW camps of 1914-1918 had a twofold function. They were both war laboratories and colonial laboratories.

After war broke out, psychologist, musicologist and physiologist Carl Stumpf, who played a decisive part in founding comparative musicology, joined forces with Wilhelm Doegen, a high school teacher and popularizer of sound recordings, to set up a Royal Prussian Phonographic Commission ('Königliche Preußisch-Phonographische Kommission') which would make sound recordings in German prisoner of war camps. With the support of the Prussian Ministry of Science, Art, and National Education and funds from the reserve funds of Wilhelm II the com-

mission commenced work in October 1915. It was composed of eight members and various voluntary workers for the subject areas of music, English, Oriental, Roman, Indian, African, and Indo-Germanic languages, and comparative linguistics. Felix von Luschan (1854-1924, Royal Ethnological Museum in Berlin, since 1911 professor of anthropology and ethnology at the University of Berlin) was the appointed ethnology expert.

Musicologist Georg Schünemann, a student of Carl Stumpf, recorded with the use of an Edison phonograph music and songs of POWs on 1,022 wax cylinders, today kept in the Berlin Phonogram Archive. The linguists, on the other hand, visited many different German POW camps from the end of 1915 through to December 1918, and they made recordings on 1,650 gramophone discs. Their aim was to create an archive or a museum 'of the voices of all the peoples'. These examples of speech and music in

This label was stuck on a load of bread sent to the British Indian occupants of Half Moon Camp in Zossen on 18 June 1917.
(© Bildarchiv Preußischer Kulturbesitz, Berlin)

Gafangenenlager 2. Münster i. W. 1916. Völkertype Nr. 43. Tirailleur Marocain.

worked. Most scholars told of cooperative and friendly prisoners who liked to cooperate for the sound recordings, and who were often rewarded with some money or cigarettes. Some of the sound recordings were published with accompanying transcriptions during the 1920s and 1930s — but after the war the academics rarely published studies on the results of their camp expeditions.

The diversity and simultaneous presence of ethnic groups in the camps of Wünsdorf were fascinating not only to musicologists and linguists, but also to anthropologists. Studies in physical anthropology on POWs from the Eastern front had been carried out by Austrian academics since 1915. Body measurements of thousands of internees and related photographic recordings had been initiated largely by the Vienna Anthropological Society and professor Rudolf Pöch and until the end of the war were mostly financed by the Imperial Academy of Sciences in Vienna. At the invitation of Felix von Luschan, anthropologist Pöch and his assistant Josef Weninger visited the camp of

about 250 languages are today kept in the Berlin Sound Archive.

Among many others, the Orientalist Heinrich Lüders recorded dozens of examples of Indian and Gurkha languages, Carl Meinhof made recordings of African and Paul Hambruch of Madagascan peoples. Before the proper process of the sound recording, the scholars wrote down the texts together with the prisoners, often with the help of a translator, to make sure that every detail on the disc was saved in a transcription, and ideally in a phonetic transcription as well as a translation. In a book called 'A new ethnography' on the various peoples in the German prison camps, published in 1925, the scholars report that many prisoners knew songs and traditional texts by heart.[4] To reassure the speakers, the professors had a little phonograph. It was used to let everybody record something and to play it back to them immediately so that the soldiers understood how the apparatus

German propaganda postcard from the series of 'people types form the prisoner of war camps'. *Völkertype* Nr 43 was the *tirailleur marocain*.

During the First World War architect and amateur photographer Otto Stiehl was a staff member of the prisoner of war camps Weinberg and Halbmond (Half Moon) in Zossen-Wünsdorf. In 1916 he devoted a booklet under the title 'Unsere Feinde' (Our Enemies) to the various types that populated the German prisoner of war camps. Shortly later the booklet was also published in Dutch. (In Flanders Fields Museum)

This photo of 1916 gives a splendid overview of the different
'types of prisoners' from the camps of Zossen-Wünsdorf.
The 'Sudanese' is a tirailleur sénégalais from present day Mali.
A Turko was a general denomination for a (North) African soldier.
(© Bildarchiv Preußischer Kulturbesitz, Berlin)

Wünsdorf from August to October 1917 to measure colonial soldiers who were not available in the Austrian and Hungarian camps. They also made plaster casts of some Africans and Indians. The findings resulting from the trip to Wünsdorf were used to write the book '100 Negroes from Western Africa' (1927)[5], Weninger took credit for having founded a dedicated school (in cooperation with Pöch, who died in 1921): the Vienna school ('Wiener Schule'), which until the 1950s continued to publish a series of books based on studies performed in POW camps between 1915 and 1918.

The German anthropological project was much smaller than the Austrian one. Felix von Luschan obtained permission for some young anthropologists to conduct studies in various German POW camps. From January 1916 until February 1917 his PhD student Egon von Eickstedt (1892-1965) travelled to 16 camps and measured a total of 1,784 individuals, whom he identified with 66 'peoples'. He numbered the individuals and took 45 measurements of each, which he noted on standardized forms. For his dissertation, which was supervised by Felix von Luschan and published in 1921 in the *Zeitschrift für Ethnologie*[6], he chose 76 Sikhs (a religious community of India) from the Eastern part of Punjab interned in Wünsdorf. His work aimed at understanding 1) the 'biotypes' or 'racial elements' and 2) the 'type groups' or 'phenotypes'. Von Eickstedt incorporated statistics and corresponding graphics to make his data tell a story. From the body measurements he calculated, for each person, 22 bodily and 9 head indices which he combined in various ways in correlation charts. Whereas he had first assumed that the Sikhs were a homogeneous group, his calculations and visualizations in the end led to the conclusion that the Sikhs were a heterogeneous population comprising two 'racial elements' and three smaller 'type groups'. In the 1930s, von Eickstedt widened the concept of physical anthropology applied in World War I by linking physical properties with spiritual 'racial characteristics' and continued to use the methods of physical anthropology in connection with geographical criteria for his chair of anthropology at the University of Breslau as from 1933 ('Breslauer Schule').

The German studies on colonial soldiers interned in the POW camps during 1915 and 1918 do not seem to have had an extraordinary methodological impact

Prizonier de gér
1 Bata 1 con
nr 11094
L093 Zo sén ale
man

La létre 30te 1917
doni le bonsore
Mons té ui é pri
zi dan de la ko
mi té maska
ran fér le gran
plé zé re avoaie
1 ko li dé man jé
tahar chaouche Kasi
3 rizi ma alséren

Camp de Zossen
"au soleil" ....

G. Gorrier. 1915.

This phonetically written letter of an Algerian is kept in the albums of Otto Stiehl. On the left we can read: 'Prizonier de gér 1 Bata 1 con nr 1093 Zosén Aleman' and on the right we can decipher: 'La létre 30te 1917. Doni le bonsore monsieui le prizidan de la komité maskaran fér le gran plézére avoaie 1 koli de manjé Tahar Chaouche Kasi 3 Risima alséren'. In other words, in this letter Tahar Chaouche Kasi ('3rd Algerian Regiment') was asking the Committee President to send him a food parcel.
(© Bildarchiv Preußischer Kulturbesitz, Berlin)

In 1915 G. Gorrier made this beautiful picture of an Islamic fellow prisoner in Halbmondlager in Zossen-Wünsdorf. The picture landed in one of the albums of Camp Commander Otto Stiehl.
(© Bildarchiv Preußischer Kulturbesitz, Berlijn)

on research. But they promoted academic careers and left data and archives that continued to be worked on — mostly without mentioning the very specific historical and political conditions that once generated this kind of knowledge.

1. See e.g. Otto Stiehl: Unsere Feinde. 96 Charakterköpfe aus deutschen Kriegsgefangenenlagern, Stuttgart 1916; Leo Frobenius: Der Völkerzirkus unserer Feinde, Berlin 1916.

2. Rudolf Martin: Anthropologische Untersuchungen an Kriegsgefangenen, in: *Die Umschau*, vol. 19, 1915, p. 1017.

3. Laura Ann Stoler and Frederick Cooper: Between Metropole and Colony: Rethinking the Research Agenda, in: *Tensions of Empire. Colonial Cultures in a Bourgeois World*, ed. L. A. Stoler and F. Cooper, pp. 1-56, here p. 5.

4. Wilhelm Doegen (Ed.): Unter fremden Völkern — Eine neue Völkerkunde, Berlin 1925.

5. Josef Weninger: Eine morphologisch-anthropologische Studie. Durchgeführt an 100 westafrikanischen Negern, Wien 1927.

6. Egon von Eickstedt: 'Rassenelemente der Sikh', in: *Zeitschrift für Ethnologie*, Vol. 52, 1920/21, P. 317-394.

German propaganda photo with 'characteristic prisoner types of the last battles in Flanders', 1917-18.
(© Bildarchiv Preußischer Kulturbesitz, Berlin)

Berliner Illustrierte Wochenschau
Jg. 1924, Nr. 9

Ein Madagaffenchor
(Leute aus Madagaskar) fingt ein Heimatlied

Der Schweizer Humanist Morf läßt sich von einem Sü...
(rechts) das Lied „Ma bergère", „Meine Schäferin", vorfing...

Stimmen der Völker

Am 30. Mai hält der Direktor der Lautabteilung der Preußischen Staatsbibliothek,
Prof. Wilhelm Doegen, in der Funk-
stunde A.-G. einen Vortrag über die
Stimmen der Völker. Bei diesem antro-
phonetischen Vortrag wird Prof. Doegen
den Rundfunkteilnehmern die von ihm
auf der Lautplatte festgehaltenen Sprachen
und Gesänge fremder Völker zu Gehör
bringen. Die hier wiedergegebenen Bilder
veranschaulichen die in diesem Vortrag zu
Wort kommenden fremdländischen Sprecher,
Sänger und Musiker.

*

Ma bergère (Gesprochen...
si kun jets ma b...
k ei b.ro kum tu...
w.ro w.ro . . .

Connaissez-vous ma ber...
Elle est belle comme l'ét...
Regardez . . .

Kennt ihr meine Schäf...
Sie ist schön wie der ...
Seht! . . .

Der Franzose links spricht...
der Fabel vom Raben un...
„Maître corbeau sur un arbre...
en son bec un fromage" . . .

Balaleika-Orchester
Kleinruffen (Ukrainer) spielen ein Liebeslied: „Mein Feuer"

*

Schottischer Dudelsackpfeifer
bläst Heimatlieder

Zwei Gurkhas
der eine (links) singt ein Volkslied

Kongoneger
singt ein Ruder...

ETHNOGRAPHIC AUDIO RECORDINGS
IN GERMAN PRISONER OF WAR CAMPS DURING THE FIRST WORLD WAR

JÜRGEN-K. MAHRENHOLZ

Between 29 December 1915 and 19 December 1918 the *Royal Prussian Phonographic Commission* collected a total of 2677 /samples/audio recordings of approximately 250 languages, dialects, and traditional music among the Prisoners of War of the German Empire. With the exception of Austria, this form of gathering ethnographical material was unique during World War I. In Germany, the activities of the Phonographic Commission were kept secret during wartime.

In total, the commission comprised thirty academics working in the fields of philology, anthropology and musicology and included such prestigious scholars as Felix v. Luschan, Alois Brandl, Otto Dempwolff and George Schünemann.[1] Between 1915 and 1918 members of the commission visited 31 of the 175 prison camps that existed in Germany.[2] In total the commission undertook 49 field trips to prison camps.

With eleven trips, the most frequently visited camp was Wünsdorf, also known as 'Halfmoon-Camp' (Halbmondlager) due to the large number of Muslim prisoners. Situated merely 40 kilometres south of Berlin, Wünsdorf was especially interesting for the researchers due to its rich diversity of cultures, many of which were associated with the colonial powers of Great-Britain and France. Languages spoken and recorded by the interned soldiers were:[3] Hindi, Gurmukhi, Rai, Bengali, Khasi, Magar, Garhwali, Old-Hindi (India), Panjabi (Pakistan, India), Baloshi, Pashto, Urdu (Pakistan), Limbu, Nepali (India, Nepal), Magari, Gurung (Nepal), English, Vietnamese (Vietnam), Baule (Ivory Coast), Dahomeen, Bariba (Benin), Mosi, Bobo, Samogo (Burkina Faso), Wolof, Pulaar (Senegal), Zarma (Mali, Nigeria), Kwa (Togo), Malinka, Soso (Guinea), Swahili, Mwali, Ngazidja,

Ndzwani (Comoros), Somali (Somalia), Bambara, Mandara, Kanuri, Haussa, Ful (Mali), Yoruba, Anyin (Ghana), Arabic, Berber (Algeria, Tunisia, Morocco), Malagasy (Madagascar), Maltese (Malta), Sardinian (Italy), Tatar, Avar (Russian Federation), Kirghiz (Kyrgyzstan).

The foundation of the Phonographic Commission is closely linked to philologist Wilhelm Doegen.[4] He was born in Berlin in 1877, the same year Edison invented the phonograph. Doegen studied modern language at the Friedrich Wilhelm University in Berlin and at Oxford University in 1899-1900 with Henry Sweet, who is considered to be one of the pioneers of modern phonetics.

Doegen later described his meeting with Sweet and the latter's system of phonetic transcription as a defining influence on his own work. In 1904, Doegen qualified as a teacher of English, French and German with his dissertation on the use of phonetics in the teaching of English to beginners. With great enthusiasm he pursued the use of phonetic transcription in teaching materials to be used in conjunction with texts spoken onto records.

As from 1909 Doegen compiled teaching materials, publishing several volumes in co-operation with the Odeon Recording Company in Berlin. In addition to this, he published material using native speaker actors reading from classical English and French literature. Encouraged by the success of his sound recordings, Doegen developed ideas for a 'voice museum'. In February 1914, he submitted an application to the Prussian Ministry for Education, entitled 'Suggestions for the establishment of a Royal Prussian Phonetic Institute'. According to his application the following sound examples were to be collected:

In 1924 the *Berliner Illustrierte Wochenschau* (Berlin Illustrated Weekly) made considerable publicity for a lecture by Wilhelm Doegen on sound recordings of prisoners of war made during the Great War. Doegen would continue to use these sound recordings for many decades.
(Lautarchiv der Humboldt-Universität zu Berlin, Berlin)

1. Languages from around the world.
2. All German dialects.
3. Music and songs from around the world.
4. Voices of famous people.
5. Other areas of interest.[5]

This application led to the creation of the *Royal Prussian Phonographic Commission* on 27th October 1915. Carl Stumpf, audio-psychologist and founder of the *Phonogramm-Archiv* was appointed as chairman of the Commission. Doegen was responsible for the technical production of the gramophone recordings. Together with the subject experts and a technician he made 1650 recordings on gramophone discs, which were for the most part recordings of languages and dialects and more rarely also featured music. Musicologist Georg Schünemann made musical recordings exclusively with the phonograph. His collection consists of 1022 wax cylinders.[6]

Recordings on gramophone discs were made in the following manner: first the members of the Commission looked for different languages spoken by the prisoners in each camp. They sent lists of languages to the camps' commanders. Based on their response, a language expert from the commission decided who would be recorded. Before each recording extensive written documentation was prepared on the informant and on the content of the recording.

Apart from documenting the recording, the questionnaire included detailed information about the personal circumstances of the speaker as well as his linguistic heritage and contained questions used to define the social background of the speaker. Furthermore, no recording could be made before the text was written down in the normal handwriting or typeface typical of the speaker's country. Since speakers and singers did not always stick to the agreed text, in some cases new text transcriptions had to be made after the reproduction of the shellac discs. Musical transcriptions were only made once the records had been pressed.

The language recordings can be classified according to the following themes, which were identified by members of the Phonographic Commission:

1. Word groups of relatively unknown
languages containing words which are easily
confused were recorded for use in dictionaries.

Camp Commander Otto Stiehl took this photo of what he referred to as an 'Indian Spring Feast' in February 1917.
(© Bildarchiv Preußischer Kulturbesitz, Berlin)

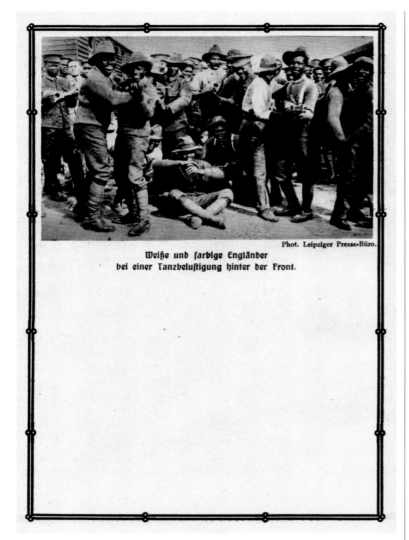

Phot. Leipziger Presse-Büro.

Weiße und farbige Engländer
bei einer Tanzbelustigung hinter der Front.

2. *Fairy tales, stories and anecdotes.*
3. *Prisoners of war, in particular from Great Britain and France, but also from other European countries, reading the Parable of the Prodigal Son (Luke XV, 11ff.) in their own dialects. In this way dialects were documented and could be compared with each other.*

The majority of the music recordings are vocal, only a few recordings are purely instrumental. About two thirds of the recordings are spoken and about one third comprises music.

The activities of the Phonographic Commission not only extended to acoustic recordings. As well as simply transcribing the recorded texts, so-called palatogrammes were made by dentist Alfred Doegen, a brother of Wilhelm Doegen, in order to determine the exact tongue position that is responsible for pronunciation. X-ray photographs of the larynx were made to enable scientific research into certain speech sounds.

The ethnologist and curator of the Berlin Ethnological Museum, Felix von Luschan, undertook anthropological studies and made measurements of the prisoners. A photographer took pictures of nearly every speaker and singer. About 50 of these photos still exist in the Lautarchiv. The photos show a person from the front and in profile, in keeping with the contemporary ethnological practice.

In the confusion of the November 1918 revolution, Doegen obtained control of the gramophone recordings through the Ministry of Education and established the collection as the basis of the sound department of the Prussian State Library (*Lautabteilung an der Preußischen Staatsbibliothek*), founded on 1 April 1920.[7] The wax cylinder recordings made by the Phonographic Commission became part of the *Berlin Phonogramm-Archiv*, and the collection was split according to the recording medium. The collections have been kept in two different locations ever since.

When Doegen became director of the *Lautabteilung* in 1920, he remained accountable to the *Lautkommission* (sound commission) which, just like the Phonograph Commission, decided what recordings were to be made and which partly comprised the same researchers. In 1934 the *Lautabteilung* was incorporated into the Friedrich Wilhelm University as the Institute for Sound Research (*Institut für Lautforschung*). Today this collection is known as the *Lautarchiv* and is located at the Department of Musicology at the Humboldt University in Berlin.[8]

The activities of the Phonographic Commission were unprecedented, particularly in terms of the highly detailed documentation that accompanied their recording programme. Although information on the informants was collected, the Phonographic Commission is today criticized for not respecting the prisoner's individual identity. According to the positivistic scientific climate of the day, the prisoners'

A page from the propagandistic book *Der Völker-Zirkus unserer Feinde* (The people's circus of our enemies) by German anthropologist Leo Frobenius. The caption reads: 'White and coloured English at a dance party behind the front'. They were probably men belonging to the South African Native Labour Corps with some white colleagues and/or guards. (In Flanders Fields Museum)

identities were treated instead as a pre-established classification system and, thus, ultimately ignored. As research on language and music became increasingly independent pursuits and thus detached from cultural considerations, obvious political and ethical concerns, such as colonialism and the ongoing war, were overlooked in pursuit of scientific objectivity. In addition to his ambitions for establishing a voice museum Doegen also openly pursued commercial interests, identifying potential markets for the recordings outside the academic world. He envisaged, for instance, a demand for the recordings among the colonial staff of the German Empire, who, in the event of a victorious outcome to the war, would need the discs for their education in the native languages of the new German colonies.

— Bibliography

Doegen, Wilhelm (Ed.), *Unter fremden Völkern. Eine neue Völkerkunde*, Berlin, Otto Stollberg, Verlag für Politik und Wirtschaft, 1925.

Mehnert, Dieter, 'Historische Schallaufnahmen. Das Lautarchiv an der Humboldt-Universität zu Berlin', in: *Elektronische Sprachsignalverarbeitung* — Siebente Konferenz Berlin. Studientexte zur Sprachkommunikation, Heft 13, 1996, pp. 28-45.

Ziegler, Susanne, 'Die akustischen Sammlungen. Historische Tondokumente im Phonogramm-Archiv und im Lautarchiv', in: Bredekamp, Horst, Brüning, Jochen and Weber, Cornelia, *Theater der Natur und Kunst*, *Essays*, Berlin, Henschel, 2000, pp. 197-206.

Inbianer = Häuptlinge aus Kanaba mit ihren Enkeln, die in moberner Kriegsausrüftung — zur Front gehen.

1. Some famous members of the commission were: Felix v. Luschan, Andreas (Iranian languages), Alois Brandl (English dialects), Otto Dempwolff, (Malaian), Adolf Dirr (Caucasian languages), Helmut von Glasenapp (Sikh, Hindi), August Heisenberg (Greek), George Schünemann (Musicologist), Heinrich Lüders (Bengali, Pashto, Gurung).

2. All the figures quoted are based on the documentation of 1650 shellac recordings of the Phonographic Commission, today held by the Lautarchiv of the Humboldt-University of Berlin.

3. Between brackets are the names of present states.

4. Wilhelm Doegen: born 17.03.1877, died 03.11.1967.

5. W. Doegen, 1925, p. 9.

6. The shellac discs of the Phonographic Commission carry the seal 'PK', whereas the Edison wax-cylinders bear the signature 'Phon. Komm.'.

7. This was based on Doegens 'memorandum on the establishment of a sound department in the Prussian state library' ('Denkschrift über die Errichtung einer Lautabteilung in der Preußischen Staatsbibliothek').

8. D. Mehnert, 1996, S. 35-38 and S. Ziegler, 2000, p.197.

   The Humboldt-University of Berlin has been renamed several times. To avoid confusion here are the names in chronological order:

   1810-1827 Berliner Universität,

   1828-1945 Friedrich-Wilhelms-Universität,

   1945-1947 Universität Berlin,

   1948-today Humboldt-Universität zu Berlin.

Another page from *Völker-Zirkus unserer Feinde* by Frobenius. The translated caption reads 'Indian chiefs from Canada with their grandchildren going to the front with modern war equipment'. The photo shows recruits from File Hills Colony in Saskatchewan, compare with page 93. A copy had apparently landed in German hands. (In Flanders Fields Museum)

THE FORGOTTEN FRONT

THE MULTICULTURAL WAR OF 1914-1918 IN EYEWITNESS ACCOUNTS FROM FLANDERS

NIELS VAN ECHTELT

The colourful mix of cultures, ways of life, religions and customs during the First World War temporarily turned Flanders' West into a multicultural patchwork. Until then such a concentration of various cultures had never been seen here. It is therefore not surprising that many diaries and letters from that period mention the contacts between the various cultures.

Not only did the Belgian population write about the presence of these multiple groups in their country, the soldiers of many nationalities also commented on the habits of the Belgians. They all did so with their own individual approach. As you read these accounts bear in mind that they express the opinion and interpretation of a specific person. It is at times quite hard to determine to what extent one person's opinion was shared by his contemporaries.

Local witnesses speak of troublesome, obtrusive or even impolite soldiers, but also about more positive aspects, such as soldiers falling in love, being polite and curious. The local population also greatly welcomed the financial boost given by the soldiers to the failing and paltry economy of Flanders. On the whole the relationship between the troops and the population behind the lines is generally described in a favourable manner. In any case, the interaction with the various cultures played an important role in life in war-stricken Flanders. More specifically highly educated people like clergymen and medical staff behind the front described the customs of the various nationalities with some degree of regularity. Their opinion is often more refined than that of the ordinary man. They considered the foreign peoples around them from a more social-anthropological and inquisitive standpoint.

When studying the testimonials about coloured troops we must consider the fact that xenophobia has existed since the beginning of time. Not only had very few inhabitants of the Flanders ever seen a coloured person in 1914, most of the soldiers from e.g. France and Great Britain had never met their coloured brothers in arms. Furthermore, not everyone was inclined to write about these foreign cultures. For instance, the Flemish sub-lieutenant Raoul Snoeck hardly even mentions the North African troops in his diary, even though he had posed with them on a photo. He may not have found their presence sufficiently noteworthy to write about it at length.

Others had gathered a very extensive collection of descriptions about the various nationalities in Flanders. The diary of Father Achiel Van Walleghem stands

Priest and diarist Achiel Van Walleghem between a French officer (left) and the British Captain H.M.L. Mansfield (right).
This photo, taken by the British Lieutenant T.D. Murray, was published in Stonyhurst War Record.
(In Flanders Fields Museum)

Two French colonial soldiers cooking their midday meal. Northern France, 24 May 1917. (© Musée départemental Albert Kahn, Boulogne-Billancourt)

A group of Spahis playing music and listening somewhere behind the front in Flanders, 1914-15. (© In Flanders Fields Museum)

head and shoulders above other documents. The priest took an interest in almost all aspects of life and reported on many nationalities. He specifically left us information about their external characteristics and customs. Obviously, he was also interested in the religious background and way of life of these men, while his diary simultaneously reflects his own mentality and thoughts.

Most diaries have a common denominator, thus, e.g. after an initial sudden confrontation between the inhabitants and the soldiers they soon became accustomed to one another. It is equally remarkable how the frame of mind and the opinions of the troops present in Belgian Flanders changed after 11 November 1918, as once the war ebbed away the population wanted to return to its former way of life as soon as possible. The presence of soldiers and more specifically of colonial troops often caused irritations in the first post-war years.

For this chapter we have made a selection of the many quotes from diaries, letters and eye witness re-ports adopting as criterion the experience of the Belgian population behind the front. These quotes are occasionally supplemented with quotes of soldiers of various nationalities or of other personnel active behind the front.

— Colours and kilts

The diversity of uniforms was frequently the first impression given by the various troops. Not only did the splendidly colourful appearance of the Sene-galese, Goumiers or Spahis draw a lot of attention, the traditional Scottish kilts were also a 'crowd puller'. Ypres priest Caesar Gezelle remembered that the Scots themselves laughed at the attention they drew:

> *From time to time a regiment of Scottish*
> *Highlanders marched past; people on*
> *the streets called them the skirt men,*
> *with legs as thick as hams, broad-shouldered,*
> *thick-necked. They laughed at the great*
> *success of their skirts.*

Scottish soldiers in a well-built trench in or
near the frontline, around 1915 (© Imperial War Museum, London)

Not everyone was equally charmed by the 'skirts'. Thus Father Edmundus of the Abbey of Saint Sixtus entered in his diary on 13 June 1915:

> *Immoral clothing of the Scots, a short skirt instead of trousers, some say they wear short pants under it, others claim they don't.*

The Germans also wondered whether the Scots wore anything under their kilt. On Christmas Day 1914 some received an answer to this question. Lieutenant Johannes Niemann left an extensive testimony of an unofficial Christmas truce near the Lys:

> *Shortly later a Scot suddenly appeared from nowhere with a football […] It was difficult to play on the hard soil […] Everyone played full of enthusiasm […] We, Germans, roared with laughter when a gust of wind suddenly showed us that the Scots did not wear any underwear under their kilt. We shouted and whistled whenever we saw the bare backside of one of 'yesterday's enemies'.*

During the course of the war a growing number of troops arrived in the Westhoek from overseas territories. On 7 September 1915, Belgian nurse Jane de Launoy described the diversity of troops in her work environment:

> *Colonial troops on exercise are also interesting: saffron yellow Anamites with cruel slit-eyes, tanned Hindus with long black hair hidden under their turban, proud and contemptuous. Tall, straightforward and healthy Australians with a balanced physical build. Beautiful Canadians, outdoor people.*

The 'exotic' soldiers from far away countries drew the greatest attention from the local population. Their at times splendid, colourful uniforms stood out against the grey surroundings of the front. Some rode small white horses through the streets and spoke an unintelligible language, and this made them all the more mysterious. Maurice Duwez (who wrote under the pseudonym Max Deauville) was a doctor in the Belgian army. In 1915 he was greatly impressed by

With full messtins, two French infantrymen return to their post through the ruins of a Flemish village, around 1915.
(© ECPAD – Médiathèque de la Défense, Paris)

On 31 May 1915, Ypres photographer Maurice Antony took this group photo of convalescing French soldiers and the nursing staff of "Villa Massabille" in Wimereux. A Spahi is seated in the middle at the front.

(© Antony d'Ypres, Ostend – Collection Municipal Museums Ypres)

a unit of North Africans marching towards Steen-straete;

> *A strange mixture of races. Arabs and Jews*
> *with tanned skin, black beard and the profile*
> *of an eagle. They march gracefully and stretch*
> *out like cats. The French, small and broad,*
> *with a determined gait. Some negroes with a*
> *swaying walk, smile at all the passers while*
> *humming long monotonous chants to lull their*
> *childish dreams to sleep. Behind them follow*
> *the mitrailleurs drawn by high mules with long*
> *ears and bare teeth, behind them a colourful*
> *procession of Arabs on small white horses.*

The local population thought up collective names for all these different nationalities. For instance there were Turcos, Hindus, Blacks and Tsjings. Many Flemings became acquainted with the soldiers and were often able to guess their country of origin from their faces, even though they were quite wrong at times. Even the soldiers and officers themselves weren't always skilled at immediately guessing the country of origin of their comrades-in-arms. This was also the experience of Japanese speaking Major Piggott:

> *Riding along the Ypres-Poperinghe road one*
> *day, I overtook what looked like a company of*
> *the Chinese Labour Corps; somewhat to my*
> *surprise an N.C.O. called the men to attention*
> *as I came abreast, and gave the command,*
> *'Eyes right!'; I then recognized them as*
> *Japanese. I reined in, and had a short chat*
> *with the sergeant in charge; he was to hear his*
> *mother tongue in Flanders, and told me that*
> *his company was one of the Japanese units*
> *serving with the Canadian Corps.*

The most extensive and detailed reports on the diversity of troops in Flanders were written by Achiel Van Walleghem. In 1914 he was the 35 year old curate of Dikkebus, a village some 5 kilometres to the West of Ypres. By June 1915 he was acting parish priest and the acts of war made him move to Reningelst, just a stone's throw away. There, amidst the army camps just behind the front, he had ample opportunity to observe the many groups marching towards the front or deployed to work. As a priest he was particularly interested in the Lord's strange folk. He described the religion of the soldiers, their 'level of civilization', their behaviour and some special characteristics. On 26 May 1917 he described some West Indian soldiers in the following words:

> *Negroes have arrived at the farm of Alouis Adriaen and '3 Goên' (from West India, Jamaica) to work. [...] The blacks are terrified by the gunfire. They stare shy and distraught when they hear a bomb coming and if it does not fall too far away they run like the damned.[...]Many of them are Catholic [...].*

— Prejudices

Van Walleghem's descriptions are rarely harsh. However, his diaries do display the general feeling of white superiority that prevailed at the time, and the prejudice that helped create a certain image. This is how he described the massive influx of French Colonial troops in December 1914:

> *Here we now see many types of troops, many Zouaves with their wide red puffy pants, short jacket and Turkish cap. Also the tirailleurs algériens, with their semi-black appearance, grey puffy pants and cape (as the latter were half-wild they could not be left alone for any period of time and their dirty tricks were often reported in the region).*

Father Van Walleghem made similar comments about the West African troops, but he also tried to find out about their background:

> *The French have had to retreat a little near Zillebeke. The Senegalese are mainly to blame for this. They are courageous and fearless of death, yet they are afraid of the sound of gunfire and according to their superstition being disfigured by a shell will prevent them from going to heaven. (30 December 1914)*

Ignorance and xenophobia gave rise to the wildest stories at the front. For instance the soldiers from the French colonies were the subject of violent, bloodthirsty stories and myths. It was generally believed that the French colonials cut off the ears and noses of the Germans to take them as souvenirs. In her diary Jane de Launoy mentioned such a story on 29 December 1914:

> *Night duty.*
> *Germans...French...Goumiers...They bring*

	— 34 —	
Billets for officers	Kwartieren voor officieren
Billets for men	Gebouw voor soldaten
Stables for horses	Paardenstallen
Garage or shelter for motor-car	Plaa's voor auto's

You are bound by military law to billet the troops	Gij zijt door de krijgswet verplicht deze mannen slaping te geven.
How many soldiers were billeted here last time ?	Hoeveel man waren hier laatst ingekwartierd ?
Where were the officers billeted ?	Waar woonden de officieren ?
Have you any stables for the horses ?	Hebt gij paardenstallen?
I want a large room	Ik zou eene groote kamer willen hebben.
How many beds are available ?	Hoeveel bedden kunt gij geven ?
Where does the Mair live ?	Waar woont de burgemeester ?
Where is the town-hall?	Waar is het stadhuis ?

in a German on a stretcher. He is accidentally placed in a room occupied by an Arab, who looks at him with burning eyes saying: 'Just leave him here, I will slit his throat tonight'. We must put him somewhere else. Another Arab goes through his pockets and asks: 'Who wants a German nose?'

Bear in mind that for many peoples instilling fear was a major part of warfare. Just think of the traditional *Haka* of the New Zealand Maori. The rumours about the wild warriors from the colonies were not always denied by the authorities, on the contrary they were often used for propaganda purposes. Both the Germans and the Allies believed these stories. After the war Marie Beck remembered;

> *Spahis. They had joined the French. Cavalrymen. [...] With their red coats. They were quite beautiful to watch. Their eyes popped out whenever they saw a woman. The best you*

To communicate with the local population and with their foreign language speaking allies many lexicons were published for the benefit of the soldiers. This is a page from a lexicon for British soldiers in Flanders. (In Flanders Fields Museum)

Ruines de Dickebusch 1914-18 Cimetière du Village.
The ruins at Dickebusch   Cemetery of the Village

could do was to get out of their way. They attacked at night their knives clenched between their teeth. They jumped into the trenches. The Germans were terrified of them because they could get through anything.[...] Sometimes you could even hear them howling. They howled when they attacked, they were savages. One morning I was standing outside with a brush in my hands, scrubbing. They were passing and looked at me. One extended his arm from beneath his red coat. It held a wire. He showed it to me and there were four or five human ears attached to this wire. He covered his arm again, looked at me and laughed.

In spite of the fact that the colonial troops were considered to be wild and dangerous they also aroused some sympathy among the population. For instance Jozef Ghesquière showed his compassion for the colonial troops who went to battle so far from home:

There are about eight hundred of them. On their heads they wear a red fez with a black tassel. With their tanned faces, their jet-black hair, black moustache and eyebrows, they look quite scary. They are looked at with a degree of fear. And yet they smile at the bystanders in a friendly manner and the fear soon dwindles away. Indeed, they have come to help liberate our country. Poor boys! So far from their home country. How many will never see it again?

— Tsjings'

The Chinese Labour Corps was an outsider among the 'colonial' troops. Not only because of their large numbers, but also they were the only auxiliary troops that were not subjects of the French or British Empires. They had been hired and had not received any military training. The Chinese remained in Belgian Flanders for the longest period of time. Until 1920 they cleared the front and did all kinds of odd

A Chinese coolie sitting amidst destroyed graves at Dikkebus cemetery, 1919.

jobs for the armies of the British Empire. The attitude of the local population towards the Chinese
changed drastically after the war. During the war
they had been considered in a critical but fairly neutral manner. Father Van Walleghem wrote about his
first meeting with the Chinese on 6 August 1917:

> *Many Chinese have arrived in the region to*
> *work for the English [sic]. I do not know from*
> *where or how these men arrived here. Many*
> *seem very young. They are strange and their*
> *manners are very childish, no better than our*
> *boys of 10 or 11. Their favourite occupation is*
> *to gawp at shop windows, preferably those of*
> *sweet and fruit shops, and if they see some-*
> *thing they like they will enter 10 at a time and*
> *start asking the prices of everything and if they*

Buses and trucks of the 2nd Australian Division passing
Vlamertinge on their way to and from the front, 26 October 1917.
(© Imperial War Museum, London)

Together with some Australians soldiers of the British West Indies
Regiment are stacking 8-inch shells near an ammunition dump on
'Gordon Road' near Ypres, October 1917. (© Imperial War Museum, London)

do decide to buy something, they are very suspicious of being diddled. However, many shopkeepers are tired of their attitude and sometimes they get mad and then they all run out like sparrows. They are yellow in colour, have a flat nose and slanting eyes, and they almost always have a silly smile and almost constantly look around, so that it is quite astonishing that none have yet been killed on our busy roads. They wear a blue linen outfit and also one in a thicker grey fabric, raincoat and hood, they wear a straw hat or brown skullcap with earflaps yet they are particularly mad about civilian clothes and if they manage to get a civilian cap or hat they will never remove it from their heads. They walk in an ungainly manner and it is obvious they are not used to wearing such heavy shoes. [...] They are not lazy and work at least as hard as our citizens and English soldiers. But what a commotion when a group of these men passes you. They are boisterous and try to outdo one another.

I prefer it when they sing a song, their singing is pleasant. They already know a few words of English but virtually none of them can speak the language. For instance, as I was passing them shortly before noon one day, they kept on saying 'Watch, watch?' What time is it? I believe their stomachs were grumbling, because when I showed them there were only five more minutes until midday, they nodded contentedly as they would soon be filling their bellies with their beloved rice. ... They are big children and should be treated like children. To keep them in order you must use convincing arguments and this is why their sergeants have a thin iron rod, which occasionally comes into contact with the men's skin; this does not disturb them, they laugh and are again well behaved. They also use other punishments and recently as I was passing along one of their camps I saw one of them wearing a yoke around his neck (a kind of toilet seat) while another had a block and chain around his neck, and they had to dig a dyke ringed in this way. They are not allowed to visit inns. They probably have little understanding of the war. When they hear a shell they just stand there gawping, and when it explodes they clap their hands and laugh.

After a while the British decided the Chinese would no longer be allowed in shops and bars. The priest mentions this order in his diary on 5 November 1917:

An order has been issued prohibiting the Chinese from entering into shops. Civilians are no longer entitled to sell them anything. Nobody knows the reason for this. Some claim that in the coffee houses Australian soldiers had poured rum in the coffee of some Chinese and had made them drunk. Others claim that they give too much away to women and children. However, after a while the order was attenuated for them. The Chinese are childish but not stupid. They do know the value of things and you will not be able to deceive them easily. They always look for the best and most beautiful items and will not readily buy trash . They pay but like to haggle about the price. They like the most beautiful shops and that is where they usually do their shopping. I have no idea what they earn but some of them seem to have a great deal of cash on them. They buy many watches and rings. Some shopkeepers have learnt a little Chinese to draw them and keep them as customers, and have found this to be an effective tool.

Two unidentified black British soldiers washing their clothes, September 1916. (© Imperial War Museum, London)

The Chinese in Flanders were soon called 'Tsjing', a corruption of the English term of abuse Chink. It is remarkable that right up to the day of their departure Van Walleghem referred to them by their nationality. During the war there seems to have been some sympathy for the Chinese. Margareta Santy from Poperinge remembered:

> It was winter and my mother was ill and lay on a mattress next to the hot stove. At a certain moment a tsjing entered; he was a regular visitor. He saw my mother lying there and put his hands to his head saying 'Madam ouch ouch madam, madam' and quickly ran away. Mother thought he was scared of becoming ill. But he soon returned with a few bags, in which there were amongst others oranges. Here madam, madam, he said. The tsjing showed compassion towards my mother.

After the war the attitude towards the Chinese Labourers changed and became distinctly negative. Even Father Van Walleghem had a different opinion in 1919:

> The region had become unsafe because of all kinds of foreign front drifters and mainly the Chinese. The small number of English officers no longer had any authority over them. They escaped from their camps and armed with the weapons and grenades they found lying around they started marauding. For instance, at the beginning of June Jules Bailleul, domiciled on the Canada, was assaulted in his own home and as he was running away he was shot and died a couple of weeks later.

Countless such stories of crimes committed by erring Chinese are still imprinted on the collective memory of Flanders' Westhoek. For the sake of clarity it should be said that very few of them are true. However, there was in fact a problem: the Chinese had been more or less abandoned by the British government. They had been promised they would be able to return home as soon as the war ended, yet by mid-1919 still no attempt had been made to repatriate them. Furthermore, there were indeed relatively few British officers left to supervise them. Citizens who returned in 1919 after years of virtual exile had in fact lost everything. Furthermore, in their fully destroyed, unrecognizable and lawless region they found droves of these very strange blokes. This turned the Chinese into their ideal scapegoat onto which all unsolved crimes were heaped.

— Consumers

The many troops represented a new group of consumers for the inhabitants. The soldiers posted behind the front had also spent their pay there. Therefore even though the billeted soldiers caused considerable inconvenience, they also provided a flow of money in war-stricken Flanders. Not everyone received the same pay and consequently some soldiers were more welcome than others. On 1 October 1915 Father Van Walleghem wrote about the Canadian units:

> On the Scherpenberg there is a whole battalion of French Canadian soldiers who usually speak French but who are difficult to understand. The Canadian army includes men from different countries, French, Dutch, Italians and also some Belgians. The latter claim that they were more or less obliged to join up. They earn a lot of money some 5, 6 or 7 fr. a day. They like to enjoy themselves, many get drunk and many have sticky fingers. Yet they are reputed to be courageous soldiers.

The Australians were liked for the same reasons: they also had a large pay packet which they eagerly spent.

> The town [Poperinge] is full of Australian soldiers', Van Walleghem wrote in his diary on 28 August 1916. 'The Australians have a lot of money, it is not surprising that they are liked by the population. Yet they seem to be more

Similarly to many other foreign missions an official Japanese delegation visited the Belgian war zone in the immediate post-war period. Here we see the Japanese Crown Prince (and future Emperor) Hirohito in front of the south porch of the Ypres Cathedral, 13 June 1921. Japan was an ally during the First World War.
(© Royal Army and Military History Museum, Brussels)

Embroidered cards were a favourite souvenir among all soldiers. This card carries the badge of the Australian Imperial Force. (In Flanders Fields Museum)

decent than the English, and are particularly more polite and less pretentious. They are also far less suspicious. They are clean, yet they do not wash more than once a day as opposed to the English who do so three or four times. I met two drunken Belgians, 1 soldier and 1 civilian, in-between two drunken Australians. I heard the Belgians say: 'Belgium good, Australian very good. Belgium no money, Australian plenty money!' The trick is to get them to buy drinks.

Other soldiers who had much less money to spend did not benefit from the same level of sympathy from the Belgian population. Also the priest did not understand all the English he heard. The soldiers did not always hold Belgium, where they had experienced so much misery, and the Belgians in high regard. After a fight between Belgians and British on 16 January 1916 Van Walleghem noted: 'There are troublemakers in both armies. The habitual abuse hurled by the English at the Belgians is "Fake Belgium"'. This was quite probably a different monosyllabic term of abuse starting with f and ending with k, which the priest neither knew nor understood.

— 'All they ever eat is rice'

The people in the Westhoek not only discovered the other clothing habits and languages of the various nationalities, they were also struck by the different eating habits of these peoples. In Lo they wrote on 18 October 1914:

In the afternoon some 300 French Spahis arrived on small white horses. They wear culottes, a turban and white coats like the Turks...They mainly eat mutton. Their (French) officers buy all the sheep from farmers. They bury the skins in the mud. They drink a lot of milk. Whenever you place a pot of sugar on the table they pour all their coffee in it. They do not drink any beer, but they do consume lots of alcoholic beverages.

Insofar as possible colonial units were given the food of their country of origin. In the camps special ovens were built for the flat bread of the Indians. And the supervising officer was able to read how long rice should be cooked in the manual on how to treat the *Chinese Labour Corps*. Van Walleghem wrote about them:

All they ever eat is rice. Whether in the morning, at midday or in the evening they always devour rice with their chopsticks.

The large multicultural presence in the Westhoek resulted in some men feeling the urge to convert. Jos Brutsaert, acting parish priest of Roesbrugge was one of the clergymen who preached the word of God to the unbelieving. After the war he reported to the Bishop of Bruges:

At the beginning of September 1917, not far from Rousbrugge Station (at Bombeek — 6 km from Rousbrugge) a large number of French soldiers were quartered. They were negroes

*from the island of Madagascar…. After having
made all the necessary arrangements with their
superiors, French officers, I was allowed to
visit them regularly outside working hours in
order to instruct them in European civilization. I went to instruct them in the Christian
Religion three or four times a week. Sergeant
Romarohova, who had been baptized a Catholic
and was a catechist in Madagascar, served
as an interpreter…*

The priest was successful and in October 1917 no
fewer than forty Madagascans aged between 18 and
43 were baptized. In his report the priest wrote:
*The French officers were exceedingly satisfied
with the boys who had followed the lessons in
European civilization: they were zealous and
very obedient.*

Yet only individuals or small groups converted to
Christianity. Most of the troops kept their own faith.

— The diary of Jane de Launoy

Jane de Launoy worked as a nurse in De Panne
during the war. In her above-mentioned diary she
reports extensively on the different troops that were
looked after in 'l'Océan' hospital or about the troops
posted nearby. She was particularly impressed by the
North Africans. In between her shifts Jane often
walked in the dunes and she described what she saw.
At times she was under the impression she was in
Africa. On 23 December 1914:
*A vision from the desert! A black dune
rises against the light of the waning sun.
Behind it the sky turns a fiery red. The
silhouette of an Arab becomes visible on the
dune crest. He seems to be walking through
fire. He raises his arms…kneels…straightens
up…kneels again. Time to pray to Allah.*

The following day she witnessed a mock attack:
*Arabian fantasy on the beach. At least
fifty horses in a row take off at a gallop
in various successive waves. With their
bright coloured uniforms it is indeed
a fabulous spectacle.*

Their interaction with other women also struck Jane.
With a somewhat jealous undertone she described
the commotion created in the field hospital by an
Algerian cavalryman on Christmas Day 1914:
*Yesterday a woman with a diabolical facial
expression showed us how an Arab had tried to
buy her…for one frank! She ran to the window,
dying to speak, she knocked puffing and
blowing and repeated: For one frank…one
frank…one frank! I had to laugh at her precise
indications concerning this delicate subject.
An older woman of almost 70 is almost proud
to report that they offered her two franks while
a young slut struts about: twenty-five franks!
A very honourable "lady" with a high collar
tells me with comical indignation how a
Belgian officer had whispered into her ear:
'Are you looking for someone, Madam'.
Strange, I probably do not look kind enough
as no one has propositioned me.*

Jane soon became used to the other customs of the
North Africans. Even though the 'buying of women'
had shocked her she noted on 29 December 1914 that
it was slightly more subtle than that. That night,
curious she entered into conversation with various
Muslims:
*One third told me that in their country women
were bought…sometimes in kind…a palm tree
for an ugly woman…a camel for a pretty
woman. Our floor looks like the tower of
Babel.[…] During the past nights a handsome
Goumier has been asking me for coffee at one
in the morning. Wearing his burnoose he comes
up into my office from outdoors. I am not
easily disconcerted but when that tall devil
with his darned seductive eyes appeared before
me, I was a little out of sorts. He enjoys his
coffee, stammers a few words and looks at me
like a sacred object, incomprehensibly taboo!…
On the whole Muslims have great respect for
women in uniform. Whenever you come across
such a Goumier in the two-metre wide corridor
he flattens himself against the wall with
outstretched arms to let you through. Belgians
should follow their example.*

— Language barriers

Cultural differences and language barriers were not only found among the various nationalities. The language situation in the Belgian army illustrated this. Here it must be stated that it would be a misconception to assume that the French speaking officers were genuinely French-speaking, as experienced by Jozef Vermeiren:

> Then a coarse, mean guy from Antwerp joined our company, I can't remember his name [...] He then stood before the company and shouted in French: 'You lot this and this exercise and that and that inspection'. When he had finished speaking French he always added in Flemish: 'All of you who did not understand me are even more stupid than pigs'. Hence his nickname: our pig.

However, it was not only the Belgians who experienced language problems within their army. The Canadians too experienced a certain rivalry between the English and French-speaking soldiers, as Father Van Walleghem found on 13 June 1916:

> The harmony among the Canadians is not optimal, even between the French and the English things aren't going too well. To give you just an example, a French Canadian padre told me that a Belgian officer had informed him that the Flemings were pro-German and hostile to France [...] I told him that was untrue, in the same way as you French Canadians are not hostile towards the English. Yet he immediately answered that the comparison was incorrect as the English were not their friends.

— Conclusion

The above fragments are but a few excerpts from the enormous amounts of source material likely to offer us an insight into the multicultural society present in Flanders between 1914 and 1919. What is missing, however, are the voices of 'the other side'. Indeed, little is known about what the North Africans and Chinese thought of the Belgian population and how they experienced the First World War in Flanders. The little that has been passed on to us is often written in languages known to very few historians. Furthermore, in depth knowledge of the culture is required to be able to interpret these testimonials accurately.

Also the input of the local population is all too frequently forgotten: with the exception of a few fragments not a single Belgian diary of Flanders was ever translated into English.

The fact that because of this the historiography of the First World War displays persistent hiatuses is clearly demonstrated in this anthology.

— Bibliography:

Deauville, Max. *De modder van de Westhoek*. Brussels, 2006.

De Launoy, Jane. *Oorlogsverpleegsters in bevolen dienst.*(War nurses under orders) Ghent, 2000.

Dumoulin, Koenraad, Vansteenkiste, Steven, Verdoodt Jan. *Getuigen van de Grote Oorlog. Getuigenissen uit de frontstreek*. Koksijde, 2001.

Elfnovembergroep, *Van den grooten oorlog: volksboek*, Kemmel, 1985.

Gesquiere, Jozef. *Veurne tijdens de Wereldoorlog 1914-1918*. Bruges, 1979.

Gezelle, Caesar. *De Dood van Yper*. Amsterdam, [1916].

Matthijs, R.J. *Lo tijdens de Eerste Wereldoorlog 1914-1918. Historische bijdrage bewerkt naar onuitgegeven schriftelijke en mondelinge bronnen*. Lo, 1959.

Niemann, Johannes. *Das 9. Königliche Sächsische Infanterie-Regiment Nr. 133 im Weltkrieg 1914-18*. Hamburg, 1969.

Piggott, Francis Stewart Gilderoy. *Broken Threads: An Autobiography*. London, 1950.

Van Staten, Victor, De Cleyn, Ludovicus-Maria en Joye, Edmundus. *De Abdij-Kazerne Sint-Sixtus 1914-1918. Dagboekaantekeningen*. Poperinge, 2001.

Van Walleghem, Achiel. *De oorlog te Dickebusch en omstreken*, 3 vols. Bruges, 1964-1967.

Vermeiren, Jef. *Getuigenissen van een frontsoldaat*. Zoersel, 1981.

Furnes, Décembre 1914
Louis Dumoulin

TRACES

OF THE MULTICULTURAL FIRST WORLD WAR
IN THE LANDSCAPE OF
FLANDERS AND NORTHERN FRANCE

DOMINIEK DENDOOVEN

It is quite impossible to give a complete overview in just a few pages of all the traces of the multicultural presence during the First World War that can still be found in Belgium and Northern France. There are people of other continents in almost all military cemeteries in Flanders and beyond. To find them, simply walk along a few rows of graves and read the inscriptions. This overview is necessarily limited to just a few important or meaningful cemeteries and monuments. However, we could not limit ourselves to sites within the Belgian border, as that border hardly existed during the First World War. Indeed, the operational area behind the Ypres Salient and the Yser front extended up to the Channel. For many parts of the British Empire the twofoldness 'France & Flanders' stood for the Western front, without any precise demarcation of where France started and Flanders ended.

This explains in part why many war victims who fell on Belgian soil are commemorated on large national monuments in Northern France. Those monuments were usually erected in a symbolically meaningful place, for instance where the own troops had gained a resounding victory. This is true for the impressive Canadian monument of Vimy Ridge (between Lens and Arras). Other 'national monuments' were erected in the spot where a national tragedy occurred. The South African museum and memorial of Delville Wood in Longueval and the Newfoundland Memorial Park in Beaumont-Hamel, both in the Somme, are such instances. These monuments also mention the names of their fellow countrymen who died in Belgium. The resolutely modern monument 'Constellation de la Douleur' (Constellation of Distress) by Christian Lapie that was inaugurated on the Chemin des Dames on 22 September 2007, is particularly moving. This is the first monument to pay tribute to all West African soldiers of the First World War. Closer to the border in Neuve-Chapelle (Pas-de-Calais), literally just a stone's throw away from one another, there is the elegant monument to the Indian Army Corps and a remarkable Portuguese cemetery. In 1914-1915 the small village of Neuve-Chapelle in the Lys valley was the heart of the Indian sector and in 1917-1918 the same applied for the Portuguese, but both groups were also deployed on the Belgian side of the border. Some kilometres further, in Laventie, there is the Rue-du-Bacquerot N°1 Military Cemetery, one of the many cemeteries where Indian casualties are remembered. What makes it so special is not only that the Indian section is separated from the British section by a country road, but that within the Indian section Muslims, Sikhs and Hindus are also remembered separately.

Here we must not only mention the monuments but also the cemeteries in Northern France. Indeed, when someone was injured at the front near Ypres, he occasionally died in a base hospital on the Northern French coast. Many French soldiers who had fallen near Ypres and in the Yser region were transferred after the war to the large national necropolis of Notre Dame-de-Lorette, half-way between Arras and Béthune. Because large groups of 'native labourers' mainly worked at the docks of the Channel ports and along the supply lines that started from there, their cemeteries can also be found in these places. In Arques-la-Bataille near Dieppe in addition to some Indian, West Indian and Chinese graves, you will mainly find graves of the South African Native Labour Corps, as well as the only monument dedi-

Georges Dumoulin (1882-1959): Veurne, December 1914.
(© Musée de l'Histoire Contemporaine, Paris)

cated to them. Chinese cemeteries can be found in Saint-Etienne-au-Mont near Boulogne-sur-Mer, Ruminghem (between Calais and Saint-Omer), and especially in Noyelles-sur-Mer in the Somme estuary, with more than 800 graves of Chinese labourers. Some cemeteries near Calais and Boulogne-sur-Mer offer an unequalled diversity of nationalities, like Les Baraques Military Cemetery in Sangatte (Calais), Terlincthun British Cemetery in Wimille (Boulogne) and the British military graves in the municipal cemetery of Boulogne-sur-Mer. Over three hundred Indians and Egyptians lie buried in Meerut Cemetery, regrettably a frequently vandalized and therefore usually locked cemetery situated in the middle of a residential area of Saint-Martin-les-Boulogne.

There are also some monuments that could qualify as 'national' in Belgian Flanders. The impressive Island of Ireland Peace Park in Messines is an outsider: not only because it was built fairly recently (1998), but also because it commemorates all the dead of the

Irish island, whether they originated from Northern Ireland or from the Irish Republic. Another new memorial is the Scottish monument of Frezenberg (Zonnebeke) inaugurated in the summer of 2007.

The most important and greatest monument of all is without doubt the Menin Gate in Ypres: all the missing soldiers of all parts of the British Empire having fought near Ypres are commemorated here, except for the Newfoundland Regiment whose missing are commemorated in Beaumont-Hamel, and the New Zealanders who are mentioned on their own monuments in Zonnebeke (Buttes New British Cemetery), Messines (Messines Ridge Cemetery) and Passchendaele (Tyne Cot Cemetery). Of the almost 55,000 names over 40,000 are from the United Kingdom (including the Irish, the Channel Islanders, etc), almost 6,200 Australians (including aboriginals), 6,830 Canadians (including Quebecois, Flemings, Japanese and First Nations), 560 South Africans, 413 Indians and 8 belonging to the British West

This German bunker near Zonnebeke, known as the ANZAC bunker, was captured by Australian troops on 20 September 1917. The actual photo was taken one week later. The abbreviation ANZAC has become a well-known concept and stands for Australian and New Zealand Army Corps. (© Imperial War Museum, London)

Indies Regiment. The gate is supplemented with two other great monuments for missing soldiers of the British Empire, i.e. that of Tyne Cot Cemetery in Passchendaele and that of Ploegsteert.

Various monuments commemorate the efforts of the troops during a specific battle. Thus, the Canadians have their 'Brooding Soldier' in Sint-Juliaan, Hill 62 in Zillebeke and Crest Farm in Passchendaele. New Zealand monuments can be found in Messines (New Zealand Memorial Park) and Zonnebeke ('s Graventafel). There is an Australian divisional monument in Buttes New British Cemetery in Zonnebeke. Oudenaarde and Kemmel have the only American memorials and the only Newfoundland monument in Belgium is located on the municipal border between Harelbeke and Kortrijk. Two small, recent Indian monuments are respectively located on a lawn at the Menin Gate and on the Sint-Elooisweg in Hollebeke.

The cluster of monuments and cemeteries near the Langemarkseweg in Boezinge is remarkable because of the Celtic connection: you will find the Breton memorial park Carrefour des Roses, a monument to the Irish poet Francis Ledwidge and the British Artillery Wood cemetery with amongst others the graves of Ledwidge and of Welsh poet Hedd Wyn.

In the Ypres Saint Martin's Church there are two large commemorative plaques honouring the great empires on the side of the allies: one for the French armies and one for the British Empire with the various coats of arms of the United Kingdom, British India and the various dominions.

In Belgium all in all there are very few military cemeteries exclusively dedicated to one nationality. On the French military cemetery in Saint-Charles-de-Potyze the many steles of the Muslims and the solitary gravestone of a Jewish Captain stand out among the hundreds of crosses. Another French military cemetery in Machelen-aan-de-Leie, was built to bury the dead of the Final Offensive in the Lys region. There are many 'tirailleurs sénégalais' and North

A parade of travailleurs indochinois on the market square of Kassel, probably on the occasion of Chinese New Year, in early 1919. (© Musée de Flandre, Kassel)

African soldiers among them but also a 'travailleur chinois' (Chinese labourer), a 'travailleur annamite' (from Viêt Nam) and a 'Malgache' (from Madagascar). Just a few kilometres further in Waregem, is the only American military cemetery of the First World War in Belgium. War graves of many different nationalities can also be found in some large municipal cemeteries, including the Ghent West cemetery, the Antwerp Schoonselhof or the municipal cemetery of Mons, where a large number of Russians are buried amongst others.

Almost all British military cemeteries in the West-hoek include graves from the dominions and colonies. An exceptionally large variety can be found in the Lijssenthoek Military Cemetery near Poperinge, where almost all parts of the British Empire are represented, next to two American and tens of French and German graves. Close by, also in Poperinge, Nine Elms Cemetery gives a complete picture of all British dominions and colonies present in the Westhoek in 1917 and 1918. Of almost 1600 graves, 961 belong to soldiers of the United Kingdom, 299 to Canadians, 150 to Australians, 117 to New Zealanders, 26 to South Africans, 8 to Guernseymen, 7 to Newfoundlanders, 2 to West Indians, 1 to a Bermudian, 1 to an Indian and 37 to Germans. Bedford House Cemetery in Zillebeke and to a lesser extent Tyne Cot Cemetery in Passchendaele have a very great diversity of representatives of the British overseas territories. On a smaller scale there is Grootebeek Cemetery in Ouderdom (near Reningelst). This beautiful cemetery that forms an island in a brook, also comprises an Indian plot. It was exactly on this spot that an Indian camp was set up in April and May 1915. In another almost idyllic spot, Ramparts Cemetery near the Lille Gate in Ypres, ten members of the New Zealand Maori Pioneer Battalion lie buried. The graves of the Indians Isaac Clause, Alexander Decoteau, Peter Ouelette and Reuben Sero can be found in Passchendaele New Military Cemetery. For the sake of completeness I must also mention the German cemeteries where many Poles and some Danish names stand out. This is particularly true for the German cemetery in Wervicq-Sud, on the French side of the Lys near Wervik.

In the polders near Groigne (Oudekapelle) stands a half-concrete and half-brick shelter.
Arabic characters have been scratched in the pointed horseshoe arch that translate as follows:
'There is no greater God than Allah. If you believe in Allah you will be victorious like
the victory over Tadmoor and Namar'. (© Daniël Leroy)

I would also like to mention two other sites. In the courtyard of the town hall of Poperinge you can view two cells and an execution pole from the First World War. Among the condemned men who spent their last night here there was probably the Chinese Wang Junzhi, but quite definitely the 17 year old Jamaican Herbert Morris. British court martials were usually less lenient for people with a different skin colour. The strangest and most original site is the shelter in the Oude Beverdijkstraat in Oudekapelle, near Diksmuide. The construction is unmistakably Belgian: yellow bricks reinforced with concrete and sheets of corrugated iron, were it not for a horseshoe-shaped Moorish arch in the middle of the door opening in which Arabic characters are engraved. And so, in a wide and ancient Flemish polder landscape stands a silent witness to the presence of North African soldiers on the Yser.

On the whole the traces of the multicultural presence in the landscape of the Westhoek during the First World War are not very spectacular: a couple of individual graves in a cemetery, some usually fairly modest monuments and some names on the Menin Gate. However, the relative absence of a number of colonial troops is noteworthy even though it simply shows how much history has forgotten them. Sources tell us that hundreds of West Africans died near Diksmuide in November 1914. There is nothing to remind us of this and in the French cemeteries in all only a few tens of graves belonging to 'tirailleurs sénégalais' can be found. Often the situation is hardly better on the British side in spite of thorough methodology and the noble intention of the War Graves Commission to remember every soldier who died in a suitable manner. One such telling example: the regimental history of the 47th Sikhs, an Indian infantry unit, reports that on 26 April 1915, 444 men launched an attack to the north of Ypres and the next morning it appeared that 348 of them had not returned. Only fourteen names of the 47th Sikhs are remembered, all are mentioned on the Menin Gate.

— Useful tips

Many British cemeteries display an information panel at the entrance with amongst others an overview of the different nationalities. British India and the dominions are mentioned separately, however, the colonies are included in the United King-

dom. The register of the cemetery, which can be found in a cabinet near the entrance, allows you easily to locate graves. Via the website of the In Flanders Fields Museum www.inflandersfields.be you can gain access to the data files of French and Belgian soldiers who died and/or were buried in the Westhoek. The website also offers links to the data files of the Commonwealth War Graves Commission (all fallen soldiers of the former British Empire, the present day Commonwealth) and the Volksbund Deutscher Kriegsgräberfürsorge (for the German graves). In addition to news about the First World War, the website www.wo1.be offers the largest database of war sites in the Westhoek and links to all major data files of war victims.

Ypres, 1919. Some early war tourists, civilians that had already returned and British soldiers, posing in front of a wooden hut converted into a café-restaurant. At the rear on the left some members of the Indian Labour Corps are standing.
(© Provincial Library & Documentation Centre, Bruges)

THE GREAT
ALIENATION
IN THE GREAT WAR

Moi mon colon cell' que j'préfère
C'est la guerr' de quatorz' dix-huit
GEORGES BRASSENS, 1962

MON STEYAERT

For many it was the strangest unforeseen death. For those who had been brought to the battle-fields of Europe from very distant countries during the First World War, it meant becoming lost and experiencing what philosophers referred to as *Verfremdung* at the beginning of the nineteenth century. All 'worldly philosophers' described how as a direct consequence of the industrial revolution the proletariat lost humanity by becoming involved in a labour process whose sole purpose was to maximize profit. Work as such was no longer meaningful. Something that made sense. The machine *verfremdete* the plebeian ... At the beginning of the twentieth century that proletariat was massively faced with a totally new phenomenon: the industrialized war ... And for the first time in history hundreds of thousands of people were brought to the battlefields of Europe from colonial territories. People who had never even seen a factory, who had never lived in a suburb. There was no other option but for them to become even more *Verfremd* from themselves.

What did the Inuit — let us call him Tapiritsat — who had travelled from Kiltikmeot (Victoria Island, Beaufort Sea) in the polar night feel when he disembarked near Boulogne-sur-Mer on a sunny spring day early in 1917, to be transported to the front near Ypres, where it was raining cats and dogs? What was he thinking?

French philosophers referred to this *Verfremdung* as *alienation*, using a word that also meant 'madness'. In the same way as the English *alien* was on a par with *lunatic*: mad. This is why the following queries the pure madness within contemporary civilisation, where 'war' has become so intangible that there are no clearly defined front lines. Why does the number of dead through suicide in the two world wars remain an open question? Antiheroes, who did not care to see their names inscribed on a monument. Destabilized people who had fallen victim to specific pathologies that often went undetected, like shell-shock. No statistics were kept of the suicides and other acts of despair. At the most there are harrowing stories of self-inflicted wounds, which was tantamount to desertion and was punished as such. It is this particular aspect of the First World War that we will discuss here. What effect did *alienation* have on many hundreds of thousands?

What was different and unprecedented in 14/18 about the presence of so many people of non-European origin on the battlefields?

— Racism, discrimination and xenophobia

A first question that should be answered is how crazy and *alienated* the spirit of 'la belle époque' was even before war broke. There was a great deal of seemingly scientifically founded racism. This was true for both sides throughout the war. It played a part in major political decisions that had to be taken to decide whether or not colonial troops should be recruited and deployed in Europe. Racism did not prevent the French and British from doing this. On the German side racist motives and logistical problems prevented them from following suit. Nowhere in Europe were troops brought in from German colonies deployed, although war was waged in Africa and in the Pacific Ocean with the deployment of local armed forces. What did (and does) this racism imply?

What is racism? Why must racism be distinguished from discrimination and from xenophobia? In the spirit of the period racism was claimed to be scientif-

A cook of the *tirailleurs sénégalais*. Northern France, July 1917.
(© Musée départemental Albert Kahn, Boulogne-Billancourt)

ically founded. A distinction is made between peoples and races. However, the concepts are never clearly defined. It would appear that a number of 'human races' were demonstrably inferior simply because it was claimed their alleged backwardness was linked to their most striking physical properties. A larger cranial capacity meant superior intelligence. The very shape of their skulls was a valid criterion to ascribe criminal tendencies to some races, a tall stature was sufficient to have the biggest and hence the best sperm. All this finally produced something like Lebensborn, breeding farms created by SS-führer Himmler for a new superior Germanic race, but the trend had already been set before the start of the twentieth century. For instance before the First World War Sweden had already passed a law aimed at preventing marriages of 'Aryan' citizens with Lappish fellow citizens. However, if we apply the 'Aryan' theory then today the Polynesians are the most superior people, as they are direct descendents of 'Aryans' who did not travel West, but proceeded up the Pacific Ocean. They are the largest humans with the heaviest build. With the Tutsis in Rwanda and Burundi the Germans had access to such a dominant aristocratic people. In short, there is racism whenever a series of measurable characteristics of a group of people results in the 'special' treatment of all the members of that group. Racism leads to apartheid. And even worse to ethnical cleansing and genocide. The source of all this evil was to be found in what many academics had proclaimed at the beginning of the nineteenth century. As from the nineteenth century no form of colonization or missionary work can be exonerated from racism. That racism naturally evolved into discrimination. However, let us be quite clear: not every discrimination is a manifestation of racism.

Total abject racism that prevailed had already been refined before the start of the First World War as inferior races were no longer entirely inferior. This was demonstrated, used and abused. 'Genetic' explanations were thought up. Some races provided good warriors. Others were deemed to be hard, stupid workers. Therefore within all the overseas groups discrimination mainly occurred on the basis of ethnicity, without there necessarily being any racial characteristics. A Sikh was allowed to carry a weapon whereas the Chinese coolie was not. There was also discrimination within the European armies that

A group of *tirailleurs sénégalais*. Northern France, July 1917.
(© Musée départemental Albert Kahn, Boulogne-Billancourt)

could not be described as a form of racism. Within the French armies the Corsicans amongst others experienced this type of discrimination. For them there were no exemptions during recruitment, like the status of 'père de famille'. At the front they were often given the worst chores. On the British side the Irish were often the victims. In the Belgian army not only the Flemish rural youth but also the Walloon small farmers were the victims of discrimination on the Yser as both were unable to understand the French spoken by their officers.

And so we arrive at the third relevant concept: xenophobia — fear and mistrust towards anyone considered foreign because of language, religion, skin colour or way of life. Xenophobia has always existed and has given rise to conflicts in all cultures, without there being any racist motives. Xenophobia is one of the most elementary forms of social life. The Ancient Greeks called anyone they could not understand barbarians. The Cree Indians and Iroquois call the Dakota 'Sioux', or generation of vipers. Many pejorative names have thus become common so that quite frequently a great people continue to be humiliated by this sort of denomination. The peoples around them called the Bamana of Mali, heirs of the library of Tombouctou, Bambara or stutterers. Why did they not call them by the name they had given themselves, Bamana: human beings? Many names simply mean 'human being' in the own language. Roma, Manouche, Romanichel, as many Gypsies call themselves have the root of the Indo-Germanic 'man' for our 'human being', whereas Gypsy, Bohemian,... almost always has a negative connotation !

— War

Now that we have made a clear distinction between racism, discrimination and xenophobia we still need to define the concept of 'war'. Indeed, not every conflict is a war.

This phenomenon seems related to the civilization pattern focused on irreversible globalization. Because of this many hundreds of cultures are disappearing, many of which were brought to Europe during the First World War. Today this is still considered a normal almost natural issue, but is this likely to generate even more conflicts in the long term? Should philosophers not have gone much further in the foot-

steps of the anarchist Pierre-Joseph Proudon and the libertarian Jean Jacques Rousseau with his *Bon Sauvage*, and grasped the absurdity of a blind faith in unending progress? They should have shouted out that nothing justifies the force of arms. Racism and discrimination were highly dependent on the positivism of the nineteenth century: the sole true faith in science and progress ... Even though xenophobia has always existed, in its most objectionable form i.e. racism it is only present in the Western world.

Our so-called 'primitives' never went to war for geopolitical reasons. Throughout history only the so-called civilized human beings organized in states and nations went to war. The Japanese and Chinese eventually joined in although the latter first built a

This 'Iron Landsturm man' was erected in Sønderborg, a Danish town that was German territory from 1864 until 1920. It is a so-called *Nagelfigur (Nail Figure)*. By buying a nail and driving it into the figure you not only contributed to the victory financially but also morally. (Museum Sønderjylland – Sønderborg Slot)

gigantic wall to keep war out of their Heavenly Empire and Japan, the Empire of the Rising Sun, managed to remain in total isolation for a very long time. The North American Indians were rarely faced with armed conflicts because they had never known stringent forms of individual property and had lived for many centuries in a static 'ecological' world. They never made history before the arrival of the palefaces! Proportionally there were very few of them in their immensely large virgin environment: it is estimated that in the days of Columbus there were eight million Indians. Indian wars first originated in the United States when the palefaces started appropriating plots of land of one square mile and fencing it in. Indians and bisons were no longer allowed to enter and were simply shot!

— Alienation

Let us now return to our imaginative Inuit Tapiritsat from Kiltikmeot. For all the colonial troops the climatological and geographical circumstances in Europe were quite different from those in their homeland. Furthermore, the situation near Ypres could at best be described as hell on earth. From his earthly paradise Tapiritsat had arrived in hell. His paradise would disappear forever even if he survived and returned to Kiltikmeot. Not because of a climatic change in the Arctic Ocean, but because he would have become *alienated* from himself. Thus the long presence in Europe of this colonial and other non-white units would trigger or strengthen a worldwide desire for independence among many peoples. Whether they liked it or not many war veterans, from wherever they came, contributed to the decolonization that would only be completed after the Second World War. Life near Ypres was degrading. It was degrading for both man and beast. A shrapnel shell could explode at any moment and end your life, in the same way as until recently a car bomb could explode on every market day in Iraq.

There is a documented case of unrests on Christmas Day 1917 at Reningelst, 10 kilometres from Ypres, in which two foremen were killed in a camp of Chinese coolies. While quashing the 'uprising' British soldiers killed three more Chinese. They are buried in Westouter British Cemetery. What had been the problem? Were they about to go on strike, did they want to

break the strike by force? In other words, were purely logistical and military interests at stake? Or did far stronger, underlying frustrations rise to the surface? Why did they shoot unarmed labourers? Was this 'tirer dans le tas' (random shooting), as frequently occurred during labour conflicts at the end of the nineteenth century, or does this highlight the conflicts or the 'being different' of the 'cultural entities' that were present in the Westhoek? At the time, i.e. during the war such an occurrence was never considered from a purely socio-anthropological standpoint.

Every Gurkha was not only a Nepalese mercenary but also an inhabitant of high mountains, and every Brit was well aware that he always carried his 'kukri', the traditional large knife, and that he would be well-advised to respect it. Many forms of apartheid originated. We can assume that the Gurkhas and the many Sikhs were slightly more familiar with British military tradition, but what about the numerous 'Tirailleurs Sénégalais', who originated from all the corners of West Africa and spoke tens of different languages, without actually speaking more French than any of the Flemish soldiers at the front? What about the Spahis from Morocco and Algeria? Anyone with a little expert knowledge who runs through the lists of names of the 'French' dead will see all the tribes of entire Sub-Saharan Africa, from Niger to Mauritania file past. White New Zealanders fought alongside the Maori and the Irish from North and South Ireland, in Messines and in Wijtschate. If ever there was a veritable tower of Babel then it was in Flanders during the First World War.

Alienation was even more extreme for overseas people if in addition to the language and way of life they

Winter 1914: British Indian soldiers try and keep warm the best they can in their primitive trench near Neuve-Chapelle

were faced with a kind of warfare that was at odds with what they knew about fighting and weapons in their own traditions. They were also usually unfamiliar with the concept 'enemy'. In traditional cultures usually the stranger is not just a human being. Like Pygmies among the Bantus he may be something like an ape. The distinction was often quite harsh: human being, not a human being. But this does not make him an enemy. That type of 'enemy' can only be found in the history of civilization when conflicts about territories, about natural resources and roads arise. 'Enemy' then depends on where you live. Here we are and there is the enemy. Headhunters would raid another village, cannibals would 'hunt' another clan. But that does not turn the others into enemies. The image of the enemy is typical of a 'civilized culture'.

Tenacious myths claim that the Senegalese would cut off the noses of the Germans they killed, that Germans crucified a Canadian near St Juliaan and that 'black cannibals' never took prisoners in spite of their white officers. There are a number of variations on the above: Maria Beck from Westouter claimed that when she was a young woman a Spahi had once shown her a number of ears of German soldiers he had killed suspended from a wire. The story may be true. There are more than enough examples in cultural anthropology to support such facts with ancient customs in which virtually all the parts of the human body are mentioned. However, such criminal deeds will only have occurred very sporadically in Flanders. As from 1917 circumstances certainly did not favour 'wanton' atrocities. Whoever wanted to recover the scalp of a killed enemy would find it impossible to

There were many colonial troops among the victims of the first gas attack of 22 April 1915. This photo of a gas victim of 1 RMT ended up in the photo collection of a German officer.
(© In Flanders Fields Museum – Collection von Kanne)

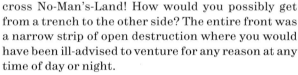

cross No-Man's-Land! How would you possibly get from a trench to the other side? The entire front was a narrow strip of open destruction where you would have been ill-advised to venture for any reason at any time of day or night.

As opposed to this it is a known fact that the deepest human dignity of many soldiers and auxiliary troops from overseas was offended by the manner in which their bodies were handled. How could a suitable funeral be arranged for deceased comrades in the unknown, hierarchical structures of the French or British army, in a very unisexual world, without women, children or clan structures? Hindus and Sikhs cremated their dead, the Chinese buried multiple bodies under a burial mound. To some going missing on the actual battlefield meant their souls would never find peace. And more specifically for the colonial troops many people disappeared entirely anonymously: not even an approximation of the total number of dead in many colonial units is known. Therefore you were treated as a *foreigner* without a traditional religious framework.

There were also all kinds of forms of animism and superstition, like fetishism adapted to the circumstances, in the shape of a Glécult originating from Senegal, that became popular among the 'tirailleurs'. This involved the questionable belief in a form of invulnerability which continues to make victims during civil wars throughout Africa: with such a Glé on your head no bullet could touch you! This corresponded to a very common practice among white soldiers in which you wore the bullet or shrapnel that injured you as an amulet so as not to be hit a second time. In such circumstances both white and black magic are always involved. This was not only true for the 'primitives': on 4 September 1915 a gigantic wooden statue of Hindenburg was erected in Berlin. Whoever drove a nail in it not only made a financial contribution to the war effort but was also deemed to promote the final victory. Remarkably we notice a partial parallel with the ritual objects from the area around the estuary of the Congo River, known as 'nail statues', even though the traditional Majombe name for this type of statue should be translated as 'power statue'. In a positive sense. The figures are almost

This woman of the Wé people of the Ivory Coast is wearing a gle on her head and is holding a tassel in her hand. She is about to perform a fortune telling ritual. The gle culture originated on the Ivory Coast around 1928 through the intervention of a soldier who had served in Europe during the First World War. This explains the denomination of the cult objects: the head is called *commandant* and the tassel is referred to as the *tirailleur*.
(© Ethnographic Museum, Antwerp)

The Bwa from Burkina Faso and Mali wear such masks during ceremonies like transition rites amongst others. The masks have special powers that are kept in check by the persons wearing them. They also convey messages about mythology and morality. In 1915 the Bwa revolted against French recruitment. Unruly Bwa villages were destroyed in retaliation.

always masculine or they are figures of a dog with at times two heads. The magical force that is believed to be concealed in this type of statue and which can be used for both good and evil purposes, lies in the 'bill-ogos': all kinds of ingredients in a sticky mixture on the head or in the abdominal cavity of the statue, which is often closed with a piece of mirror glass. The forged nails and plates, which in the course of many years of use gradually covered such statues, are merely a payment for the use of these magical forces. This is typical magical thinking in which there is a direct link between the actions and their inevitable consequences.

Moreover, many facts show that the *alienation* experienced at the front accelerated the *acculturation process* of and in the homeland and more specifically in Africa. The reserves of smaller museums that believed they could supplement their collections quickly and cheaply immediately after the First World War, are now full of junk they don't know what to do with. Indeed, at the time the paraphernalia of traditions that had disappeared as a result of the First World War were copied on a large scale by skilled sculptors, who had never even seen the originals and who were not familiar with their 'use'. They simply copied from reproductions and books. This illustrates the serious consequences of the First World War for the traditional culture and personal identity of many inhabitants of what would later be called the 'Third World'.

Alienation is also used in court terminology. First, when you want to indicate that someone has misappropriated something, second when a right on something is transferred to someone else due to rental or sale. In this sense *alienation* during the First World War refers to a form of human trafficking. Chinese coolies, sometimes used for hazardous work, were not aware of what they were in for when they were recruited. Many colonial soldiers were removed by force from their traditional way of life and attempts were made to talk them into false patriotism. Whether or not this was successful is another matter. However, it is certain that this brutal contact with another world had a decisive influence on the development of emancipative currents that would result in decolonization after the Second World War.

There are very few testimonies of non-Western First World War veterans. And those who were here often experienced too great *acculturation* and the loss of the best of themselves to still be relevant.

— Strange objects

An object can explain how remote the traditional way of thinking could be from warfare during the First World War. The most common word to designate the most sacred object of the Plains Indians originates from French Jesuits, who already did missionary work among them in the seventeenth century. Thus the Canadian-French 'calumet' has become ethnological jargon for what Karl May calls a peace pipe in his Cowboys and Indian stories. A calumet could be such an item that illustrates how many misconceptions would need to be cleared up before unprepared people of totally different cultural backgrounds meet, this will continue to be so in the future. Just step into a pub where someone at the bar turns round and blows his cigarette smoke in your face: this might well cause a fight. Yet this is precisely what a tribal chief of the Woodlands always did when he welcomed a guest with the greatest respect. A pipe ceremony among the Plain Indians was described in 1673 by French Jesuit Jacques Marquette among the Quapaw,

A German *Nagelfigur*. By buying a nail and driving it into the figure you not only contributed to the victory financially but also morally. This unfinished nail figure of 1916 originates from South Jutland, a Danish province that was incorporated in the German Empire between 1864 and 1919. (Museum Sønderjylland – Sønderborg Slot)

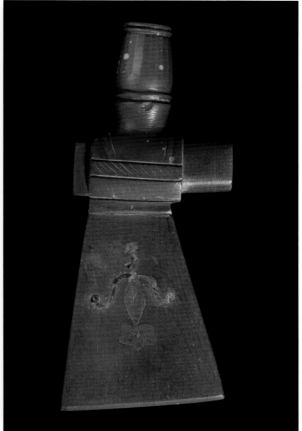

a small tribe that has since died out. The host circulated his *Canupa:* if you were handed the pipe to smoke you were accepted in the community. This could imply that you had unknowingly been accepted into a life-and-death alliance based on the principle that the friends of my friends are my friends also. In the Dakota this pipe is called *Canupa Wakan,* in which *wakan* simultaneously means large and erect. *Tatanka* means bison, *Tanka* spirit, *Wakan Tanka* Great Spirit. You could not be more ecological in any other language: *Tanka* spirit, the intangible, *Tatanka,* the bison who virtually provides everything. The erect, large pipe, *Canupa Wakan,* interconnects everything. Why 'erect'? Because the root of the *Canupa,* the erection, is the male element in a highly complex picture of the cosmos. Indians do not kneel to pray, they stand. The pipe head in which only tobacco and no other herb is burnt, is the female ele-

ment. During official ceremonies the pipe is shown to the four points of the compass with the pipe head pointing downwards, i.e. to Earth. The smoke will rise so that everything is spiritualized and connected by offering tobacco. Even though the Indians lived in the Stone Age their spirituality will stand up to modern times.

A remarkably pure counterpoint in the racist cacophony of the period under consideration can be heard from the artists of that period. They acknowledged the superiority of the art of one so-called primitive man. Western art had run aground in impressionism, the last convulsions of any realism, and the invention of photography was hailed as making art as a reproduction of reality superfluous. When Picasso wanted to immortalize ladies of the night on canvas in an entirely different way he used as models a Bambara

Both sides of a *calumet.* This calumet is both a 'tomahawk' and a 'peace pipe': opposite the blade of the axe there is a pipe head. The calumet is a sacred item full of symbolism to the Indians of the North American plains. (Private Collection, Kemmel)

mask, one from Salampasu and a Senoufo mask, as well as a couple of statues of the Baoule. And he made Les Demoisselles d'Avignon. The artists of his generation discovered that sculptors of the peoples fighting beside them at the front had long resolved the form problems they had just discovered ... And they took their hat off to that. Some decades later this would also result in the exhibition of Entartete Kunst in Munich and elsewhere!

Various publications of the period show how black Africans, Indians, North African soldiers taken prisoner of war were considered by the Central Powers: in fact most frequently as curiosities! Cultural anthropology has started with curiosity cabinets in the eighteenth century, not in the least in Germany. There is no country in Europe with as many Völkerkundemuseums and old ethnographic collections. The strange person was initially an odd person, who had strange morals and habits. A big child? Possibly. Dangerous? Possibly, but not entirely uncivilized! This was not a problem at first. Serious questions were first raised around the middle of the nineteenth century. To find answers unbridled science was immediately let loose on everything explorers told and on everything they brought back from around the world: anthropometry. Well into the twentieth century they believed they had found the right answers by measuring as many physical elements on human beings as possible.[1] In parallel they attempted to conclusively demonstrate the inferiority of women. No example of discrimination is more universal than the discrimination of which women throughout the world

have been the victim for many centuries merely on the basis of their female genitals, which are as different as a fingerprint from one person to the next!

— Gott mit uns

From Cato, who kept repeating his 'Carthago delenda est' you can draw a direct line to the statement of Carl von Clausewitz that war is merely the continuation of politics by other means. Both statements fit in with the typically Western way of thinking and imply major questions in respect of the morality and legitimacy of warfare. For centuries and up to the present day the vital importance of a state or nation is used to justify deadly violence against everything that is considered hostile about that state. Going to war is a holy duty. Anyone who backs out of it is criminalized and until recently was given the death penalty in wartime. Here I would like to stress that all parties involved in conflicts invoked and continue to invoke the same divine support: 'Gott mit uns', 'God bless...'. This is quite different from what the non-white, non-Westerner thought, insofar as he had not been introduced to another opinion through contact with the Mediterranean world, the imperialism of Western Christianity or any other form of colonialism. He had no need for a notion of God. The origin of a Western vision on warfare was closely related to the creation of city-states at the end of the Neolithicum and the necessity from then onwards to control the surrounding area of such cities and to keep their trade routes open. Warfare became a geopolitical issue and soon acquired a religious dimension. Whereas in all civilizations with far

A trench club from the First World War found during excavations in Boezinge (© In Flanders Fields Museum)

— Toi baïonnette à dents!.. moi couteau dans les dents..

more ancient animistic roots, which we continue to refer to as 'primitive', there have always been uses and customs specifically intended to avoid confrontations. Thus the 'primitive' man knows many forms of imposing behaviour, which similarly to the imposing behaviour of primates and animals of prey seldom or never develop into an actual fight. The oldest forms of coexistence did not originate to be stronger in the event of conflicts with other groups but to survive better together in an open and wide world. Recent research at American universities, both in the field of depth psychology and in that of distant prehistory has irrefutably shown that our earliest ancestors did not kill one another!

Obviously, the non-Western man also made weapons. The most sophisticated like the Australian boomerang or the throwing knives of Central Africa were essentially hunting weapons intended to strike wild animals running loose in the dry Savannah region from a greater distance than would be possible with a spear or arrow. Most ironware from Central Africa collected today is no longer a genuine weapon but a status symbol with a fixed currency value. No one would want to risk losing it in a fight. The man-sized shield of the Asmat, the most fearsome headhunters in the world, is colourful and very strikingly decorated with totem signs. It is used in group to impress and thus to prevent 'attacks', i.e. to quash any fight.

This French cartoon seems to be asking 'Who is the barbarian?':
the West African soldier holding a knife between his teeth or
the German soldier with his sawtooth bayonet (that inflicts terrible injuries).
(© BDIC-Musée de l'Histoire Contemporaine, Paris)

The *wakahuia* of Victor Spencer. For the Maori the wakahuia is a wooden, sculpted container in which a person's most precious possessions are stored like the heitiki, the personal pendant in nephrite. The actual wakahuia is considered to be a holy object handed down by ancestors to the next generations. Young Victor Spencer was half Maori, half Pakeha (white). He was executed on 24 February 1918 near Dikkebus. In 2000 the New Zealand government granted him a posthumous pardon. Some years later his relatives brought this wakahuia to his grave. It contains a biography, the pardon by the New Zealand government and a heitiki. (In Flanders Fields Museum)

The non-Western man does go on raids, he is a canni-bal, kidnaps women, takes slaves, plunders. But that is precisely why he never goes to war in the sense of Cato to Clausewitz.[2] There may be blood feuds, revenge may be taken on certain members of a tribe or clan, but seldom on the entire society to which they belong! The elements invoked to justify modern wars are not known to so-called 'primitive ' man. Whoever travelled from the North West Coast and disembarked in Le Havre or Calais was faced with something he more or less knew was typical of the paleface, but quite definitely not on that scale. In their culture many conflicts are avoided with things like a Potlatch: a huge feast you organize to convince your competitors that you are indeed the greatest and the best.

— The superiority of the 'primitive' man

Before concluding I would like to add something about the Dogon, an internationally famous people from Mali with a particularly rich cosmology in which quite exceptionally Sirius, the morning star, and not the sun is at the centre of the universe. There is a remarkable connection between the First World War and the manner in which between the two world wars and shortly after 1945 most information about the Dogon was gathered, with stories of extraterres-trial beings, who are claimed to have visited earth, about the smallest of all grain seeds, the digitaria, which it is claimed the extraterrestrials brought along from the invisible sister star: small but extraor-dinarily dense and hence ten times heavier. These stories are still causing controversy among special-ists. Nonsense for some and a particularly intriguing myth for others. The main informant of Marcel Gri-aule, the Dogon expert, was a veteran called Ogotem-mêli. He or his interpreter had been in France suffi-ciently long to embellish their stories! Maybe! All the great anthropologists of that period, of which Mar-garet Mead is the best known, have dealt with inform-ants who wanted to answer questions that had not yet been put.

The fact remains that Dogon indeed died near Ypres and that therefore two years after their death the so-called 'Dama's' were held in their beautiful country of origin. This is a traditional transition cer-emony to the world of the forefathers, during which something of the deceased is always transferred

to future generations. You are always part of your ancestors: a remarkable reincarnation theory!

This brings us back to the heart of the matter: what is the meaning of life and death, own identity in the eyes of someone who arrives here in wartime from a very distant country, usually an animist for whom in principle everything is highly symbolic and who would have taken life and death extremely seriously? The reason for a slaughter like this war can only have escaped the underestimated wisdom of the so-called 'primitive'. He would not have been able to make any sense of it, he would have felt repulsed and depressed. Deep down did this ultimately give him a feeling of superiority? We may assume it did.

I started with a text by a great French chansonnier, Georges Brassens, and I will end with a question put by another great chansonnier, Léo Ferré: 'Est-ce ainsi que les hommes vivent?'

1. Until the 1970s at the entrance of the Musée de l'Homme in Paris you could see which shape the breasts of European and Asian women should have.

2. This is still remarkably expressed in Carolingian law. An organized armed action is only a war if at least thirty men are fighting on either side. If there are fewer belligerents common law applies and any armed action is considered a criminal offence.

Native Canadians under the Menin Gate in Ypres. In October 2005 the Canadian Department of Veterans Affairs organised a 'Calling Home Ceremony'. During the ceremony representatives of native Canadian communities (Indians, Inuit and Métis) called home the spirits of their ancestors that had remained behind on the European battlefields. (© Tijl Capoen, Ypres)

DYING IN A DISTANT COUNTRY, IN A FOREIGN WAR

ABOUT WAR AND CULTURE

RIK PINXTEN

A recent count performed by the In Flanders Fields Museum totalled over 50 different cultures, whose young people lay buried in the Westhoek. I aim to highlight how the concept of war should be further examined. Even though comparative research did not yield a great deal of information about death and war in other cultures, we can list a number of basic insights.

— War

The a-cultural approach claims that 'war is an integral part of the human nature'. However, this does not stand up to a comparison of the different cultures. In the last decades of the twentieth century some research focused on the anthropology of war. Otterbein (1977) in particular acquired a reputation in this field. The work of Foster and Rubinstein (1986) gives an intentionally comparative perspective. What do we know for certain from this and other studies?

Aggression is undoubtedly a universal phenomenon in man. This aggression is caused by the action of the adrenaline gland and is influenced by diet; however, these biological conditions do not tell us anything about war. A special finding in anthropological studies is namely that some 'peaceful societies' are known to us, like the Hopi Indians in Arizona, USA, where the expression of aggression is systematically interrupted during the education process and tabooised. In such societies the individual is socialized to ensure he fully empathizes with the processes of growth and interdependence of all species in nature. When a member of such a society commits an act of aggression, he or she causes great shame among the entire group. In other societies (like the Yanomami) the life of the male is entirely structured by successive periods of initiation and aggressive encounters as warrior. The same biological structure thus clearly results in a different behaviour. The famous saying of war ideologist von Clausewitz: "war is a continuation of politics by other means" is therefore an improper generalization. People have aggressive impulses, but no direct causal relationship can be inferred from this regarding the cultural aspect of acts of war: the organic predispositions are 'culturalized' by traditions, values and educational routes that can be found in various cultures. This is why the impulse in society A will lead to war whereas in society B it will e.g. generate rituals. This clearly outlines the subject of this paper as an attempt to explain war in a different manner in compliance with the cultural identity of the population involved in a war.

— The West and other cultures

Let us first consider the Western approach. Obviously, a huge amount of literature on war has been written. I will only use one general work, which apparently is considered to have some authority: Jones (1987). The author gives an overview of Western warfare from the ancient Greeks and Romans to the guerrilla warfare at the end of the last century. As the author is a strategist and military historian the approach is fairly typical in the sense that war is considered an art that evolves in a linear historic development. Jones expounds the Western (cultural) vision on war, i.e. territorial expansion, the acquisition of loot and the elimination of as many enemies as possible. He does note that this has gradually increased over the past two centuries with the dwin-

This poster showing a *tirailleur algérien*, advertised the war loan of the Compagnie Algérienne. Its creator Lucien Jonas (1880-1947) was an official French war artist. (Collection Philippe Oosterlinck)

preparing for warriorship, warrior initiations and the like, but the following elements are missing from each genuine encounter: no territory is occupied (as the ownership of land is pointless), and they tend to steal women rather than goods. Homicide is considered to be a serious misfortune for which the enemy is entitled to compensation. Lévi-Strauss suggests distinguishing the ritual character of these acts of aggression from the concept of war. Recent comparative research (Ember & Ember, 1994) somewhat qualifies this while maintaining the overall distinction: war as the action of an entire community against another is at least more unusual in small survival societies (desert or primeval forest inhabitants) than in the larger agricultural groups. And its character changes: land does become important. The proposition that a shortage (e.g. of protein, of women ...) causes war in other cultures is definitively rejected. Highly belligerent communities are driven more by the fear of a possible misfortune, which they try to prevent or control through war. Also, the more evolutionary cultural approach of Carneiro (1994) supports this proposition and shows that the expansion of the scale of a population is a major factor: agricultural societies display greater concentrations of people, with a greater interest in property (land and other goods). States are a late emanation of this, and the war incidence in states increases as the states grow (Carneiro 1994, and also Jones 1987). Cohen, who focused his entire career on the anthropological

dling of the tactical meaning of acts of war as such (Jones: 639). This reasoning is accurate as long as you remain within the historic cultural beacons of the West. Once you abandon these beacons and start discussing 'war' as a general human phenomenon you are on the wrong track.

Claude Lévi-Strauss, the founder of structuralism, wrote a famous article on this subject. His starting point does accept culturally different concept meanings. In 'Guerre et commerce' (1943) he shows how none of the 'obvious' war characteristics can be found in typical 'belligerent' societies: the members (males) of those societies occupy a great deal of their lives

The native people on the American North-West coast (Canada and Alaska) celebrate impressive winter feasts called *potlatch*, during which a rival is given enormous amounts of food and valuable items such as blankets. The other party is not only overwhelmed but is also challenged to hold an equally impressive potlatch at a later date. The givers and the recipients thus became dependent on one another while remaining competitors. A potlatch is amongst others a subtle manner of avoiding conflicts. The ceremonial clothing for a potlatch comprises amongst others a coat/blanket and a woven hat.

A blanket/coat as worn and given away by the Haida of the American North –West coast at a potlatch.
(Royal Museums for Art and History, Brussels)

study of states, describes states as 'war machines' (Cohen, 1986). We can safely claim without exaggeration that this scientific sector is convinced that the onset of war with territorial expansion and death of the enemy only appeared with the creation of states. Furthermore, it would appear that the number of conflicts and the number of victims increase in line with the growth of the states. In this sense the contemporary concept of 'war' should preferably be reserved for state-related conflicts.

— War and other cultures

Here I return to the soldiers of the First World War, who originated from various non-Western cultures. Touaregs, Dogon, Malagasies, Indians and Chinese, and also inhabitants of Samoa and Canadian Indians lay buried in Flemish soil. To them war could only have meant the strange and virtually endless killing of their colonizer's enemy in a remote country. The purpose or meaning of this battle must at least have made an exotic impression on the colonial subjects: the arguments were namely nationalistic: you died for the fatherland and the enemy was considered repugnant, barbarian and immoral. But what did this mean for the colonial subject? Was the enemy

Feather headdress of the Indians of the Great Plains.
(Royal Museums for Art and History, Brussels)

like them in the eyes and arguments of 'their' colonizer? Or was there some difference? If we attempt to understand what the so-called Great War could have meant for these people in the light of the above described concepts we are faced with a riddle: their understanding of conflict or war was almost certainly entirely different from that of the 'masters' in whose service they had travelled to Flanders from the colonies. The 'numerical' approach of the conflict with millions of soldiers, the heroism of sacrificing your own life for a country and a sovereign with no biological kinship with the 'hero', the striving for a maximum number of casualties among the enemy, the fighting and dying for the occupation of some metres of territory: all of these must have been equally strange and unreal notions for the colonial subjects. The prospect of being buried would have been culturally alien to some of them (like some Indian groups and also others). More specifically the certainty that after being killed in battle in a foreign country they would remain eternally remote from their own population, captive in this clay soil overhung with a leaden sky, must without doubt have been terrifying for most of them. As I have demonstrated that 'the nation states at war' is simply a highly specific concept complex that is not at all obvious for people of a different culture and who therefore have a different concept framework about conflict and war, it must also be clear that dying in this uprooted empirical situation would be a daunting prospect. Needless to say that dying was not a particularly appealing proposition for the European soldiers in this war, yet it is hard to grasp the uprooting and the total lack of horizon of understanding which the colonial subject experienced in his role as auxiliary soldier of the colonial master. The simple fact that the graves of these people are often geographically separated from those of the European soldiers is in my mind all the more poignant. You could reach the conclusion that even in death they were not fully considered as fellow men. They died in 'our' war, a war that must have been entirely alien to them.

The last subject that I will briefly discuss is death. In a technical sense we call death a life crisis, in the same way as birth and puberty. All known cultures have developed transitional rituals to cope with these crises. It is striking that all these transitional rituals have the same three-part structure: discarding of the identity, display of the 'sacra' in the boundary phase and reconstruction of the new personality to be adopted. The fact that this is a universal occurrence with a same format indicates the fundamental importance of transitions for man in crisis situations. In our regions we find these ritualizations in a religious liturgy or in a state ritual for soldiers. This is where the meaning or positioning is defined for the deceased and obviously also for and by the survivors. Yet again we must try and imagine what this dying must have meant for the soldier of a different culture and his relatives. We are not longer able to ask them and to the best of my knowledge no studies were carried out on this subject. I suggest we humbly acknowledge our human shortcoming in this respect.

— Conclusion

In the abstract to this paper I indicated that war is not a universal concept. Multiple and at times radically different cultural meanings can be found. Dying for the fatherland during the First World War is also a highly specific concept. The dignity of men can only be recognized if we are capable of coping with this diversity.

— Bibliography

Carneiro, R.L., 'War and Peace. Alternating Realities in Human History', in Reyna, S.P. en Downs, R.E. (eds.), *Studying War. Anthropological Perspectives*, Philadelphia, 1994, pp. 3-29.

Cohen, R., 'War and Peace Proneness in Pre- and Postindustrial States', in Foster, M.L. en Rubinstein, R.A. (eds.), *Peace and War. Cross-Cultural Perspectives*, New Brunswick, N.J., 1986, pp. 253-267.

Ember, M. en Ember, C., 'Cross-Cultural Studies of War and Peace', in Reyna, S.P. en Downs, R.E. (eds.), *Studying War. Anthropological Perspectives*, Philadelphia, 1994, pp.185-208.

Foster, M.L. en Rubinstein, R.A. (eds.), *Peace and War. Cross-Cultural Perspectives*, New Brunswick, N.J., 1986.

Honigmann, J. (ed.), *Handbook in Social and Cultural Anthropology*, New York, Columbia University Press, 1977.

Jones, A., *The Art of War in the Western World*, Chicago, University of Illinois Press, 1987.

Lévi-Strauss, C., 'Guerre et commerce chez les Indiens de l'Amérique du Sud', in *Renaissance*, vol. 1, 1943.

Otterbein, K., 'The Anthropology of War', in Honigmann, J. (ed.), *Handbook in Social and Cultural Anthropology*, New York, Columbia University Press, 1977, pp. 923-958.

Reyna, S.P. en Downs, R.E. (eds.), *Studying War. Anthropological Perspectives*, Philadelphia, 1994.

Lucien Jonas: The three races, 1915. Here the artist aligns three soldier types of 'exotic' appearance in a dune landscape: the Belgian with the dog cart, the Indian sepoy and the West-African *tirailleur sénégalais*.
(© BDIC-Musée de l'Histoire Contemporaine, Paris)

LES TROIS RACES

Tableau de Lucien JONAS.

Djemba Dialo · St. Louis-Senegal.

Amin · Moskana-Algier.

Rabah Kheta · Nagara-Senegal.

Abdullah Ahmed · Timbuktu.

N. Baye Gode Sene. · Senegal.

Personalia

DOMINIEK DENDOOVEN
is a historian and assistant curator at In Flanders Fields Museum in Ieper (Ypres), Belgium.

PIET CHIELENS
is co-ordinator of In Flanders Fields Museum in Ieper, Belgium.

NIELS VAN ECHTELT
is a historian and studied military sciences and military history at the University of Amsterdam.

GWYNNIE HAGEN
is a sinologist and lives in Belgium.

CHRISTIAN KOLLER
is Senior Lecturer in Modern History at Bangor University, Wales.

BRITTA LANGE
has a PhD in Cultural Sciences and is currently a post-doc research fellow at Berlin's Humboldt University.

JÜRGEN MAHRENHOLZ
is a musicethnologist, responsible for the Sound Archive at Berlin's Humboldt University. He also works for the German Music Archive.

RIK PINXTEN
is Senior Lecturer in Comparative Anthropology and is chairman of the Centre for Intercultural Communication and Interaction (CICI) at Ghent University, Belgium.

MON STEYAERT
is a cultural philosopher, was an art dealer and might remain a politician somehow.

PHILIP VANHAELEMEERSCH
is a research fellow at the Ferdinand Verbiestinstitute of the Catholic university of Leuven, Belgium.

Colofon

This book was published on the occasion of the exhibition
Man – Culture – War.
Multicultural Aspects
of the First World War.
In Flanders Fields Museum, Ypres.
1 May – 7 September 2008

Authors:
Piet Chielens, Dominiek Dendooven,
Niels van Echtelt, Gwynnie Hagen,
Christian Koller, Britta Lange,
Jürgen Mahrenholz, Rik Pinxten,
Mon Steyaert, Philip Vanhaelemeersch

Editing:
Dominiek Dendooven and Piet Chielens

Graphic design:
Dooreman
Image correction:
Stijn Dams

Typesetting:
Karakters, Ghent
Translations:
Altair Vertalingen bvba, Aalst

Printed and bound by
Die Keure nv, Brugge, 2008
This book is printed on
Tatami Ivory 135 gr

www.lannoo.com

www.inflandersfields.be

© Uitgeverij Lannoo nv, Tielt, 2008
ISBN 978-90-209- 7727-1
D/2008 /45/225

The photographs on the cover and on p2, 206 and 207
are mainly portraits of prisoners of war in Germany.
They were made by Otto Stiehl, at one time camp
commander in Zossen-Wünsdorf near Berlin.
The photographs are now kept at the Museum
for European Cultures in Berlin. (© Bildarchiv
Preußischer Kulturbesitz, Berlin)

The words 'man culture war' on Page 1 have been repeated in
the languages spoken at the front in Flanders during the First
World War. (The list is probably incomplete)

On the end leaves:
The World in Hemispheres. From: *Johnston's Royal Atlas of
Modern Geography*. Edinburgh & London, 1918.
(Talbot House, Poperinge)